ROUTLEDGE LIBRARY EDITIONS:
HISTORY OF MONEY, BANKING AND FINANCE

Volume 4

THE EMERGENCE OF THE TRUST COMPANY IN NEW YORK CITY 1870–1900

THE EMERGENCE OF THE TRUST COMPANY IN NEW YORK CITY 1870–1900

H. PEERS BREWER

Routledge
Taylor & Francis Group
LONDON AND NEW YORK

First published in 1986 by Garland Publishing, Inc.

This edition first published in 2018
by Routledge
2 Park Square, Milton Park, Abingdon, Oxon OX14 4RN

and by Routledge
711 Third Avenue, New York, NY 10017

Routledge is an imprint of the Taylor & Francis Group, an informa business

British Library Cataloguing in Publication Data
A catalogue record for this book is available from the British Library

ISBN: 978-1-138-70169-4 (Set)
ISBN: 978-1-315-10595-6 (Set) (ebk)
ISBN: 978-1-138-09028-6 (Volume 4) (hbk)
ISBN: 978-1-315-10870-4 (Volume 4) (ebk)

THE EMERGENCE OF THE TRUST COMPANY IN NEW YORK CITY 1870–1900

H. Peers Brewer

Garland Publishing, Inc.
New York & London ★ 1986

Library of Congress Cataloging-in-Publication Data

Brewer, H. Peers, 1934–
The emergence of the trust company in New York City, 1870–1900.

(American business history)
Thesis (Ph.D.)—New York University, 1974.
Bibliography: p.
1. Trust companies—New York (N.Y.)—History—19th century. I. Title. II. Series.
HG4356.N5B74 1986 332.2′6′097471 86-9942
ISBN 0-8240-8352-0

All volumes in this series are printed on acid-free, 250-year-life paper.

Printed in the United States of America

THE EMERGENCE OF THE TRUST COMPANY IN NEW YORK CITY: 1870-1900

H. Peers Brewer

A dissertation presented to the Faculty of the Graduate School of Business Administration, New York University, in partial fulfillment of the requirements for the degree of Doctor of Philosophy.

1974

Dedicated to My Parents

Margaret and Harrison Brewer

PREFACE

Several years ago Fritz Stern's Varieties of History was recommended if not required reading for graduate students and history majors. I recall the fascination of this book--descriptions of the uses to which the study of history had been put, of the techniques and schools of historians. The implication of Stern's discourse was that intelligent men saw a purpose in history and historians were advocates of one or another of these purposes. This came as a surprise (and a rebuke) for then, as now, the reading of history was to me largely a matter of personal enjoyment and intellectual expansion. And this is the rubric under which the following chapters have been written.

I would not deny that the study of history has a more utilitarian function. From the pages of virtually any historical narration, including the following, it is apparent that the market (so to speak) goes down--and up, and not many men know which a priori, and none know omni tempore.

The subject of this dissertation is exciting in its own right. Between 1870 and 1900 the trust companies grew at a rapid rate and emerged as a major financial intermediary. The purpose has been to determine how and why this came about. Prior efforts in this direction have been sound but sketchy. As a consequence I have relied almost entirely on original sources and documents of the time. The dissertation benefited immensely from the patient counsel of Dr. Herman Krooss, whose contributions to the fields of business and financial history are both extensive and exacting.

It is a blunt fact, but writers of histories are at the mercy of librarians and archivists. Since I may wish to do something of this character again, I lubricate the hinges of welcome with a statement of supplicant gratitude to Miss Ann Little, Librarian of Manufacturers Hanover Trust Company, Jack Evans, Executive Vice President of Manufacturers Hanover Trust Company, and the appropriate individuals of Bankers Trust Company, the New York Public Library, the New York Historical Society, the libraries of New York University, the Library of Congress, the National Archives, the Boston Public Library, Widener Library, and the New York State Banking Department. And of course, though she would scarcely expect it, a word of thanks to my good lady Carolyn.

July, 1974

H. Peers Brewer

TABLE OF CONTENTS

LIST OF TABLES

LIST OF CHARTS

CHAPTER I

AN OVERVIEW OF THE TRUST COMPANY MOVEMENT: 1870-1900

Object of the Dissertation

Between 1875 and 1900, the assets of trust companies in New York City grew at a compound annual rate of 9.6%, compared with 4.1% for national banks and 5.4% for state banks located in the City.[1] At the least, the superior growth rate of trust companies would quicken one's curiosity, but more important, from the aspect of financial history, the trust company movement was the primary channel through which the state banking system reestablished a competitive position with the national banking system. As Table 1:1 indicates, the trust companies moved from 13% of the City's banking assets in 1875 to 33% by 1900. Combined, the state banks and trust companies held 26% of the assets in 1875 and 46% by 1900.

The purpose of this dissertation is to bring to light the entrepreneurial, economic and political forces which

[1] Aggregate data for the trust companies is not available for years prior to 1874.

TABLE 1:1

Distribution of Assets in the New York City Banking Sector

	1875 Assets (000)	1875 %	1900 Assets (000)	1900 %
National Banks	$389,758	74%	$1,067,356	54%
State Banks	66,632	13	251,031	13
Trust Companies	67,032	13	662,114	33
	$523,422	100%	$1,980,501	100%

Source: Data for national banks from Annual Reports of the Comptroller of the Currency. Data for state banks and trust companies from Annual Reports of the New York State Superintendent of Banking. See footnote number 3:7.

prompted the growth of the trust companies and, step-by-step, resolved the movement into a well-defined financial intermediary and eventually led to the merging of the trust movement with commercial banks.

Some years, of course, are more important than others. An historical analysis is the process of imputing meaning to time--of recognizing which years and events are important for an understanding of the present. One day (December 7, 1941) is more important than another day (December 7, 1931) because events occurred on that date which moulded lives and institutions, changing thereby the alternatives people would have in the future.

Although the first New York trust company (Farmers

Fire and Loan Company) was chartered in 1822, and a half-dozen or so were chartered in the next forty years, it was not until the years following the Civil War that the formation of trust companies reached the proportion of a movement, drawing the attention of a broad range of entrepreneurs, challenging the equilibrium of the established financial community, and demanding the protracted attention of legislative and regulatory bodies.

The period between 1870 and 1900, therefore, is especially significant because events occurred in these years which moulded a scattered group of moneyed institutions into a financial intermediary with well-defined economic and behavioral properties. Accordingly this study focuses on the 1870-1900 period.

The study also focuses on New York City. This is particularly appropriate first because of the primacy of New York City in the nation's financial and commercial structure--its central position in the payments mechanism, the size and quality of the stock and bond exchanges, and the sheer size of all financial intermediary groups. If the trust companies penetrated the New York financial structure, then the movement was of consequence in the over-all financial history of the nation. A second reason for concentration on New York is the richness of the surviving data on

New York financial institutions of this period which facilitates the pursuit of a broad spectrum of issues.

Defining a Trust Company

By the mid-1870's the phrase "trust company" was widely employed in the titles of specific companies and, to a lesser extent, as a generic term referring to a class of companies.

Of the eight operating New York City trust companies formed prior to 1870, all had the phrase "trust company" in their corporate name. Of the forty-seven companies which sought charters between 1870 and 1873, twenty-two had the phrase in their corporate name. Unlike national banks, that had to have the word "National" in their title, a company could be a trust company whether or not the phrase appeared in the corporate name.

By the mid-1870's, national banks, state banks, savings banks and insurance companies all had specific enabling legislation. As financial intermediaries, these companies were well defined by legislation and function. All other financial intermediaries were classified under the residual term "moneyed corporations." Trust companies were a subset of "moneyed corporations." The first general legislation in New York State, (Laws of 1874, Chapter 324) dealing with trust companies was entitled "An Act relative to Moneyed Corporations, other than Banks, Institutions for Savings, and Insurance Companies." The title of this Act, as passed, varied slightly from the title of the bill (Number 88) as introduced into the State Senate: "An Act for the regulation of trust companies, and certain other moneyed corporations."

Trust companies in the 1870's were by far the largest segment of the "moneyed corporation" classification. As the century drew to a close, other companies emerged from this classification to become identified as distinct financial intermediaries; specifically, building and loan societies, safe deposit companies and investment corporations. As the century moved on, companies initially called by the residual phrase "moneyed corporations" gradually acquired specific legislative, judicial and economic identification points, which taken together served to define separate financial intermediaries.

From approximately the end of the nineteenth century, the term "trust company" connoted to most observers a bank with authority to engage in personal and corporate trust business. For the 1870-1900 period, however, this definition was entirely too specific.

An examination of the charters acquired or sought by trust companies between 1870 and 1873 indicates that most were not even interested in personal or corporate trust business.

TABLE 1:2

Summary of Corporate Powers of Trust Companies Based on Charter Provisions

	Number of Companies Having Power				
	1870	1871	1872	1873	Total
Number of Companies Seeking Charter	11	20	7	9	47
Powers:					
Mortgage	1	5	5	7	18
Mercantile	1	8	0	3	12
Pawning	3	0	2	0	5
Debt Guaranty	5	12	4	6	27
Receive Deposits	7	19	6	7	39
Lending on Collateral	11	20	7	9	47
Personal Trust	1	7	1	2	11
Corporate Trust	1	8	2	4	15
Warehouse	5	4	3	4	16
Insurance	2	9	1	0	12
Investments	3	13	3	3	22
Agency	5	13	4	5	27
Borrowing	4	6	1	3	14
Branching	1	5	0	3	9

Source: Charters of respective companies (see Chapter 2, Table 2:14:A-D) in Laws of New York, 1870-3, or Bills Introduced (Bill Jackets) in New York Legislature--1870-3.

As Table 1:2 illustrates, out of the 47 companies seeking charters in the 1870-3 period, only 11 requested personal trust powers and only 15 requested corporate trust powers. Clearly, the personal-corporate trust theme is too narrow a definition for the trust companies of this period.

What, then, did the term "trust company" mean?

The term "trust" referred to a debtor-creditor relationship. More exactly, to the function of lending on collateral. Bouviers Law Dictionary (1874), the definitive law dictionary of the time, wrote under the topic "Trusts":

> Express trusts are those which are created in express terms in the deed, writing, or will.... Express trusts are usually found in preliminary sealed arguments, such as marriage articles, or articles for the purchase of land; in formal conveyances, such as marriage settlements, terms for years, Mortgages, assignments for the payment of debts, raising portions, or other purposes.[2]

Chaplin in Express Trusts stated that express trusts might be created for four purposes, one of which was "to sell real property for the benefit of creditors."

Chaplin's language in discussing this type of express trust is revealing:

> If, under a trust of the first class, the beneficiaries (i.e., the creditors of the creator of the trust) release their claims against him /the creator/ in consideration of his releasing to the trustee all his revisionary interests in the subject of the trust, the trust itself thereupon ceases. For there are no longer any debts to be paid, to furnish the basis of a trust.[3]

---

[2]John Bouvier, Law Dictionary, 1874, Vol. 2, 615. Italics mine.

[3]Stewart Chaplin, A Treatise on Express Trusts and Powers, Baker, Voorhis and Co., New York, 1897, 28. Italics mine.

Chaplin also makes it clear that the above purpose of express trusts relating to the sale of real property also applies to personal property.

It was important for the trust companies to have explicit power in their charters authorizing them to enter into a trust relationship with borrowers. Chaplin stated:

> There is a class of artificial persons--that is corporations--which cannot be trustees unless specifically empowered in their charters, or by way of necessary incident to the powers and rights given,...

Overwhelmingly, the term "trust company" referred to a debtor-creditor relationship and this in the function of lending on collateral.[5] Whether or not the words "trust company" appeared in the title was immaterial.

Seen in this light, it is apparent that trust companies were basically lending institutions. It is a curious fact of financial history that this definition has been so widely misunderstood.

If trust companies were interested in commercial banking business, how was it that they were each chartered by special, individual legislation and were not chartered under the New York State General Banking Law of 1838? The

---

[4]Ibid., 68.

[5]Ibid., 309.

<u>Constitution of the State of New York</u> (Article 8, Section 4) did prohibit the special chartering of financial companies that could be chartered under the Law of 1838.

The legal loop-hole which allowed trust companies to come into existence without being under the Act of 1838 was an almost incidental by-product of a case at law in 1855. In this case (U.S. Trust Company vs. Brady), Brady (the defendant) had taken a loan from Knickerbocker Savings Institution and secured the loan with hypothecated stock. Knickerbocker became insolvent. The receiver, U.S. Trust Company (the plaintiff), sought to recover the loan from Brady. Brady argued, among other things, that U.S. Trust could not bring action because its charter was illegal under Article 8, Section 4 of the <u>State Constitution</u>; that the Trust Company should be chartered under the Act of 1838. The New York State Supreme Court held that the charter was constitutional, that the Legislature could at its discretion grant special charters, just as long as it did not grant special banking powers.[6]

In point of fact, the U.S. Trust charter (April 12, 1853) did permit several functions which could be regarded as banking--making loans and investments, receiving

---

[6] "U.S. Trust v. Brady," 20 <u>Barbour</u> 119.

deposits--but it did not allow the issuance of circulating notes. The judges hearing the case apparently felt the ability to issue circulating notes was a critical feature in bringing a company under the Act of 1838 and under Article 8, Section 4 of the State Constitution.

None of the trust companies ever had the authority to issue circulating notes, although their charters permitted virtually every other type of banking function.

Statutory and Regulatory Background

In the 1870-1900 period, trust companies were created and regulated by state law. In New York two pieces of legislation during this period were especially important for the trust company movement: (1) The Act of 1874, and (2) the Act of 1887.

The Act of 1874. In 1874, the New York Legislature passed the first general legislation relating to trust companies.

The Act provided in substance that all trust companies would in the future report to and be examined by the State Superintendent of Banking. Most of the sections of the Act concerned the mechanical aspects of the examinations and reports and the recourses available to the Superintendent if companies failed to cooperate. The Act also required all trust companies that received deposits to place with the Superintendent government bonds in the amount of 10% of paid-in capital. And finally the Act provided that deposits or loans could not at any time in any trust company exceed ten times paid-in capital and surplus.[7]

The Act as passed on May 5, 1874 was quite different in several interesting respects from the bill as introduced on February 18, 1874. Apparently, the trust companies themselves felt the bill as introduced on February 18 prescribed more stringent regulations than they deemed to their advantage. On March 12, 1874, for example, the Executive Committee of Mercantile Trust Company resolved that a committee

> be appointed to act upon the matter of proposed legislation in reference to Trust Companies, with power to take such measures as will in their judgement be judicious to prevent oppressive requirements from the Companies and that the views of the Committee be presented by Counsel or otherwise to the Legislature if deemed desirable.[8]

Apparently the Committee (or others) did reach the Legislature, because changes were made in the bill. In the original bill, Section 2 provided that all trust companies

---

[7]New York State, <u>Laws of 1874</u>, Chapter 324, Section 8.

[8]Mercantile Trust Company, <u>Minutes of Executive Committee: February 10, 1874-June 4, 1875</u>, meeting of March 12, 1874.

should deposit with the Superintendent of Banking, securities in an amount equal to one-fourth of capital stock. This would have required for the New York City trust companies about $2.8 million in securities as of June, 1874. This section, however, was amended in the final bill to read an amount equal to one-tenth of capital and surplus. By comparison, this required only $1.7 million in securities for the New York City trust companies. But more, the original bill was also amended to provide that only trust companies receiving deposits would be required to place securities with the Superintendent of Banking. At the time, Mercantile Trust was withdrawing from the deposit receiving business.

The original bill also provided a penalty clause of one to five years imprisonment for any trust company officer who applied the company's deposits or securities to his own use. In the final bill, this penalty clause was deleted.[9]

The critical aspect of the Act of 1874 was that for the first time all trust companies were brought under the systematic survey of one regulatory authority.

---

[9]New York State, Bills Introduced into Senate, 1874, Number 88, Section 8.

The reasons prompting the State to pass this legislation were three-fold.

First, prior to the passage of the Act of 1874, the regulatory responsibility for trust companies, if it existed at all, was scattered among various state agencies and very passive in nature. The charter of each trust company might provide for some regulatory relationship with the state. In such cases, however, the charter would usually merely provide that the company would report annually to a certain state agency. In most cases, however, no provision was made for any active response or initiative on behalf of the agency. The state agencies designated by individual charters to receive reports included: the Comptroller of the State, the Superintendent of Banking, the Superintendent of Insurance, and the State Supreme Court. Of course each company which had some reporting provision in its charter, reported to only one of the agencies. There was no coordination among the agencies, no clearing house for industry problems, and no central mechanism for devising and recommending critical trust company legislation to the Legislature. The agencies receiving reports from trust companies served little more than an archival function.

But the charters of most trust companies made no provision for any regulatory relationship whatsoever, even of the most superficial kind. Of the 47 applications for trust company charters in the 1870-3 legislative sessions, 30 made no provision for reporting to any state agency.

One of the objectives of the Legislature in passing the Act of 1874 was to create a uniform system of accountability.

Second, the rash of formations of trust companies in the 1870-73 period suggested to the Governor and the Superintendent of Banking that trust companies were going to be an increasingly important portion of the New York financial sector.

Superintendent of Banking, D. C. Ellis, arguing for general trust company legislation, said in his Annual Report (December 29, 1873):

> A new class in institutions in rapidly multiplying in the State....There is no obvious reason why such institutions should be privileged by exemption from the safeguards which the State has set about similar financial corporations;...

A few days later (January 6, 1874), Governor John A. Dix, echoing Ellis' suggestion for general trust company legis-

[10] D. C. Ellis, Superintendent of Banking New York State, Annual Report, December 29, 1873, Assembly Document No. 7, 97 Session, 14.

lation observed that trust companies:

> ...have, as a general rule, greater powers than the /banks/, under less restriction, with no uniform external supervision, and with equal liability to hazardous risks and ultimate loss... they are, to a great extent, free from the operation of those laws to which it is the policy of the state to subject other moneyed institutions as custodians of the funds of the citizens of the state in order to protect the people from loss through management and fraud.[11]

Behind the Governor's message was a recognition of the primacy of New York financial institutions and the nationwide repercussions which could result if institutional problems developed in New York. The association of the Panic of 1857 and the failure of the New York office of the Ohio Life and Trust Company was well known by the financial community.[12]

Finally, the Act of 1874 was passed amid a note of urgency, because two trust companies had run into serious financial difficulty in the Fall of 1873. Both National Trust and Union Trust actually suspended for a brief period. Although the September 1873 financial crisis was instrumental in both closings, Union's probelms were ag-

---

[11]John A. Dix, Governor New York State, Annual Message, January 6, 1874, Assembly Document No. 2, 97 Session, 8-9.

[12]J. S. Gibbons, The Banks of New York, Their Dealers, The Clearing House and the Panic of 1857, Appleton and Co., New York, 1858, Chapter 19.

gravated by the discovery of a serious defalcation by one of its officers.[13]

Another critical aspect of the Act of 1874 was to bring the trust companies under the regulatory authority of the Superintendent of Banking. In retrospect this was a logical step. But in 1874 the logic was less clear. At that time, the Superintendent of Banking was a weak office. The office of the Superintendent of Insurance was far more prestigious. The Legislature could have placed the trust companies under the regulatory authority of the Superintendent of Insurance, the Secretary of State or even created an entirely new regulatory office. If any of these choices had been adopted, it is likely that the trust company movement would not have assimilated into the commercial banking industry as smoothly as it did, and the structure of American financial intermediaries would be different than it is now.

It was by no means axiomatic that the Legislature would put the trust companies under the Superintendent of Banking. In 1870, a resolution was introduced in the As-

---

[13] See: Union Trust Company, A Short History of the Union Trust Company, in manuscript collection: "Miscellaneous Data Pertaining to History of Bank." Secretary, Manufacturers Hanover Trust Company.

sembly that "the Committee on Insurance be authorized to inquire into the affairs of the life insurance and trust companies of this State, . . ."[14] And at the New York Constitutional Convention of 1873, it was actually recommended that the office of the Superintendent of Banking be abolished altogether and the functions of the office be turned over to the Secretary of State.[15] Neither the Assembly's Resolution nor the Convention's recommendations was adopted.

There were, however, several powerful factors leading the Legislature to place the trust companies under the Superintendent of Banking. For one, the basic lines of business were lending and accepting deposits--exactly the same as the state banks, for another, the Superintendent already had the personnel to conduct the examinations, and finally by 1874 the trust companies already constituted a portion of the Superintendent of Banking's business. As early as 1871, for example, the securities on deposit with the Superintendent had a value of $2.7 million, of which the trust companies contributed $0.5 mil-

---

[14]New York State, Assembly Journal, 1870, 93 Session, 51.

[15]Constitutional Convention of the State of New York, Journal, 1873, Weed, Parsons and Co., Albany, 69.

lion, or about 19%.[16]

At the time of the passage of the Act, the office of the Superintendent of Banking was not particularly distinguished. The office was originally set up by legislation passed in 1851 (Laws of 1851, Chapter 164). Prior to this time, the functions of the Superintendent of Banking were performed by the Comptroller of the State.[17] With the formation of the national bank system, and the wholesale conversion of state banks in 1865 to this system, the Superintendent of Banking was left with little more to do than regulate the State's savings banks (which had been placed under his jurisdiction in 1857).

The Superintendent of Banking was, of course, a political appointee. In the late 1870's the incumbents of both major state financial regulatory agencies--Insurance and Banking--were brought to trial before the State Senate

---

[16] John T. Hoffman, Governor New York State, Annual Message, January 3, 1871, Assembly Document No. 2, 94 Session, 8.

[17] Willis S. Paine, The Laws of the State of New York Relating to Banks, Trust, Investment, Safe Deposit, Personal Loan Companies and Brokers, Private Banks, Savings and Loan Associations, Credit Unions and the Land Bank, Baker, Voorhis and Co., New York, 1914, 32.

for negligence in duty.[18] Commenting on these trials, the editor of the Commercial and Financial Chronicle said: "The fact is that superintendence by the State, in both these departments, has proved only a deception to the public,...."[19]

The trial of the Superintendent of Banking seems to have quickened the Governor's realization that the post called for an individual of strong abilities. This in fact did come about. The next two Superintendents were of above average ability. The first, appointed April 13, 1880, was A. Barton Hepburn. While Superintendent, Hepburn was responsible for the first consolidated codification of New York State banking law (1882). Hepburn later served as Comptroller of the Currency (1892-3), as a member of Governor Hughes' 1907 Commission on Banking and in 1913 as President of the American Bankers Association's Currency Commission. The second Superintendent of note

---

[18]Banks Committee, New York State Senate, Testimony taken before the Senate Committee on Banks and the State of New York, in reference to the Charges preferred by William J. Best, Receiver, Etc., Edward Mallon and John Mack, Against DeWitt C. Ellis, Superintendent of the Banking Department of the State of New York, 3 vols., Weed Parsons and Co., Albany, 1878. Banks Committee, New York State Senate, Testimony taken before the Senate on Charges against John F. Smyth, Superintendent of the Insurance Department, 1878.

[19]Commercial and Financial Chronicle, June 12, 1877, 75-6.

was Willis S. Paine, appointed April 27, 1883. Paine, who worked as an examiner for the Banking Department as early as 1874, knew the New York banking scene from the inside, from the debits and credits up, and through the personalities of its officers. Paine was responsible for the "free banking" legislation in 1887 as applied to trust companies. Paine later followed a well traversed path for a regulator, becoming a director, president and roving entrepreneur for three trust companies in New York City. Paine's book on New York banking law underwent several editions and was for many years the definitive work in the field.

Both Hepburn and Paine were strong Superintendents and both were favorably disposed to the trust company movement.

The Act of 1887. The second major piece of legislation regarding the trust companies in the 1870-1900 period was the Act of 1887, which provided a "free banking" environment for trust companies in New York State. Prior to this time, each trust company was chartered by an act of the State Legislature. The bill passed by the Legislature and signed by the Governor was in effect the charter of the company. Powers granted to trust companies could and did vary widely from charter to charter.

The Act of 1887, however, eliminated the special legislation procedure, providing instead that all a trust company had to do to gain a charter was to make application to the Superintendent of Banking and satisfy certain standard, and rather minimal requirements. The Act of 1887 thus served the same function with regard to trust companies as the New York State Banking Law of 1838 served for state banks and the National Currency Act of 1863 served for national banks. Trust companies chartered under the Act of 1887 had standardized powers.

Structurally the laws providing for free banking for the New York state banks, trust companies and national banks were quite similar. The major exceptions to this were that the national and state bank legislation made elaborate provision for issuance of circulation, while the Act of 1887 made no such provision for the trust companies. The minimum capital constraints for a New York City based financial institution also varied ($500,000 for trust companies, $100,000 for state banks and national banks) among the respective free banking laws.[20] The higher minimum capital requirement for the trust companies does not seem to have been a critical factor in the entrepreneurial choice between forming a trust company or forming a commercial bank.

The Act of 1887 (Laws of 1887, Chapter 546) as passed by the Legislature was identical to the bill as introduced into the Senate (bill number 269), with one exception: the Act as passed contained an additional proviso that the powers granted to trust companies under existing charters continued in force without reference to the Act of 1887.

The Formation of Trust Companies

The Annual Reports of the New York Superintendent of Banking indicate that at one time or another in the 1870-1900 period a total of 41 trust companies were in operation. In the years immediately following the Act of 1874, as the Superintendent was implementing the examination requirements of that Act, a few companies that operated briefly may have been missed, but these were inconsequential in size or influence.[21]

---

[20] For national banks see: The National Currency Act of 1863, Section 6, paragraph 3. For New York state banks see: Laws of 1882, Chapter 409, Section 29. For New York trust companies see: Laws of 1887, Chapter 546, Section 19.

[21] One of the companies missed was Loaner's Bank. Failure to examine Loaner's was one of the charges of negligence

Actually the companies listed in Table 1:3 were remarkably stable as financial institutions went at the time. Only three companies went out of business involuntarily (National Trust--1877, American Loan and Trust--1890, and New York State Loan and Trust--1875) and in each case the liquidation was orderly. No mergers took place in the industry until 1900. And two of the reporting trust companies, Equitable Trust (New London) and Jarvis-Conklin Mortgage (Kansas City) were domiciled outside of New York State.

Chart 1:1 indicates the pattern of new company charters in the 1870-1900 period. The factors which influenced the rate of trust company formations were: (1) prior to 1887, the willingness of the Governor or Legislature to entertain charter legislation, and (2) the general economic conditions. As Chart 1:1 indicates, the years of low or no new company formations were fairly closely correlated with recessionary periods. Beyond this, the entrepreneurs in each new company formation would have particular economic motivations.

An interesting perspective on the rise of the trust

---

brought against Superintendent D. C. Ellis in 1877. See footnote 18 above, 331-5, 1159-73.

TABLE 1:3

New York City Trust Companies
Reporting to the Superintendent of Banking
In The Ninteenth Century

Trust Company	Date Chartered	Reporting Years
American Deposit and Loan	1871	1897-1900
American Loan and Trust	1872	1883-1890
Atlantic Trust (1)	1887	1887-1900
Bankers Trust of N.Y. (1)	1898	1899
Bowling Green Trust (2)	1898	1898-1900
Central Realty Bond Exchange	1898	1899-1900
Central Trust	1873	1876-1900
City Trust	1899	1899-1900
Colonial Trust	1873	1897-1900
Continental Trust	1890	1890-1900
Equitable Trust (New London)	-	1877-1889
Farmers Loan and Trust	1822	1874-1900
Fifth Avenue Trust	1898	1898-1900
Guaranty Trust (3)	1864	1874-1875 1882-1900
Holland Trust	1888	1888-1900
International Banking (4)	1899	1899
Jarvis-Conklin Mortgage	--	1888-1890
Knickerbocker Trust	1874	1884-1900
Manhattan Trust (5)	1871	1874-1900
Mercantile Trust	1868	1874-1900
Merchants Trust	1899	1899-1900
Metropolitan Trust	1881	1881-1900
Morton Trust (6)	1899	1899-1900
Mutual Trust	1868	1885-1889
National Trust	1867	1874-1877
New York Life	1830	1874-1900
New York Loan and Indemnity	1870	1874
New York Security	1889	1889-1900
New York State Loan	1870	1874-1875
North American Trust (4)	1885	1897-1900
Real Estate Trust of New York (7)	1890	1890-1900
Standard Trust	1898	1898-1900
State Trust (6)	1889	1889-1899
Title Guaranty Trust (8)	1882	1882-1900
Trust Company of America	1899	1899-1900
Trust Company of New York	1900	1900
Union Trust	1864	1874-1900
United States Mortgage	1871	1878-1900
United States Transfer and Exchange	1889	1889-1894
United States Trust	1853	1875-1900
Washington Trust	1889	1889-1900

(1) Merged in 1900.
(2) Was Produce Exchange Trust Company until 1900.
(3) Was N.Y. Guaranty & Indemnity until 1896.
(4) Merged 1900.
(5) Was Real Estate T. C. of City of N.Y. until 1886.
(6) Merged 1900.
(7) Was R.E. Loan and T.C. of N.Y. until 1894.
(8) Was German-American Loan & T.C. until 1884.

Source: Superintendent of Banking, New York State, Annual Reports, 1874-1901.

CHART 1:1

Trust Company Formations New York City: 1870-1900

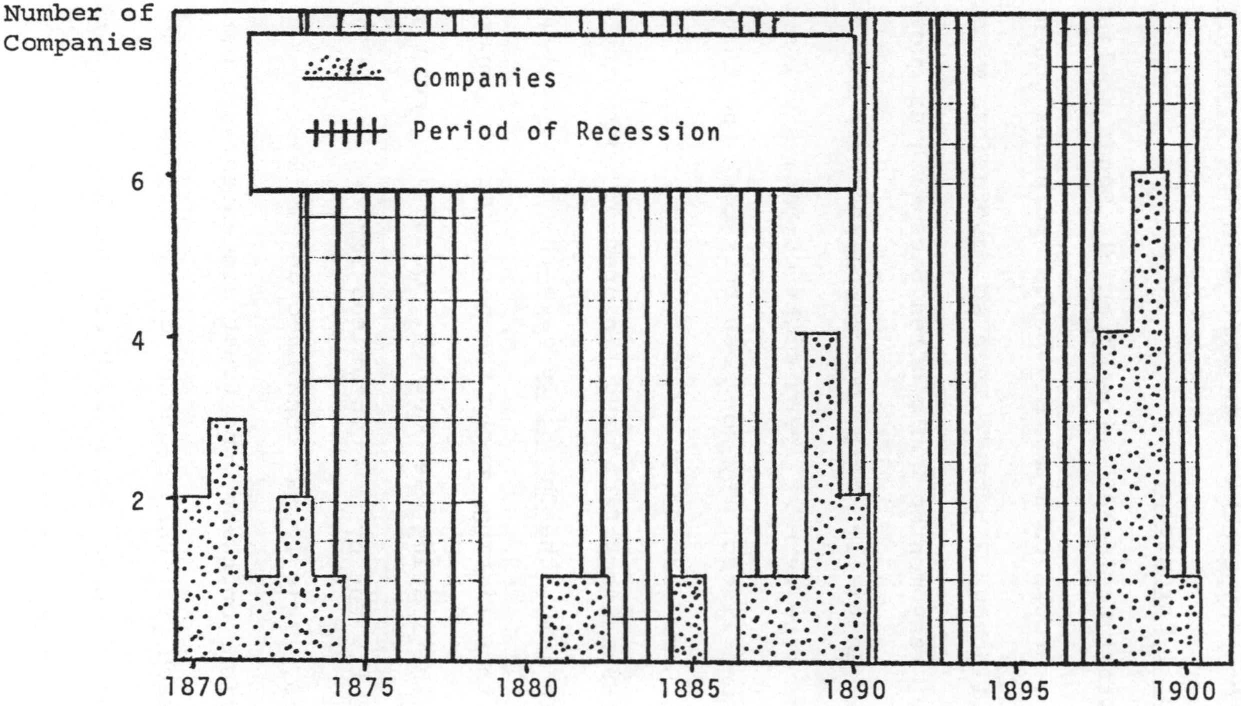

Source: Superintendent of Banking, New York State, <u>Annual Reports</u>, 1874-1901, and Geoffrey Moore, <u>Business Cycle Indicators</u>, Vol. 1, p. 670.

companies in the estimation of the financial community and their eventual blending into the commercial banking industry is gained by examining how the quotations for trust company stocks were treated in the Commercial and Financial Chronicle

Starting in 1877, the Chronicle began to list trust company stocks on a monthly basis and under the heading "Miscellaneous Stocks." Even so, quotations were infrequent. Many months would often pass with no quotation entry. Initially, only four companies were listed even though there were at least eight companies which could have been listed. By contrast both bank and insurance stocks were carried on a weekly basis and under the headings "Bank Stock List" and "Insurance Stock List."

In 1880, the Chronicle gave the trust company stocks a separate listing, under the title "Trust Company Stocks." Again the listing was monthly. Quotations were still infrequent. But by now quotations for ten companies were carried. This format continued until 1895, by which time quotations on twenty-one trust companies were carried. With each year the frequency of quotations on each company increased. Both the breadth and depth of the market for trust company stocks were steadily increasing.

In 1895, the Chronicle initiated a special monthly

"Quotation Supplement." With this Supplement, trust company stocks were integrated with bank stocks under a listing of "Bank and Trust Company Stocks."

In 1898, the Chronicle began to list trust company stocks on a weekly basis, also under the listing of "Bank and Trust Company Stocks." With this development, in terms of capital market information, New York City trust companies ranked at least on a par with other financial intermediaries. The experience of the trust companies in this regard is a reasonably close vignette of what was happening in all major aspects of their business in the 1870-1900 period.

CHAPTER II

THE TRUST COMPANY MOVEMENT QUICKENS: 1870-3

Object of Chapter

The first concentrated activity in the trust company movement came in the decade following the end of the Civil War. Table 2:1 shows the number of bills introduced in the New York State legislature each year from 1867-75, either incorporating or amending existing charters of New York City trust companies.[1]

TABLE 2:1

Number of Bills Introduced in New York State Legislature Relative to New York City Trust Companies: 1867-75

Year	Bills Introduced
1867	11
1868	9
1869	15
1870	17
1871	32
1872	22
1873	21
1874	13
1875	6

Source: New York State *Senate* and *Assembly Journals*, *1867-75*.

[1]Lists of legislation were derived from examination of indices each year of the New York State *Senate* and *Assembly*

Legislative activity increased during the latter years of the 1860's, rose radically in 1871 and declined thereafter. The object of this chapter is broadly to answer the question why the legislative activity gained and lost intensity during this period. The question will be pursued by a cross-sectional analysis of the years 1870-3, which flank the peak year of activity. The cross-sectional analysis will serve as a framework to explore four specific questions:

1. Who were the incorporators or entrepreneurs starting these companies? This question has relevance because it would be helpful, among other things, to know if the trust company movement sprang from within or without the established financial community.
2. What was the legislative and political process through which the companies passed to become chartered. Chapter I pointed out that general

---

Journals. The quality of the indexing was at times rather shoddy, but since different individuals indexed the two Journals, a lapse in one was not transferred to the other. In cases where the name of the proposed corporation did not clearly indicate a trust company, the question was resolved by consulting the text of the bill, either in the printed bill collections or the Laws.

legislation governing the formation of trust companies was not passed until 1887. But in the period prior to that date, including the years from 1870-3, charters still had to go through a legislative and political process which acted as an ad hoc filter and put a definitive stamp on the young industry.

3. What economic functions were the companies seeking? The answers to this question will indicate whether or not at this early date in the movement the companies were after the same services as the established banking system already offered.

4. What was the economic environment in the 1870-3 period? It would be helpful to know just how sensitive company formations were to economic conditions.

Each of these questions deals with forces which began the process of shaping and ordering the trust company movement.

Entrepreneurs and Corporators

In 1870 the New York State Legislature introduced 13 bills that sought to incorporate trust companies in New York City; 25 were introduced in 1871; 11 in 1872; and 13 in 1873--a total of 62 companies in all. Fortunately, Section 1 of each bill of incorporation carried a list of the company's corporators. Of the 62 bills of incorporation during the 1870-3 period, 47 moved far enough along in the legislative process to be printed. These 47 companies had a total list of 614 corporator positions representing 553 individuals.[2]

To derive an idea of the occupations of these corporators, the list of 553 individuals was checked against Trow's New York City Directory (1870/1 and 1872/3) and Rand McNally's Banker's Directory--1876.[3] These lists yielded a reasonably certain identification of 62% of the individual corporators and 67% of the corporator positions.

Table 2:2 shows the occupational distribution of the corporators of each company.

Lawyers were prominent among the list of corporators. This is hardly surprising since financial institutions in

---

[2] Some individuals were corporators of two or more companies.

[3] Other helpful documents were: New York City, Board of Aldermen, Document Number 6, April 8, 1872. (This document was prepared by A. H. Green, Comptroller, and showed the names of all recipients of drafts drawn on the City for the three months ending March 30, 1872.) The New York Times Obituary Index; The Dictionary of American Biography.

TABLE 2:2

Occupations
Corporators of New York City
Moneyed Institutions: 1870-3

Company	Total Corporators	Lawyers	Bankers	Merchants	Politicians	Other	Not Known
	Percentage Distribution by Occupation						
American Mortgage and Trust	100%	26%	22%	26%	9%	0%	17%
Anglo American Loan and Trust	100	22	0	45	11	0	22
Atlantic Guaranty and Trust	100	67	0	0	0	0	33
Bankers Life Insurance and Trust	100	21	0	32	21	0	26
Central Trust	100	22	11	28	0	0	39
Colonial Trust	100	22	22	34	0	0	22
Commercial Credit and Guaranty	100	29	0	64	0	0	7
Continental Loan and Trust	100	0	20	40	0	0	40
Corn Exchange Warehouse	100	0	0	18	9	0	73
Depositors Loan Institution	100	10	0	20	20	0	50
Equitable Loan and Trust	100	11	0	33	0	0	56
German American Loan and Mortgage	100	7	27	33	13	0	20
International Trust and Banking	100	0	12	63	0	0	25
International Trust, Loan and Investment	100	18	9	45	0	0	28
Island City Loan and Trust	100	10	5	43	5	5	32
Knickerbocker Loan and Trust	100	0	0	15	15	0	70
Manhattan Indemnity and Loan	100	12	0	32	6	0	50
Manhattan Loan and Trust Co.	100	8	0	31	8	0	53
Manhattan Loan and Trust Co. of N.Y.	100	8	0	31	8	0	53
Manhattan Trust	100	0	20	33	0	7	40
Merchantile Loan and Warehouse	100	17	0	58	8	0	17
Merchants Loan	100	6	6	55	0	6	27
Metropolitan Loan and Trust	100	0	0	43	21	0	36
Mutual Benefit Life Policy Loan & Trust	100	22	0	28	11	0	39
Mutual Trust Institution	100	7	0	43	0	14	36
N.Y. City Life Policy Loan & Trust	100	3	3	34	3	0	57
N.Y. Collateral Loan & Deposit Bank	100	0	11	33	0	0	56
N.Y. Deposit & Loan	100	10	0	50	10	0	30
N.Y. Loan and Improvement	100	18	6	23	6	0	47
N.Y. Loan and Indemnity	100	42	5	26	11	5	11
N.Y. Loan and Real Estate	100	25	8	50	0	0	17
N.Y. Loan and Security Bank	100	10	0	40	10	0	40
N.Y. Loan and Security Co.	100	20	20	60	0	0	0
N.Y. Loan, Trust Warehouse & Deposit	100	0	0	33	22	0	45
N.Y. Mortgage and Trust	100	0	20	73	0	0	7
N.Y. Mutual Loan and Deposit	100	0	0	15	54	0	31
N.Y. Real Estate Banking(1)	100	0	6	6	65	0	23
N.Y. State Loan and Guaranty	100	0	0	67	0	0	33
N.Y. State Loan and Trust	100	8	8	45	0	8	31
Phoenix Trust	100	0	10	10	35	0	45
Real Estate Trust Co. of N.Y.	100	17	11	38	17	0	17
Republic Life Insurance & Trust	100	0	6	71	0	0	23
Security Deposit Co. of N.Y.	100	9	45	9	28	0	9
Traders Deposit	100	0	0	86	0	0	14
U.S. Loan and Security	100	20	0	60	0	0	20
U.S. Mortgage	100	6	23	59	0	0	12
TOTAL %	100	11	8	37	10	1	33

(1) Introduced in 1870 and 1871.

Source: Charters of respective companies in Laws of New York 1870-3, or Bill Introduced (Bill Jackets), in New York Legislature--1870-3, Trow's New York City Directory (1870/1, and 1872/3), and Rand McNally's Bankers Directory, 1876.

general and those with mortgage and corporate or personal trust in particular were substantial generators of legal business. Of the 46 institutions, all but 14 had one or more lawyers as a corporators. A few lawyers, like George H. Carey (notary of the National Bank of Commerce and the Bank of America), Thomas C. T. Buckley (notary of Corn Exchange Bank), Frederick dePeyster and Rufus F. Andrews were men of special prominence in legal and commercial circles.

The bankers category includes representatives of trust, commercial, savings and investment banks, but does not include security brokers who merely traded issues. This category also included several prominent individuals, such as Robert Lennox Kennedy (President of National Bank of Commerce), Edward V. Loew (President of Eleventh Ward Savings Bank), William M. Vermilye (Vermilye and Co.), Emil Sauer (President of German American Bank), Frederick D. Tappen (President of Gallatin National Bank), John J. Donaldson (President of Bank of North America), Philo C. Calhoun (President of Fourth National Bank), and John A. Stewart (President of United States Trust Co.).

The number of corporators drawn from the mercantile sector was quite large. This sector--roughly synonymous with the group known in economic history as "merchants"--

included security and commercial brokers, agents, importers and principals in diamonds, drygoods, carpets, liquors, sugar, tobacco, meat, bags, watches, produce, furs, drugs, insurance, hides, railroads, manufacturing and many more. The mercantile sector also had several prominent representatives, including William Orton (President of Western Union), A. Augustus Low (importer), William T. Blodgett (paints and varnish), R. A. McCurdy (Vice-President, Mutual Life Insurance), James Talcott (merchant), and David Dows (merchant).

The political category, as shown in Table 2.2, was rather large (10%) ranking ahead of the bankers (8%) and just behind the lawyers (11%). The political category was also fairly well distributed, 25 of the 46 companies having one or more corporators with political occupations.

The category "political" refers to individuals holding elected or appointed offices in the New York City or New York County administrative, legislative or judicial structures. Four of the corporators were State Assemblymen at one point or another during the 1870-3 period, but none was in office at the time they were corporators.

The more prominent persons in the political category appearing as corporators were: G. D. Cardozo (Chief of Ordinances), Daniel D. Conover (Alderman), Jenkins Van Schaick (Alderman), William Wade (Assistant Alderman), Bernard Smyth (Receiver of Taxes--Bureau of Taxes), George W. Van Nort (Commissioner, Department of Public Works), Gilbert Palmer (Superintendent, Bureau of Street Improvement), Wilson G. Hunt (Commissioner, Department of Docks), Henry Smith (Commissioner, Police Department), James S. Hennessy (Treasurer, Fire Department), Alex Shaler (Commissioner, Fire Department)--all City Officers. Among County Officers: Walter Roche (President, County Board of Supervisors), Charles E. Loew (Clerk of the County Court), Peter Trainer (Deputy Tax Commissioner), M. C. Gross (Justice, Marine Court), Thomas Kivlen, Joseph Koch, W. J. Kane (all Justices of County District Courts), and John Cox, John Scott, E. J. Shandley, Butler H. Bixby, John McQuade (all Justices of County Police Courts).

All the political corporators held office in the 1870-2 period, right at the peak of influence of Tammany boss, William M. Tweed. It is difficult to believe that any of these men could have occupied these offices of sensitivity and influence without Tweed's approval. It was quite possible that there was a correlation between the peak in Tweed's rule and the legislative activity concerning trust companies.

To pursue this point, the basic data on the corporators can be reconstituted in several ways. Table 2:3 shows, first, the absolute number of corporators in each category on a yearly basis, and secondly, a percentage distribution of the same information.

Focusing on the politicians column, the absolute data indicates a radical decline in the number of political corporators between 1871 and 1872. But the total number of corporators showed a sharp decline also. The percentage data, however, confirms that the decline in the political category was quite abrupt relative to the totals.

The structural change in the political category participation between 1871 and 1872 is quite significant because it was at the very time that the Tweed scandals were being exposed. The State Legislature met in 1871 from January to May, hence all legislative activity for 1871 was concluded by May. In July, 1871, the New York Times began its expose of Tweed's crimes. By the Fall of 1871, the political heat on Tweed and the Tammany Ring was quite

TABLE 2:3

OCCUPATIONAL DISTRIBUTION
YEARLY BASIS

Year	Total Number of Corporators	Distribution					
		Lawyers	Bankers	Merchants	Politicians	Other	Not Known
Absolute:							
1870	137	23	4	46	18	2	44
1871	300	23	27	105	39	2	104
1872	79	9	5	33	5	2	25
1873	98	15	10	43	1	1	28
Percentage:							
1870	100%	17%	3%	34%	13%	1%	32%
1871	100	8	9	35	13	0	35
1872	100	11	6	43	6	3	32
1873	100	15	10	44	1	1	29

Source: See Table 2:2.

intense.[4]

It is possible that the other corporators who once might have thought it politically expedient to have a representative(s) of the Tammany forces among their number, no longer felt this way after the scandals became public. This much is suggested by Table 2:4 which for each year shows the total number of companies for which incorporation was proposed, the number of these companies with one or more political incorporators, and the ratio between the two.

TABLE 2:4

Companies and Political Corporators

Year	Total Number Companies	Number of Companies Having One or More Political Corporators	Percentage
1870	10	7	70%
1871	20	13	65
1872	7	4	57
1873	9	1	11

Source: See Table 2:2.

If some credence is given to a recognition lag, and to the fact that the governorship changed from Democrat John Hoffman (one of Tweed's proteges) to Republican John Dix

4 Edward Robb Ellis, The Epic of New York City, Coward-McCann Inc., New York, 1966, Chapter 26.

in the 1872 election, then the evidence is fairly persuasive that the presence of a Tammany politician was deemed less desirable by the corporators in 1873 than in 1870.

The "Other" category of corporators, the smallest in size, was composed of a stenographer, a teacher, a priest (the rector of St. Ann's Episcopal Church), and physicians.

Five observations may be set forth concerning the entrepreneurs:

1. The occupational distribution was well-balanced, with no one occupational category dominating the movement.
2. The sheer size in numbers of the corporators was impressive, indicating the depth of the New York business community and suggesting that the movement was not dominated by a handful of men, such as was the case in New York financial affairs in the earlier part of the century.
3. The large number of proposed incorporations of trust companies and the occupational balance and numerical size of the incorporators taken together implies a broad dissatisfaction with the banking facilities provided by the national and

state systems.

4. The corporators included many of the city's established financial, commercial and legal leaders, but the broad base of support was drawn from a solid, middle class mercantile level.

5. Based on an examination of the entrepreneurial structure alone, it is apparent that the formation of trust companies was a powerful movement by 1870-3.

The Legislative and Political Process: 1870-3

New York State commercial banks were chartered, in the 1870-3 period, under the free banking law originally passed in 1838. This meant that a state commercial bank could be chartered by direct application to the Superintendent of Banking without, in each case, a special Act of the Legislature.

The case was quite different with the trust companies. Until general trust company legislation was passed in 1887, each trust company was chartered by a separate act. In the same manner, trust company charters were amended by separate acts. Since the trust companies were not yet subject to systematic or effective regulation, regulation was essentially limited to the Legislature and Governor granting or denying powers at the time of incorporation. The legislative process, accordingly, was an important determinant of the scope and nature of the trust company movement at this time.

As Table 2:5 illustrates, the legislative process was a critical filter. Of all bills introduced in the 1870-3 period, either chartering or amending existing charters, 54% failed to become law.

TABLE 2:5

New York City Trust Companies
Summary of Legislation: 1870-3

Year	Number of Bills: Introduced	Passed	Failed	Percent Failing
1870	17	9	8	47%
1871	33	12	21	64
1872	22	10	12	55
1873	21	12	9	43
Totals	93	43	50	54

Source: Same as Table 2:1.

The legislative process, then, exercised a significant influence over the types of trust companies which were incorporated.

The legislative process may be divided into four distinct areas: (1) the process of introducing legislation, (2) the determination of the standing committees which reviewed the bill, (3) the actions of the Legislature (Committee of the Whole) after receiving the bill from the standing committee, and (4) the Governor's disposition of the bills reaching his office. Each of these four areas represented a filter through which a bill had to pass and each gave the Legislature or Governor the opportunity to stamp their influence on the trust company movement.

The Introduction of Legislation. The process of introducing legilsation was itself an entrepreneurial function. The organizers of a company, recognizing a risk in getting the bill successfully through the Legislature, would presumably select that sponsorship which seemed to hold the best chance of success.

There seems to have been no critical benefit in the eyes of the organizers whether a bill was introduced in the Senate or Assembly. Of the 93 bills introduced in the 1870-3 period concerning trust companies, 46 were introduced in the Senate and 47 in the Assembly. The politics, however, of the introducer was of considerable importance. Organizers would naturally tend to select those legislators whose politics reflected the dominant political party. As Table 2:6 illustrates, sponsorship of trust company legislation reflected Democratic control of both houses in 1870 and 1871, and Republican domination in 1872 and 1873.[5]

TABLE 2:6

Sponsorship of New York City Trust Company Legislation by Political Party

Year	Total Bills Introduced	Politics of Sponsor: Democrat	Politics of Sponsor: Republican
1870	17	16	1
1871	33	30	3
1872	22	8	14
1873	21	6	15

Source: Same as Table 2:1

[5]In the case of the Senate, political affiliations were listed in Senate Documents, Number 19 (1870), Number 28 (1871), Number 29 (1872), and Number 29 (1873). The Assembly produced a similar biographical document but omitted political affiliations. In 1870, 1871, and 1872, however, the World Almanac did list such affiliations. For 1873, the political affiliations of Assemblymen were derived from W. H. McElory and A. McBride, Life Sketches of Executive Officers and Members of the Legislature of the State of New York for 1873. The Sketches, written and published at the State's expense, was a delightful trial in biographical ingenuity and subaltern tact. To wit:

> George Mosher (D-Assembly) "...He has the appearance of an earnest, intelligent man of business, and he is one."

> Stephen F. Gilbert (R-Assembly) "...His record thus far, while devoid of any marked feature, has been such as to reflect honor on his constituency."

> Leonard F. Hardy (R-Assembly) "...He is an efficient and wide-awake member."

The question also arises whether the sponsorship of bills was confined to a relatively small group of legislators or was broadly based. If a small group dominated then the ratio of sponsors-to-bills introduced would be low. An analysis of the sponsorship of the bills shows a wide distribution with no small group dominating, except in 1871. In 1871 three legislators sponsored one-third of the legislation concerning moneyed institutions. These legislators, William Tweed (5 bills), Martin Nachtmann (3 bills), and James Pierce (3 bills), were all New Yorkers and prominent members of the Tammany Ring. 1871 was the apex of Tammany power.

The fact that 1871 was the peak year in the number of bills introduced and that this was also the one year of significant concentration of political sponsorship suggests that the quest for trust company charters reached a "goldrush" fever in 1871.

Some of this fever came through on the face of the legislation. The above cited Martin Nachtmann introduced a bill concerning City Loan and Trust Company. The bill was referred to the Committee on Banks--of which Nachtmann was a member, and Nachtmann voted for the bill (naturally) when it reached the Assembly floor. Martin Nachtmann was

TABLE 2:7

Number of Legislators
Introducing Bills

	Number of Legislators Introducing:					Total No. of Legislators Introducing Bills	No. of Bills Introduced	Ratio Sponsors/Bill Introduced
	5 Bills	4 Bills	3 Bills	2 Bills	1 Bill			
1870	0	0	0	1	15	16	17	94%
1871	1	0	2	5	12	20	33	59
1872	0	0	0	4	14	18	22	81
1873	0	0	0	2	17	19	21	90

Source: Same as Table 2:1

also Vice President of City Loan and Trust Company.[6]

Up-state legislators occasionally got into the act also. George Banker introduced legislation to incorporate the National Security Trust Company. Banker was also a corporator of the company. So too were three of his fellow Assemblymen--Isiah Fuller, Mortimer Wade, and Webster Wagner. All were from the Schnectady area. Banker and Fuller were Democrats, Wade and Wagner Republicans.

The Standing Committee. A bill was referred to a standing committee at the time it was introduced into the first house or received by the second house for concurrence. Accordingly each bill went to at least one and usually two committees. Numerous standing committees, each covering a special topic, were set up in both houses during the first days of each legislative session. Committee members were expected to be especially knowledgeable in the problems concerning legislation assigned to their committee and hence able to authoritatively guide the legislature. The political balance of each committee reflected the dominant party in each house.

---

[6]New York State, Assembly Bill, 1871, Number 752. Governor Hoffman vetoed the bill.

The standing committee is of interest because it was the first critical filter through which a trust company bill had to pass. As Table 2:8 indicates, a large number of companies did not pass the filter.

TABLE 2:8

Response of Standing Committee to Legislation on Trust Companies

Year	Number of Bills Introduced	Number Failing to Pass Committee	Bills Combined	Bills Going to Committee of Whole
1870	17	3	0	14
1871	33	3	1	29
1872	22	6	1	15
1873	21	2	3	16
Total	93	14	5	74

Source: Same as Table 2:1.

The standing committees killed 14 of the 93 bills, or 15%, introduced during the 1870-3 period: ranging from a high of 27% in 1872 to a low of 9% in 1871--the peak year for the introduction of such legislation. The column entitled "Bills Combined" refers to cases where identical bills were introduced in both houses. In the event one of the two bills passed both houses, the second bill disappeared from the docket. In substance this disappearance was not a defeat of the bill. The table accordingly distinguishes between such bills and those genuinely killed by committees.

The last column shows the number of bills which actually survived the committee filter and passed to the beginning of the second filter--the legislative vote.

At this point, two questions are of interest: (1) What governed the allocation of bills introduced to specific committees, and (2) what were the standards used by the committees in passing judgment on the bills?

Technically, bills were allocated to a committee by vote of the house. In practice this was probably a perfunctory matter based on the recommendation of the bill's sponsor. One might assume that all bills concerned with chartering trust companies would be allocated to the Committee on Banks. But such was not the case. The bills concerning trust companies were actually allocated among several committees. Why?

First, Article 8, Section 1 of the New York State Constitution provided that:

> Corporations shall not be created by special act, except for municipal purposes, and in cases where, in the judgement of the Legislature, the objectives of the corporation cannot be attained under general laws.

Governor John T. Hoffman, in his Annual Message of January 3, 1871, referring to this section, encouraged the Legislature not to pass so many special charters:

TABLE 2:9

Allocation of Bills
To Standing Committees

	Number Bills Considered	Committee					
		Banks	Judiciary	Insurance	Affairs of Cities	Municipal Affairs	Commerce & Navigation
Senate:							
1870	14	8	2	1	-	2	1
1871	31	14	6	2	-	8	1
1872	17	16	0	1	-	0	0
1873	16	10	5	0	-	0	1
Assembly:							
1870	14	5	0	2	3	1	3
1871	30	15	12	0	3	0	0
1872	17	10	7	0	0	0	0
1873	19	13	4	1	1	0	0

Source: Same as Table 2:1.

> Of late years /said Hoffman/ there has been a a disposition to overlook the strict intent of this limitation upon legislative power.[7]

Governor John Dix, in the Annual Message of January 6, 1873, returned even more forcefully to the same theme, stating:

> The legislature, in yielding to such applications, under a natural desire on the part of the members to gratify the wishes of their constituents, has disregarded a restriction, which was intended by the constitution as a restraint upon unnecessary legislation. Your attention is respectfully and earnestly invoked to this subject, with the assurance that much of your valuable time may be saved, and that you may avoid the hardship of transacting public business at your own expense.[8]

The subject of private legislation was actually a heated political issue at the time. Both Hoffman and Dix were mirroring a position taken by political reformers that private legislation was essentially inefficient, that it took the legislators attention and time

---

[7] New York State, Assembly Documents, 1871, Number 2. Hoffman was apparently referring to special legislation for corporations in general. Article 8, Section 4 actually contains a more explicit injunction against chartering banks:

> The Legislature shall have no power to pass any act granting any special charter for banking purposes; but corporations or associations may be formed for such purposes under general laws.

[8] New York State, Assembly Documents, 1873, Number 2.

away from more pressing and socially important public legislation.[9]

That private legislation gave rise to cause for corrupting legislators also occurred to the political reformers (and doubtless also to legislators) but the direction of the reformers here was aimed more at private legislation regarding public works (e.g., the building of a bridge in Erie County) than at the chartering of corporations.

In light of the remarks by the Governors, the explicit constitutional provision, and the presence of the General Act for Banking of 1838, it is possible that some sponsors of trust company legislation had their bills referred to such committees as Municipal Affairs or Judiciary in an effort to draw a veil over the propriety of another special charter.

The referral of bills to committees other than the Committee on Banks therefore could have been, in part, a parliamentary gambit.

---

[9] New York City Council of Political Reform--Law Committee, Proposed Amendments to the Constitution of the State of New York, Their History, Nature and Advantages. September 1, 1874. Interestingly, one of the reformers (Henry J. Scudder) signing this document had been a corporator of Real Estate Trust Company, which received a special charter in 1871.

Secondly, most of the trust companies seeking charters had multiple functions. The names of the companies are indicative of this: ...Collateral Loan and Deposit, ...Loan and Indemnity, ...Warehouse, Trust and Loan, ... Loan and Trust, ...Trust and Banking, ...Life Policy, Loan and Trust, ...Trust Loan and Investment, ...Mortgage and Trust, *et cetera*. Within twenty years the basic economic homogeneity of these companies would be well understood. But in the early 1870's it was not.

That the bills incorporating these companies were referred to so wide a range of committees may be indicative of a confusion or uncertainty among the legislators about the nature of the creature they were dealing with.

And thirdly, some of the bills may have been referred to committees other than the Committee on Banking simply to distribute the work-load.

What standards did the committees use to pass or fail bills concerning trust companies? This question will be considered in detail in the next section, along with the standards used by the Committee of the Whole. But briefly, the standing committees rejected bills for five apparent causes:

1. The charter provided for an interest rate in excess of usurious levels.

2. The "powers" section of the charter was too general, or vague, or non-existent.
3. Stipulated capital levels were too low.
4. The people listed as corporators were either unknown to the committeemen or known to be deficient in character.

It would be a mistake, however, to generalize these standards. They were not applied uniformly. There were numerous exceptions, from year-to-year, from committee-to-committee and within specific years and committees.

This lack of uniform application of standards serves as additional evidence that the formation of these trust companies was in a turbulent phase, exploding from a tranquil to a high level of activity, and that the machinery of the state had not yet developed a standard and smooth means of dealing with the movement.

Committees of the Whole. A bill passing the standing committee arrived at the floor of the house. The house would resolve itself into a Committee of the Whole to consider the bill. The house would then vote on the bill. The procedure was the same for both the Assembly or the Senate.

In the previous section, it was noted that the standing committees killed about 15% of the bills introduced in the legislature during the 1870-3 period. The Committees of the Whole, the second critical legislative filter for a prospective trust company killed about 8%.

TABLE 2:10

Response of Committees of Whole to Legislation on Trust Companies

Year	Surviving Standing Committee	Failing on Floor: Committee of Whole	Failing on Floor: By Vote	Surviving House Floor
1870	14	2	0	12
1871	29	1	0	28
1872	15	2	1	12
1873	16	2	0	14
Total	74	7	1	66

Source: Same as Table 2:1.

As Table 2:10 notes, the Committees of the Whole (the Assembly and Senate combined), killed 8 of the 74 bills coming under their preview. Seven of the bills were killed without a vote and only one was killed by vote. A bill could be killed without a vote simply by parliamentary procedures which resulted in the bill losing place on the docket. The Assembly Speaker, Senate President and majority party leaders were the main forces determining priority of bills.

Those bills which were killed in this manner probably lacked adept sponsorship, or possibly the sponsors sacrificed this legislation to secure the passage of more favored bills.

The Committee of the Whole, however, could do more than just pass or kill a bill. They could also amend a bill, which was done quite frequently. The Committee of the Whole, accordingly, could influence the chartering of a trust company in two ways: (1) by passing or killing the bills, or (2) by amending the bills.

Two issues are worth pursuing at this point: (1) what is to be learned from the actual voting record on the charters and (2) what standards did the legislature use when considering charter legislation?

Tables 2:11 A-D show the voting record on moneyed institution charters for the years 1870, 1871, 1872, and 1873. In the Senate, 16 votes were needed to pass legislation and in the Assembly, 64.[10]

The first observation to be made on the above tables is that only in one case (N.Y. Loan and Real Estate--1872) was a charter defeated by a vote. Once a bill reached the voting stage, chances were very high that it would pass.

---

[10]The voting records here listed are the primary votes. Votes in the house of introduction in response to amendments made by the other house are not included in the tables.

TABLE 2:11:A

Voting Record
1870

Company	House	Date	Republican Yes	Republican No	Republican Not Voting	Democrat Yes	Democrat No	Democrat Not Voting	Total Yes	Total No	Total Not Voting
American Trust	S	4/23	9	0	5	8	1	9	17	1	14
Company	A	4/26	28	0	28	49	0	23	77	0	51
Bankers`Life	S	4/15	9	0	5	12	0	6	21	0	11
	A	4/23	19	18	19	49	9	14	68	27	33
Commercial	A	4/18	37	0	19	50	0	22	87	0	41
Credit	S	4/25	7	1	6	13	1	4	20	2	10
Corn Exchange	A	4/25	29	5	22	49	0	23	78	5	45
Warehouse	S	4/26	6	0	8	11	0	7	17	0	15
Cosmos Life	A	4/16	(Vote Not Recorded, but bill passed)								
	S[1]	4/25	3	7	4	10	3	5	13	10	9
	S[2]	4/26	8	1	5	12	0	6	20	1	11
Fire Proof	S	2/18	11	2	1	8	3	7	19	5	8
Warehouse	A	3/29	35	1	20	39	0	33	74	1	53
National	S	3/28	11	0	3	9	1	8	20	1	11
Trust	A	4/18	(Vote Not Recorded, but bill passed)								
N.Y. Loan &	S	4/25	8	4	2	9	2	7	17	6	9
Improvement	A	4/26	36	0	20	54	0	18	90	0	38
N.Y. Loan &	A	4/18	29	0	27	54	0	18	83	0	45
Indemnity	S										
N.Y. Mutual	A	4/ 9	38	0	18	45	0	27	83	0	45
Loan	S	4/25	10	0	4	10	1	7	20	1	11
N.Y. State	A	4/22	35	0	21	50	0	22	85	0	43
Loan	S	4/25	10	1	3	8	1	9	18	2	12
Union	A	4/ 8	10	0	4	8	0	10	18	0	14
Trust	A	4/18	25	0	31	48	0	24	73	0	55

Source: Same as Table 2:1.

TABLE 2:11:B

Voting Record
1871

Company	House	Date	Republican Yes	Republican No	Republican Not Voting	Democrat Yes	Democrat No	Democrat Not Voting	Total Yes	Total No	Total Not Voting
American Mortgage	S	4/ 7	5	7	2	14	0	3	19	7	5
	A	4/18	39	0	24	52	0	13	91	0	37
American Trust	S	3/21	4	1	9	13	0	4	17	1	13
	A	4/18	36	0	27	44	0	21	80	0	48
Anglo-American Trust	A	3/16	35	2	26	51	1	13	86	3	39
	S	4/13	4	9	1	13	1	3	17	10	4
Bankers Loan & Trust	A	4/ 9	44	0	19	40	0	25	84	0	44
	S	4/13	8	3	3	12	0	5	10	3	8
City Loan & Trust	A	4/ 4	33	1	29	56	0	9	89	1	38
	S	4/19	7	2	5	15	0	2	22	2	7
City Trust	S	3/28	10	0	4	11	0	6	21	0	10
	A	4/ 8	39	0	24	39	0	26	78	0	50
Commercial Trust	A	4/19	42	0	21	46	0	19	88	0	40
	S	4/21	7	4	3	12	0	5	19	4	8
Commercial Warehouse	A	4/ 3	33	0	30	54	0	11	87	0	41
	S	4/ 4	6	7	1	13	0	4	19	7	5
Continental Loan	S	4/ 5	4	9	1	13	0	4	17	9	5
	A	4/19	46	0	17	43	0	22	89	0	39
Equitable Loan	S	3/17	6	4	4	11	2	4	17	6	8
	A	4/18	38	0	25	50	0	15	88	0	40
International Trust	A	4/12	39	0	24	48	0	17	87	0	41
	S	4/13	7	0	7	10	0	7	17	0	14
Island City Trust	A	4/ 7	35	0	28	54	0	11	89	0	39
	S	4/20	11	0	3	13	0	4	24	0	7
Knickerbocker Loan	A	3/27	39	0	24	47	0	18	86	0	42
	S	4/13	8	3	3	12	0	5	20	3	8
Manhattan Indemnity	S	4/12	5	7	2	12	0	5	17	7	7
	A	4/13	39	0	24	54	0	11	93	0	35
Manhattan Trust	A	4/ 4	31	0	32	43	0	22	74	0	54
	S		(Defeated in Senate Committee on Banking)								
Mutual Benefit	A	4/ 4	(Vote not recorded, but bill passed)								
	S	4/15	4	3	7	14	0	3	18	3	10
N.Y. Guaranty & Indemnity	S	3/16	12	0	2	8	1	8	20	1	10
	A	4/17	41	0	22	52	0	13	93	0	35
N.Y. Loan & Improvement	S	3/24	10	0	4	10	0	7	20	0	11
	A	4/ 8	43	0	20	48	0	17	91	0	37
N.Y. Loan & Indemnity	A	3/20	33	0	30	45	0	20	78	0	50
	S	4/11	13	0	1	8	0	9	21	0	10
N.Y. Real Estate Banking	A	3/23	38	0	25	58	0	7	96	0	32
	S	3/31	5	2	7	14	0	3	19	2	10
N.Y. State Loan	A	4/19	43	0	20	53	0	12	96	0	32
	S	4/20	10	1	3	11	0	6	21	1	9
Phoenix Trust	A	4/ 7	40	0	23	43	0	22	83	0	45
	S	4/20	8	2	4	15	0	2	23	2	6
Real Estate Trust	S	3/21	5	7	2	13	0	4	18	7	6
	A	4/ 8	37	2	24	50	0	15	87	1	39
Republic Like	A	4/12	32	0	31	48	0	17	80	0	48
	S	4/19	6	3	5	14	0	3	20	3	8
Security Deposit	S	4/ 6	8	1	5	13	0	4	21	1	9
	A	4/ 7	38	0	25	47	0	18	85	0	43
Traders Deposit	S	4/ 4	6	2	6	11	0	6	17	2	12
	A	4/17	43	0	20	46	0	19	89	0	39
U.S. Mortgage	S	4/12	9	4	1	10	0	7	19	4	8
	A	4/19	36	0	27	51	0	14	87	0	41

Source: Same as Table 2:1.

TABLE 2:11:C

Voting Record
1872

			Republican			Democrat			Total		
Company	House	Date	Yes	No	Not Voting	Yes	No	Not Voting	Yes	No	Not Voting
Bankers Life	A	4/25	60	5	34	14	0	17	74	5	51
	S	5/ 1	18	0	6	40	0	4	21	0	11
German American	S	4/23	14	3	7	2	0	6	16	3	13
	A	5/ 9	56	11	32	7	7	17	63	18	49
Manhattan Loan & Trust	S[1]	4/ 9	13	3	7	1	1	6	14	5	13
	S[2]	4/ 9	17	0	7	2	1	5	19	1	12
	A[1]	5/14	41	17	41	7	8	16	48	25	57
	A[2]	5/14	58	5	36	21	0	10	79	5	46
Mutual Trust	A	3/29	71	0	28	16	1	14	87	1	42
	S	4/ 5	13	0	11	4	0	4	17	0	15
National Trust	S	3/ 1	11	0	13	5	0	3	16	0	16
	A	5/ 9	52	8	39	18	2	11	70	10	50
N.Y. Bond Deposit	S	4/ 9	15	0	9	2	0	6	17	0	15
	A	5/ 4	68	1	30	14	0	17	82	1	47
N.Y. Deposit	A	4/24	71	8	20	19	2	10	90	10	30
	S	5/ 2	17	1	6	0	2	6	17	3	12
N.Y. Life	S	3/ 1	17	0	7	4	0	4	21	0	11
	A	5/10	62	2	33	16	1	14	78	5	47
N.Y. Loan & Improvement	S	4/ 9	17	0	7	2	1	5	19	1	12
	A	5/10	52	6	41	13	3	15	65	9	56
N.Y. Loan & Indemnity	S	5/ 9	16	0	8	3	0	5	19	0	13
	A	5/ 9	65	0	34	12	0	19	67	0	53
N.Y. Loan & Real Estate	A	4/25	38	25	36	13	3	15	51	28	51
N.Y. State Loan & Trust	A	5/ 8	57	2	40	14	1	16	71	3	56
	S		(Defeated in Senate Committee on Banking)								
Real Estate Trust	S	4/ 9	16	0	8	2	0	6	18	0	14
	A	5/14	53	13	33	20	1	10	73	14	43
U.S. Loan & Security	A	5/10	61	2	36	16	0	15	77	2	51
	S[1]	5/14	10	9	5	3	0	5	13	9	10
	S[2]	5/14	15	1	8	3	1	4	18	2	12

Source: Same as Table 2:1.

TABLE 2:11:D

Voting Record
1873

Company	House	Date	Republican Yes	Republican No	Republican Not Voting	Democrat Yes	Democrat No	Democrat Not Voting	Total Yes	Total No	Total Not Voting
Atlantic	S	4/22	13	2	9	4	1	3	17	3	12
Guaranty	A	5/29	45	6	40	26	1	10	71	7	50
Bankers	S	3/20	14	0	10	6	0	2	20	0	12
Life	A	4/25	72	0	19	26	0	11	98	0	30
Central	A	3/12	69	3	19	9	3	25	78	6	44
Trust	S[1]	4/30	9	8	7	3	4	1	12	12	8
	S[2]	5/20	14	1	9	3	1	4	17	2	13
Commercial	A	2/27	52	7	32	14	3	20	66	10	52
Warehouse	S	4/22	15	1	8	2	4	2	17	5	10
Fire Proof	A	5/28	49	10	32	16	6	15	65	15	45
Warehouse	S	5/29	17	0	7	3	0	5	20	0	12
Manhattan	S	5/26	15	1	8	2	0	6	17	1	14
Loan & Trust	A	5/27	54	8	29	18	7	12	72	14	41
Merchants	A	5/20	63	3	25	13	2	22	76	5	47
Loan	S	5/27	13	1	10	4	0	4	17	1	14
Mutual	A	4/17	70	0	21	16	0	21	86	0	42
Trust	S	4/21	13	0	11	4	0	4	17	0	15
N.Y. Loan	A[1]	3/12	45	31	15	8	20	9	53	51	24
& Security	A[2]	3/17	61	1	29	23	1	13	84	2	42
Co.	S[1]	4/ 4	13	7	4	2	3	3	15	10	7
	S[2]	4/15	15	3	7	3	2	3	17	5	10
N.Y. Mort-	S	5/ 9	13	1	10	4	1	3	17	2	13
gage	A	5/27	51	6	34	20	3	14	71	9	48
N.Y. Real	A	5/15	54	1	36	17	0	20	71	1	56
Estate &	S[1]	5/27	11	4	9	2	1	5	13	5	14
Guaranty	S[2]	5/29	15	0	9	4	0	4	19	0	13
Real Estate	S	5/ 9	14	0	10	4	1	3	18	1	13
Trust	A	5/27	52	4	35	23	2	12	75	6	47
Union Trust	S	4/11	15	0	9	2	0	6	17	0	15
	A	5/29	68	0	23	22	1	14	90	1	37
U.S. Mort-	S[1]	5/ 8	7	8	9	3	2	3	10	10	12
gage	S[2]	5/27	14	2	8	4	1	3	18	3	11
	A	5/29	60	2	29	20	1	16	80	3	45

Source: Same as Table 2:1.

The second is that there were very few negative votes. Apparently a negative note on legislation that was certain to pass could be a political liability. An abstention was a somewhat milder liability. Accordingly, in 1870 and 1871, when the Democrats were in power, the Republicans tended to contribute a high portion of the "Not Voting" population, and the Democrats in 1872 and 1873 when the Republicans were in power.

The third factor of note is that in several cases, legislation failed but was later reintroduced. This happened once in 1870, three times in 1872 and five times in 1873. In these cases individuals probably voted against a bill to gain political leverage, then allowed the vote to be reconsidered and, after the appropriate political agreements, voted for the bill.

The significance of this is easily overlooked. If a piece of legislation was utterly inconsequential, there was no point in isolating that bill for political maneuvering. A bill would be selected for which the sponsors would be willing to make a real sacrifice to secure passage. If this was so, then the fact that the instances in which this gambit occurred was higher in 1873 than 1872, and higher in 1872 than the previous two years suggests that special charters for trust companies became more cherished as the 1870-3 period wore on. This suggestion is strengthened by another aspect of the legislative process. It was previously indicated that some bills were introduced both in the Assembly and the Senate. This happened once in 1871, twice in 1872 and three times in 1873. The implication is that as the 1870-3 period evolved, special charters became more valuable because, among other things, opposition became more determined and consequently sponsors of the bills developed more sophisticated parliamentary techniques.

The standards used by the legislature as a whole to kill or amend the bills being considered included the standards briefly mentioned in the previous section (the standards used by the standing committees) as well as the standards of the committees of the whole.

The records of the standing committees were kept in bill jackets. Bill jackets were packets of information on bills before a committee. A bill jacket would include such information as the original bill, amendments originating in the committee, attorney's opinions, letters of support and opposition and biographical data on the corporators. Unfortunately, all bill jackets from the period have been lost.[11]

The proceedings of the committees of the whole were preserved and printed as the Journals of the Assembly and Senate. These Journals, however, were basically epitomes of the legislative process and seldom contained any of the actual debate. The Journal would indicate that a bill was amended, but say nothing about why the amendment was made.

The question of standards of evaluation, however, can be approached through the examination of the bill content. In several cases, bills which were defeated at the standing committee or committee of the whole level, were printed and hence available for examination. Moreover, the text of the bills which ultimately became law can be compared with the text of the bills as first printed. Any differences between the two would reflect amendments which the legislators thought important enough to put in.

Among the standards which appear to govern the success or failure of a bill in the legislature were:

First, in some instances the charter provided for negotiable interest rates or interest rates above the statutory maximum. In 1870, the charter of the proposed Depositors Loan Institution authorized an interest rate of

---

[11]The earliest bill jackets known to survive are dated 1905.

1½% per month, and that of New York Collateral Loan and Deposit authorized 2% per month.[12] Both of these charters were killed in the standing committee stage.

The subject of usury was an explosive political issue in New York State at this time and remained so throughout most of the century. In 1870, the maximum statutory annual interest rate was increased from 6% to 7%. Even so the New York rate was toward the low end of the range on a national scale (five states had a 6% maximum, two, including New York, 7% and the rest 8% or above--with 15 having no statutory maximum at all). New York was the only state to carry a prison sentence for violation of usury laws.[13] Although the subject of usury will come up again, at this point it is sufficient to point out that legislators were likely to be wary about passing charters authorizing rates above statutory usury levels.

Second, much of the legislation was poorly and hastily drawn. In particular the powers of the corporation were not spelled out clearly. In 1871 the New York Loan, Trust, Warehouse and Deposit Company simply asked for the powers

---

[12] New York State, Assembly Bills, 1870, Number 898, and Senate Bills, 1870, Number 298.

[13] Rand McNally's Bankers Directory--1876. "Interest Laws of the States," 32.

of "any loan, trust, warehouse or deposit company," without going into detail.[14] The company's powers were broad but vague and quite possibly the Assembly Committee of the Judiciary, which reviewed the bill, had no idea what such powers might be--and if this were the case it would be entirely understandable.

Third, the amount of capital required by charter to commence business varied widely but those companies with lower capital requirements generally fared less well at the hands of the Legislature or Governor. Charters normally specified three capital figures, one the maximum capital, secondly, the amount of capital which had to be subscribed before operations could commence and thirdly, the amount of capital which actually had to be paid in before operations could commence. In 1873 the Assembly rejected the charter of the New York State Loan and Guaranty Company, which had a maximum capital provision of $100,000, a subscription minimum of $100,000, but a paid-in requirement of only $10,000.[15]

Fourth, it is possible that the standing committees screened some companies on the basis of the people involved

---

[14] New York State, Assembly Bills, 1871, Number 538.

[15] Ibid., Number 241.

as corporators. The people might be largely unknown to the committeemen, or they might be too well known. In 1870, the New York Real Estate Banking Company, listed 17 corporators, of whom 11, or 63% were directly identified with New York City political or judicial offices. The 63% figure is over six times the average of 10% for the political occupation category of the corporators of the 46 companies seeking charters in the 1870-3 period, and far-and-away the highest concentration of politicians.

Quite possibly the Senate Committee on Banking, which killed the New York Real Estate charter, was suspicious of the preference which could result from having a company with nine of its corporators employed in a judicial system (including three as judges and two as tax collectors) when the company in the normal course of business often would be a party within that judicial system. Moreover, the charter had the unusual proviso of permitting the company to engage in business dealings with its directors and officers. Senator William M. Tweed introduced the bill.

The 1870 Senate Committee on Banking, with three members, was controlled by the Democrats, but both Democrats, William Graham (banker) and Jarvis Lord (farmer) were upstaters (as was Republican Norris Winslow--banker) and consequently less involved in the designs of the Tammany adherents.

Fifth, it is possible that committees also screened proposed charters in light of challenges made by competitor companies. Although the bill jackets for this period have been lost, existing and operating companies are known to have been sensitive to the types of charters under consideration in Albany and to have voiced their opinion. What is not known is how pervasive or persuasive was this class of opposition. But it did exist.

Sixth, the legislature seemed to have been concerned about the concentration of economic power which might develop with the trust companies. In 1872, National Trust Company sought an amendment to its charter which would expand the possible list of investments from U.S. Government stocks (i.e., bonds) to include bonds of any state, bonds of incorporated cities and counties in New York and bonds and stocks of interest and dividend paying corporations. The legislature granted as much (except "any state" was amended to "this State") but added a proviso that no investment could exceed $50,000 in any one company. The legislature also added a constraint that National could hold no more than $15,000,000 in trust accounts.[16]

Seventh, the legislature became increasingly uneasy over the "unregulated" aspect of the trust company movement. This uneasiness is reflected in the trend of "regulatory" provisions which were included in the charters submitted for approval.

TABLE 2:12

Trend in "Regulatory" Provisions

Year	Number of Companies Seeking Charter	Number of Charters with "Regulatory" Provisions	%
1870	11	3	27%
1871	20	6	30
1872	7	3	43
1873	9	6	67

Source: Same as Table 2:2.

The term "regulatory" is in quotes because the provisions usually called only for an annual reporting to some authority. That authority varied among the New York Supreme Court, the State Comptroller, and the Superintendents of Banking and Insurance. Both the fact that many charters contained no provision for regulation and those that did

16 New York State, Laws, 1872, Chapter 725 and Senate Bills, 1872, Number 48.

would be regulated by widely different authorities, with varying degrees of discretion, indicates that the trust company movement was still in a very young stage. The regulatory structures which accompany a mature financial intermediary were not yet present.

The legislature's concern in this regard is evident in the 1873 chartering of Atlantic Guaranty and Trust. Atlantic's submitted charter contained no "regulatory" provision. But the Legislature added a provision to the effect that the affairs of Atlantic would be under the "general supervision" of the Superintendent of Banking "with the same power in relation thereto as he has over the banks of the State."[17]

Also in 1873, the bill for chartering New York Mortgage and Trust Company provided for the regulation of the company by the State Comptroller. The legislature amended this, however, to read "Superintendent of Banking," suggesting a concern on the legislature's behalf with the structural and executionary aspects of regulation.[18]

On both the standing committee and committees of the

---

[17] Ibid., 1873, Chapter 783 and 1873, Number 293.

[18] Ibid., Chapter 629 and Assembly Bills, 1873, Number 840.

whole levels there were numerous exceptions to the application of these standards. Even so, the Legislature had done a rather remarkable job. Confronted in 1870 with a sudden rise in legislative activity concerning trust companies, the Legislature gradually gained some understanding of the issues involved. The legislative filter for aspiring trust companies was much more discriminating in 1873 than it had been in 1870.

The Governors (Hoffman and Dix). The third and final legislative obstacle through which legislation had to pass was the Governor's office. The Governor could veto or sign a bill. As Table 2:13 indicates, the Governors were a formidable obstacle, vetoing about 35% of the bills reaching their desks.

TABLE 2:13

Executive Action on N.Y.C.
Trust Company Legislation

Year	Number of Bills Surviving House Floor	Bills Vetoed by Governor	Bills Becoming Law
1870	12	3	9
1871	28	16	12
1872	12	1	11
1873	14	2	12
Total	66	23	43

Source: Same as Table 2:1.

John T. Hoffman, Governor from 1869-1872, was a Democrat. His political experience was confined to New York City, where he had been elected City Recorder in 1860 and Mayor in 1866. His political loyalty was closely tied to Boss Tweed and the Tammany forces. One historian describes Hoffman as Tweed's "henchman."[19]

As the above table indicates, Hoffman vetoed 25% of the bills reaching his desk in 1870 and 57% in 1871. 1871 was, again, the year of the "gold rush." Hoffman's determined refusal to sign such legislation was one primary reason why legislative activity peaked in 1871 and declined thereafter.

Hoffman's reasons for vetoeing these bills are not always clear. More often than not, bills would be vetoed with no accompanying explanation.

Although Hoffman probably sympathized with all the critical standards developed in the Legislature (he may even have told the Legislature that no bills would pass his desk which did not meet these standards), two standards stand out.

First, several charters which reached his desk would have permitted the companies to charge interest rates

---

[19] Ellis, op. cit., 333.

above the legal maximum. The 1870 charters of Commercial Credit Guaranty and Corn Exchange Warehouse were vetoed on this basis.[20]

Secondly, objection was raised to the "multiple function" aspect of the charters. The charters normally requested a wide range of functions. Often also the language of the charter was vague and an enterprising banker could have found statutory grounds to move in virtually any direction profit was to be had.

The Governor's position in this regard bears influence of the State Banking Department. For many years the primary regulatory trend had been toward strengthening the safety of deposits by narrowing the functions of the bank or savings bank. Indeed, it was precisely this trend that had created the fertile ground for the rise of a new financial intermediary.

In 1871, Hoffman vetoed a bill to charter the Knickerbocker Loan and Trust Company. The bill reached his desk on April 3. On April 4, he returned a strongly worded veto message to the Legislature. Objecting to (and listing) the multiple functions requested by the charter, Hoffman said:

---

[20] Messages, op. cit., 196, 215.

> The incorporation of companies for any single object, not forbidden by law and in accordance with public policy, is well enough, but I respectfully submit that it is against public policy to confer upon any company the power and privileges granted by the bill herewith returned.

The Governor went on to generalize:

> My attention has been called to the fact that, at the last session, I approved a bill /the New York State Loan and Trust Company/, the provisions of which were similar to those now objected to. It was an error on my part, committed through inadvertance, and perhaps inexcusable. It would certainly be inexcusable to repeat it. The public interests demand that such legislation should be stopped, whatever precedents there may be for it.[21]

Ten days later (April 14) Hoffman signed a bill incorporating the Real Estate Trust Company; which charter permitted almost exactly the same functions denied to Knickerbocker Trust, except Real Estate Trust had no limit on interest rates and Knickerbocker did. The Real Estate Trust bill was sponsored by Senator William M. Tweed of New York City. In fact, of the twelve trust company bills signed by Hoffman in 1871, four were introduced by Tweed.

John A. Dix, a Republican, was Governor from 1873-1875. Dix was 75 years old in 1873, with a varied and quasi-notable record. He had been active in the War of

---

21 Ibid., 305-6. Italics mine. Also in: Assembly Journal, 1871, 1102-3.

1812 (as an ensign) and in the Civil War (as a general). At other times he served as a New York Canal Commissioner, State Assemblyman, Secretary of State (New York), U.S. Senator, Postmaster of the City of New York, U.S. Minister to France, President of the Union Pacific Railroad Company, U.S. Secretary of the Treasury (under Buchanan, 52 days). To his contemporaries he was also known for his statement: "If any one attempts to haul down the American flag, shoot him on the spot!" Dix had a learned bent too, being classified by one contemporary as "an extremely elegant classical scholar."[22]

Dix vetoed only two of the fourteen bills concerning trust companies which reached his desk. One of these (Merchants Loan) was vetoed on the grounds that the charter allowed the company to charge a usurious interest rate.[23] In the other case, the United States Mortgage Company requested an amendment to its charter to allow trustees and corporations to invest in bonds issued by the company. Dix vetoed the bill on the grounds that the savings banks were corporations and hence "they would be released from the most essential restrictions in regard to

---

[22] Life Sketches, op. cit., 7-15.

[23] Messages, op. cit., 588.

their investments."[24] Exactly what the "most essential restrictions" were is not spelled out, but presumably the Governor referred to the laws which confined savings bank investments to U.S., state and political subdivision bonds.

Although Dix may have been, and probably was, concerned with the safety of savings bank investment, the veto had some interesting undercurrents. U.S. Mortgage was a mortgage banker. Mortgages were bought from around the country and bonds, backed by the mortgages, would be sold by the company. The company would make its money on the geographical rate spread between the West and the East, by the credit quality rate spread between unknown names and their name and by the liquidity rate spread between essentially unmarketable mortgages and marketable bonds. If the savings bank had been able to buy these bonds then they would in effect have been using New York savings to finance mortgages in other states. Also savings banks were prime purchasers of New York State and political subdivision bonds. No state official was anxious to see this source of funds diverted to other investments; moreover there

---

[24] Ibid., 580.

has always existed an isolationist bias.

As Table 2:5 indicated, of the 93 bills concerning trust companies introduced in the 1870-3 period, only 43 became law. The legislative process was a critical and on balance wholesome filter. The Legislature and Governors did turn aside weaker companies and encourage charter restrictions which promoted sound banking. The companies which emerged from this early wave of formations were solid institutions and afforded a good base of prosperity and public acceptance for the trust company movement.

Economic Functions of the Trust Companies

Financial intermediaries are usually differentiated one from another by their characteristic economic functions. Fortunately, the texts of the bills to incorporate included an enabling section or sections listing the functions which the companies wanted to perform. Although the language of the bills was often vague, an analysis of the appropriate sections yields an understanding of which functions were common and which less frequent.

Tables 2:14:A-D (which were summarized in Table 1:2) set forth as closely as can be determined the functions

TABLE 2:14:A

Charter Provisions for Corporate Powers
1870

Company	Powers: Mortgage	Mercantile	Pawning	Guaranty	Deposit	Lending on Collateral	Personal Trust	Corporate Trust	Warehouse	Insurance	Investments	Agency	Borrowing	Branches
Bankers Life & Trust					X	X	X	X		X	X			
Commercial Credit				X	X	X						X	X	
Corn Exchange				X		X			X			X	X	
Depositors Loan			X			X								
Mercantile Loan (1)						X			X	X			X	
N.Y. Collateral Loan			X		X	X			X		X			
N.Y. Loan & Improvement				X	X	X					X	X		X
N.Y. Loan & Indemnity				X	X	X			X			X		
N.Y. Mutual Loan			X			X								
N.Y. Real Estate Bank	X				X	X							X	
N.Y. State Loan & Trust		X		X	X	X			X			X		
Total 11	1	1	3	5	7	11	1	1	5	2	3	5	4	1

(1) Introduced as Fire Proof Warehouse

Source: Same as Table 1:2

TABLE 2:14:B

Charter Provisions for Corporate Powers
1873

Company	Powers													
	Mortgage	Mercantile	Pawning	Guaranty	Deposit	Lending on Collateral	Personal Trust	Corporate Trust	Warehouse	Insurance	Investments	Agency	Borrowing	Branches
American Mortgage & Trust	X				X	X	X	X			X		X	
Anglo-Am. Loan & Trust		X		X	X	X			X			X		X
Continental Loan & Trust	X	X			X	X			X			X		X
Equitable Loan & Trust		X		X	X	X			X			X		
International Trust		X		X	X	X					X	X		
Island City Loan & Trust				X	X	X					X			
Knickerbocker Trsut		X		X	X	X			X			X		
Manhattan Indemnity & Loan				X	X	X			X		X	X		
Manhattan Trust		X		X	X	X	X	X	X			X		
Metropolitan Loan & Trust		X		X	X	X		X	X		X	X		
Mutual Benefit Life Policy				X	X	X	X	X		X		X		X
N.Y. City Life Policy				X	X	X	X	X		X		X		X
N.Y. Loan, Trust, Warehouse	X	X		X	X	X	X	X	X	X	X	X	X	X
N.Y. Real Estate Bank					X	X					X	X	X	
Phoenix Trust					X	X	X	X						
Real Estate Trust Co.	X			X	X	X					X	X		
Republic Life & Trust					X	X	X	X		X	X		X	
Security Deposit						X			X					
Traders Deposit					X	X							X	
U.S. Mortgage	X				X	X							X	
Total 20	5	8	0	12	19	20	7	8	4	9	13	13	6	5

Source: Same as Table 1:2.

TABLE 2:14:C

Charter Provisions for Corporate Powers
1872

Company		Powers													
		Mortgate	Mercantile	Pawning	Guaranty	Deposit	Lending on Collateral	Personal Trust	Corporate Trust	Warehouse	Insurance	Investments	Agency	Borrowing	Branches
German-American Loan & Mortgage		X			X	X	X							X	
Manhattan Loan & Trust		X			X	X	X		X	X		X	X		
Mutual Trust Institution		X				X	X	X	X			X			
N.Y. Deposit & Loan Co.				X		X	X			X		X	X		
N.Y. Loan & Real Estate		X			X	X	X						X		
N.Y. Loan & Security				X	X		X			X			X		
U.S. Loan and Security		X				X	X				X				
Total	7	5	0	2	4	6	7	1	2	3	1	3	4	1	0

Source: Same as Table 1:2.

TABLE 2:14:D

Charter Provisions for Corporate Powers
1873

Company		Mortgage	Mercantile	Pawning	Guaranty	Deposit	Lending on Collateral	Personal Trust	Corporate Trust	Warehouse	Insurance	Investments	Agency	Borrowing	Branches
		Powers													
Atlantic Guaranty & Trust					X		X						X	X	
Central Trust		X				X	X	X	X			X			
International Trust Loan		X	X		X	X	X			X			X		X
Manhattan Loan & Trust		X			X	X	X		X	X		X	X		
Merchants Loan		X	X			X	X		X	X			X	X	
N.Y. Loan & Security					X	X	X			X			X		
N.Y. Mortgage & Trust		X				X	X	X	X					X	X
N.Y. Real Estate & Guaranty		X			X	X	X					X			
N.Y. State Loan & Guaranty		X	X		X		X								X
Total	11	7	3	0	6	7	9	2	4	4	0	3	5	3	3

Source: Same as Table 1:2.

or powers sought by companies in the 1870-3 period.[25]

Some of the powers listed in Tables 2:14:A-D play largely ancillary or supportive roles. The ability to borrow, to branch (!), investment authorizations (in effect, categories of permitted investments), agency functions (e.g., managing real estate property) are included in this class of powers.

The "Mercantile" proviso was a vague, grape-shot request, stating that the company had "power to grant, bargain, sell, buy or receive all kinds of property, real, personal, or mixed,..." The proviso was included in the successful charter of the New York State Loan and Trust Company in 1870 and in numerous charters thereafter, but none of the other charters containing the provision passed in Albany.

The Personal and Corporate Trust functions are listed for those companies which had specific and detailed charter provisions in this regard. They provided mainly for acting as a trustee under court appointment (including receivership) and as corporate registrar, transfer agent or

---

[25]The powers were deduced through analysis of the appropriate sections of the charters. The charters were printed as Assembly or Senate Bills, or in the event they passed, also as Laws, for the respective years.

trustee in indenture.

The central function running through all the charters, however, was lending on collateral. A few companies were purely pawning operations, a few stressed lending on life insurance collateral, a few aimed at lending on bulk merchandise collateral (warehousing), some on financial collateral (stocks and bonds) and some on real estate (mortgages).

The "Guaranty" proviso permitted corporations to guaranty the payment of debt of another party. It was an off-balance sheet transaction. The fee which the corporation charged the issuing company would theoretically be slightly less than the spread between the rate of interest paid by the issuer with the guaranty and what the rate would have been without the guaranty.

The data in Tables 2:14:A-D argues persuasively that the trust companies seeking charters at this early date were mainly interested in functions which were currently the mainstay of the existing commercial banking system. The one exception, of course, was note issue. The trust companies could not by law issue circulating notes, and none showed the slightest interest in doing so. In Chapters III and IV, the balance sheet is examined item by item to show the advantages of pursuing a banking business by the trust company route rather than the national or state bank route.

Economic Conditions and Trust Company Formations

Section III of this chapter pointed out that the legislature and political process served as a filter, whereby only 47% of the bills concerning trust companies which were introduced into the legislature in 1870-3 actually became law.

It further develops, however, that of the 21 bills that did become law and which authorized the incorporation of a trust company, only five were activated by July 1, 1874.[26]

---

[26]The "yes-no" designation is somewhat problematical. The list of companies was checked against the list of reporting trust companies as of July 1, 1874. By virtue of a law (Chapter 324) passed in 1874 all trust companies had to report annually (mid-year at this period) to the Superintendent of Banking. With regard to the July 1, 1874 list, Superintendent D. C. Ellis reported (December 31, 1874):

> In the endeavor to procure reports from this class of companies, it was discovered that many of them incorporated during the last few years have made no organization, while some others which have been organized have languished and failed in the end. It is believed that every company which is subject to the provisions of the law mentioned is embraced in the reports which are elsewhere given. (See: Assembly Documents, 1875, Number 5, 10).

Ellis's statement might have been too comprehensive; see

TABLE 2:15

Activation of Charters Passed in 1870-3 Period

Charter Granted	Company	Activated by July 1, 1874
1870	Bankers Life Insurance and Trust	No
	Fire Proof Warehouse	Yes
	N.Y. Loan & Improvement	No
	N.Y. Loan & Indemnity	Yes
	N.Y. State Loan and Trust	Yes
1871	American Mortgage and Trust	No
	Mutual Benefit Life Policy, Loan & Trust	No
	Real Estate Trust	Yes
	Security Deposit	No
	Traders Deposit	Yes
	U.S. Mortgage	No
1872	German-American Loan and Mortgage	No
	Mutual Trust Institute	No
	N.Y. Deposit and Loan	No
	U.S. Loan and Security	No
1873	Atlantic Guaranty and Trust	No
	Central Trust	No
	Manhattan Loan and Trust	No
	N.Y. Loan and Security	No
	N.Y. Mortgage and Trust	No
	N.Y. Real Estate and Guaranty	No

Source: Superintendent of Banking, Annual Report, 1874.

Several of the charters were activated later, sometimes

---

footnote 1:21.

The list of charters in the 1870-3 period was also checked against Trow's City Directory, 1874/5. Those companies reporting to the Superintendent or listed in Trow's were given a "yes" designation.

with a name change. Traders Deposit, for example, was activated in 1897 as American Deposit and Loan. Mutual Benefit Life Policy, Loan and Trust changed its name in 1884 to Commercial Trust (still a dorman charter) and again in 1900 to New York and London Trust, at which time the charter was activated. And several of the charters were never activated at all. Why the delay?

The answer appears to rest in the fact that the only major hurdle to activating a charter, once passed, was the capital subscription requirement. Each charter provided for a specific stated maximum capital level, and minimum subscription and paid-in levels before operations could begin. Although a company could begin operations as soon as the minimum constraints were met, in practice the corporators appear to have regarded the stated maximum as the normal objective. No companies are known to have operated longer than a brief period at minimum capital subscribed and paid-in levels.

As the years moved from 1870 to 1873, however, monetary conditions eased slightly, then tightened and the raising of capital progressively became more difficult and expensive. The volatility and tension of the New York money market during the 1870-3 period is shown in Table 2:16.[27]

TABLE 2:16

Monthly Average Call Loan Rates
New York Money Market

	1870	1871	1872	1873
March	6.0%	5.2%	20.7%	35.7%
June	5.0	4.2	5.5	6.0
September	6.0	5.2	12.2	200.0
December	6.5	21.2	30.6	14.8
Average	5.9%	8.9%	17.2%	61.6%

Source: Commercial and Financial Chronicle, 1870-3.

Both the levels of rates and the volatility of rates increased alarmingly during this period. The averaging process used in the above table actually buries the true extent of the variation. In the week ending September 19, 1873, the call loan rate reached a per annum value of 554%! The next week there was no rate at all, because money was not to be had at any price.

How could this be? There was a usury law (7% maximum)

---

[27]The basic data for this table was derived from the Commercial and Financial Chronicle. The Chronicle, in the first or second week of each year, reported a summary table of weekly call loan rates existing in the previous year. These rates represent charges by banks to stock brokers on a secured, demand basis. The rate could structurally vary with the quality of the collateral and whether or not the loan was denominated in gold or currency. See: Joseph Hedges, Commercial Banking and the Stock Market before 1863, John Hopkins Press, 1938, 44.

in New York State and prison penalties and fines for violation. The banks did not charge more than 7%, but they did add a per diem rate. The per diem rate, when imposed, varied from a low of 1/32 (11.4% annually) to a high on September 19, 1873, of 1½% (547% annually). Normally the per diem rate would appear in September or October and May as correspondent funds flowed to the interior in response to agricultural demands.

Specific economic and monetary conditions influenced the duration and intensity of these seasonal patterns. Accordingly, another way to measure the condition of the money market would be to count the number of weeks per diem rates were in force during the year.[28]

TABLE 2:17

Per Diem Rates

Year	Number Weeks Per Diem Rate Charged	Per Diem Rate Range (%)
1870	0	0 - 0
1871	6	1/32 -1/8
1872	15	1/32 -1/4
1873	31	1/32 -1½

Source: Commercial and Financial Chronicle, 1870-3.

[28] Ibid.

Table 2:17 confirms the supposition that the market conditions become progressively less favorable for raising capital as the period moved on.

The data correlates inversely with the experience of those trying to activate their newly granted charters. In the class of 1870, 3 of the 5 charters were activated. The corporators of these companies would have approached the market in a fairly tranquil period, June 1870, to June, 1871. In the class of 1871, two of the six companies successfully raised capital. These corporators would have approached the market in a still largely reasonable period of June 1871, to June 1872. But none of the 9 charters granted in 1872 or 1873 are known to have been activated by July 1, 1874.

The market conditions characterizing the Fall of 1873 abated very rapidly. In 1874, call loan rates declined markedly. In the Fall of 1874, the call loan rate was characteristically 3%; and only one week (the first in January) had a per diem charge. The primary reason for this, however, was a weak demand for funds. The shock of the panic had been so extreme that entrepreneurs were cautious to engage in capital utilizing projects. As late as August, 1875, a commentator in the Commercial and Financial Chronicle spoke of the prevailing "depression" and said:

> ...there is an ample supply of free or loanable capital to put in active motion all the industrial forces of our whole people. It awaits only those conditions which shall inspire its owners with confidence,...[29]

The difficulties in the capital market lingered considerably beyond the Panic of 1873 and prevailed to the end of the depression in 1878.

The capital market itself acted as a regulator of the trust company development in the 1870-3 period. Ironically, but quite logically, the economic prosperity which made it attractive in the first place to form a trust company also begat the conditions which would keep some companies from beginning operations.

The Founding of Central Trust Company--A Case Study

This chapter closes with a study of the founding of Central Trust Company. The study illuminates the actual process of organizing one of the most successful financial intermediaries in the nation. Central Trust was far and away the most important and successful company to emerge from the 1870-3 period.

---

[29] B. F. Nourse, "The Crises of 1837 and 1873," Commercial and Financial Chronicle, August 7, 1875, 122-6.

The bill to incorporate Central Trust was introduced in the Assembly on January 29, 1873, by Bradford Prince (R), a lawyer from Queens County.[30] The bill was referred to the Committee on the Judiciary, presumably because the text of the bill had reference to the Surrogate Court system.

Every aspect of the bill suggested that an organization of good tone and potential was in the making. The board of corporators was spectacular, including among its eighteen members prominent merchants William H. Aspinwall, William Turnbull and William T. Rosenkrans; lawyers George H. Carey, Anthony L. Foster, Edwin A. Post, N. Dana Wells, and Charles M. Wiley--all closely associated with Wall Street. Carey was also prominent in banking circles as the notary for two banks--the National Bank of Commerce and the Bank of America. Mortimer Fowler and Henry W. Gray, prominent brokers and investment bankers, were also listed. Topping the corporators was Robert Lenox Kennedy, president of the National Bank of Commerce--the largest (by far) bank in New York City. Only one (Henry W. Gray)

---

[30] The legislative history of Central Trust Company is found in the Senate Journal, 1873, 362, 690, 720, 774, and 1155; and in the Assembly Journal, 1873, 132-3, 161, 194, 372, 414, 442, 532, 2103, and 3136.

of the Central Trust corporators was known to have been a corporator of any other trust company chartered or proposed in this period. The text of the Central Trust bill emphasized personal and corporate trust functions, with provisions for receiving deposits, lending on collateral and investments. The bill closely followed the language of the charter of the Mutual Trust Institution, granted in 1872. Mutual Trust's charter, in turn, had closely followed the language of the Phoenix Trust Company charter--which failed to pass in 1871.

In spite of the standing of the corporators and even though the language of the charter had been tested legislatively, Central Trust's bill had a difficult time in Albany. When the bill reached the Assembly floor on March 12, Smith Weed (D), a Plattsburgh attorney, moved to have the bill recommitted to the Committee on Local and Special Laws to determine if there was a need for further companies of this kind. The motion, although defeated, was indicative of the toughening legislative environment for trust companies in 1873. On March 13 the bill passed the Assembly, 78 to 6 with 44 Not Voting. A year earlier Mutual Trust Institution had passed with a much wider margin.

In the Senate, the bill was referred (March 13) to

the Committee on Banks. On April 30, the Senate defeated the measure 12 to 12 with 8 Not Voting. The Senate then agreed to a motion by Townsend Cock (D) of Queens County to reconsider and table the bill.

The Senate's action on Cock's motion showed that the original defeat had elements of political maneuvering, but there was also real opposition. When the bill came up for reconsideration on May 27, only 4 of the 12 No's of the original vote switched to the Yes column. The bill passed the Senate 17 Yes, 2 No and 13 Not Voting. Governor Dix signed the bill on June 25, 1873.

Among the bill's original provisions that the legislators amended by addition or deletion were:[31]

1. Deleted a provision whereby the company was excluded from giving bond on court-ordered deposits.
2. Deleted a provision permitting the company to invest in bond issues of other states and political sub-divisions.
3. Deleted a provision for a staggered (three year cycle) trustee election system.
4. Added a provision requiring annual reporting to the State Superintendent of Banking.

---

[31] New York State, <u>Laws, 1873</u>, Chapter 832, and <u>Assembly Bills, 1873</u>, Number 61.

Given the great agonies of birth, one would assume the corporators would be quick to give their company the full measure of life sustaining capital--fully subscribed and fully paid-in. But this was not the case.

Two years passed before the company was formed in 1875. Why the delay? Probably because the money market was tight and capital was expensive. Central Trust's total proposed capitalization ($1,000,000) was not excessive, but the minimum subscription and paid-in level ($300,000) necessary to begin operations was on the high side compared with the other trust companies. The Panic of 1873 impaired business confidence enough to deter the company's formation. Moreover, the well-publicized troubles of Union Trust Company and National Trust Company, two of the important established trust companies, in the Fall of 1873, may have made investors wary of trust company charters in general.

The corporators, however, were still serious about the company. On April 30, 1874, the Governor signed an act giving the company an additional year in which to organize.[32]

Nothing is known to have been done toward furthering the organization in 1874. The corporators, however, knew

[32] New York State, Laws, 1874, Chapter 306.

the charter had value, particularly after the 1874 Fall elections which passed even more pointed and inflexible constitutional prohibitions against special charters for banks than had existed previously.

On March 30, 1875 Assemblyman Shiel introduced a bill to extend the time for organization for another year.[33] By then the principal corporators of Central Trust must have seriously considered the sale of the charter, because on April 12, the law firm of Foster and Thompson sent a brief message to William Allen Butler, saying:

> Our party accepts your offer of $10,000 for the Charter of Central Trust Company.[34]

William Allen Butler was the senior partner of the prestigious law firm of Butler, Stillman and Hubbard. Butler represented a group of eleven, including himself and Samuel D. Babock, A. A. Low, James B. Johnston, David Dows, Jonathan Thorne, Martin Bates, Adrian Iselin, J. M. Fiske, James P. Wallace and Isaac N. Phelps. Each of these indi-

---

[33] Ibid., 1875, Chapter 250.

[34] Data regarding Central Trust Company's founding is found in a manuscript collection entitled Central Trust Company--Miscellaneous Historical Papers. The collection is reposited under the jurisdiction of the Secretary of the Bank, Manufacturers Hanover Trust Company, New York City.

viduals was prominent in New York social and commercial circles.

Within the financial community, Samuel Babcock, who apparently led the group of eleven, was an enormously powerful figure. He was the founder in 1864 of the New York Guaranty and Indemnity Company (later, Guaranty Trust Company), the founder in 1874 of the United States Mortgage Company, and Chairman of the Finance Committee of Mutual Life Insurance Company.[35] Each of these companies, along with Central Trust, was quite successful and Babcock was actively identified with each through the balance of the nineteenth century.

Who the "our party" of the Foster and Thompson note might be is not known, but it probably refers to those of the company's corporators who led the way in 1873 (the entrepreneurs) and incurred real and opportunity costs in the process.

The Foster of Foster and Thompson was Anthony L. Foster, one of the corporators. Foster was probably one the "our party" group. Others most likely to be included were George H. Carey, Mortimer Fowler and William Rosenkrans, all of whom had been designated in the original

---

[35] Guaranty Trust Company, <u>One Hundred Years of Banking Service: 1839-1939</u>, New York, 1939, 20.

1873 Act as commissioners for the subscription of stock. The commissioners of subscription were in one of the most critical positions in the organizational process and probably included the primary entrepreneurs. That Carey and Fowler were closely identified with the selling party is reinforced by the fact that each served on the board of trustees only 24 days, from April 20 when the books of subscription were opened until May 13 when the minimum level of subscription had been achieved.

On April 13, the day after the Foster and Thompson note, the Butler eleven entered into an agreement:

> ...to subscribe in equal sums for the entire capital stock of the Central Trust Company of New York--being $1,000,000 divided into shares of $100 each...

The agreement contained an interesting additional provision:

> It is also understood that all the stockholders of the New York Guaranty and Indemnity Company are to have the privilege of taking from the undersigned an amount of stock of the Trust Company equal to one half the amount of stock standing in the names of such stockholders respectively on the books of the N.Y. Guaranty and Indemnity Company on the day when the subscriptions to the Trust Company shall be made by the undersigned, but this privilege is not assignable and must be availed at once.[36]

The relationship between Central Trust and New York Guaranty and Indemnity is quite revealing. At least five

---

[36] See footnote 2:34.

of the Butler eleven (Babcock, Johnston, Thorne, Bates and Wallace) were directors of New York Guaranty and Indemnity. Moreover, Wallace was president.

Why did this relationship exist? Indirect evidence suggests that the directors of N.Y. Guaranty and Indemnity considered their charter too restrictive to permit them to engage in the types of business they would like to pursue. Since the legislative route to a more liberal charter was all but closed (at least to their belief), the alternative was to purchase a dormant charter with broad powers--and this was Central Trust's.

Since the N.Y. Guaranty and Indemnity Company had 20,000 shares outstanding, and the Central Trust would have 10,000, the proviso of the Butler eleven that the subscription ratio would be one Central Trust for each two N.Y. Guaranty and Indemnity shares meant that the shareholders of N.Y. Guaranty and Indemnity would probably also control Central Trust.

The proviso was actually an ingenious mechanism for acquiring more liberal banking powers. The existing business of N.Y. Guaranty and Indemnity could be transferred to Central Trust, thus immediately making Central Trust a profitable operating company. The capital of the N.Y. Guaranty and Indemnity could be reduced (e.g., distributed) to the minimum operating level ($100,000), if necessary, to pay for the capital investment of the Butler eleven in Central Trust. And finally, the N.Y. Guaranty and Indemnity charter was a saleable item.

In practice this is pretty much what happened. On July 1, 1874, N.Y. Guaranty and Indemnity had assets of $4,285,000 and capital of $2,089,000. The company's basic business was lending on collateral. The collateral was, in part, stocks and bonds and in part merchandise stored in a warehouse that the company had purchased for that purpose. The collateral-to-loan ratio was 122%. The annualized profit margin was 55% and dividends were 75% on paid-in capital. A year later, July 1, 1875, assets had shrunk to $2,029,000. The company still had a profit margin of 55%. There were no financial difficulties. But loans on collateral were down radically, to $560,000, and the warehouse had been converted into office space.[37] That most of the business was picked up by Central Trust is suggested by the fact that on July 1, 1876, Central Trust's first reporting date, assets were a husky $5,263,000, with an annualized profit margin of 64%!

---

[37]New York State, Assembly Documents, 1875, Number 108, Superintendent of Banking, "Annual Report Relative to Savings Banks," 335.

N.Y. Guaranty and Indemnity continued to operate, but at a very low level. The primary asset was the warehouse-now-office, and capital was reduced to the book value of the property. Since no deposits were held, the company ceased reporting to the State Superintendent of Banking with the 1875 report.

The Central Trust's books for subscription opened on April 20. On the same day the Butler eleven sent a letter to N.Y. Guaranty and Indemnity stockholders setting forth the subscription ratio and stating:

> As the recent amendments to the /State/ Constitution forbid the creation of corporations by special acts, the advantages under the /Central Trust/ charter above referred to are apparent. Its provisions are similar to those contained in the charters of the leading Trust Companies of this city, and the business to be conducted will be strictly that of a Trust Company.[38]

The Butler eleven immediately subscribed $90,000 each and paid-in an initial 15% installment of $13,605. Carey and Fowler, of the selling party, as required by the Charter, subscribed to $1,000 stock each. A second installment of 15% was paid on April 23, bringing total paid-in capital to $300,000 the minimum to begin operations.

The initial 30% paid in, of course, was not paid out of the subscribers' pockets. On April 23, the Butler

---

[38] See footnote 2:34.

eleven addressed a note to N.Y. Guaranty and Indemnity stating:

> Please advance for us respectively an additional 15 per cent of the amount of our respective subscription to the Capital Stock of the Central Trust Company of New York and charge same to us respectively as a call loan at 4% per an.[39]

The rate was fair, since the call loan rate in the New York money market was at that time 4%. But since the money from the subscription was deposited at N.Y. Guaranty and Indemnity, and the bank paid the depositor (Central Trust) an interest rate thereon of 3%, the net spread to N.Y. Guaranty and Indemnity was 1%--which again was in line with open market experience.

However, at the time (April 20) that the Butler eleven began paying 4% to N.Y. Guaranty and Indemnity, the letter they sent to N.Y. Guaranty and Indemnity stockholders stipulated that from the date of the letter (April 20), those who availed themselves of the subscription privilege would be charged 5% interest on the initial subscription 15%, until such 15% was paid-in, since the eleven had already paid the subscription.

Before the Central Trust could begin operations the

---

[39] Ibid., In effect the sellers were financing the transaction.

charter provided that $100,000 of securities (U.S. Government or N.Y. State) had to be deposited in Albany with the Superintendent of Banking, at which time a certificate authorizing operations to begin would be issued by the Superintendent. The securities were for the protection of depositors and creditors.

On April 26, James Wallace took the securities to Albany and wired Butler:

> Certificate received. You might print receipt and transfer some Guaranty deposits if deemed best to commence business.[40]

Central Trust was legally organized. The next few months were devoted to operational organization--seals, by-laws, office space, etc., and of course a board of trustees. By August 31, the full board had been selected. The list was impressive.

Trustees of Central Trust Company:
August 31, 1875

Abernathy, Charles	Merchant
Appleton, William H.	Merchant
Babcock, Samuel D.	Banker
Bates, Martin	Importer
Butler, William A.	Lawyer
Corlies, Edmund W.	Importer
Cossitt, Frederick H.	----
Dows, David	Merchant
Eno, Amos R.	Merchant
Fiske, Josiah M.	Merchant

[40] *Ibid.*

Iselin, Adrian	Banker
Lane, George W.	Importer
Landon, Charles G.	Importer
Low, A. A.	Importer
Miller, George McC.	Lawyer
Morgan, J. Pierpont	Banker
Phelps, Isaac W.	----
Pyne, Percy R.	Banker
Schwab, Gustav	Merchant
Skeel, Roswell	Merchant
Sherman, Benjamin B.	Banker
Spaulding, Henry F.	President
Thorne, Jonathan	Banker
Vermilye, Jacob D.	Banker
Wallace, James P.	Banker
Webb, W. H.	Merchant

That a list of trustees of this quality could be drawn together is indicative of the reputation of the founders within the financial and commercial community.

On April 20, 1875, Central Trust shareholders paid in $100 per share. By 1900, the stock would be selling at 21 times this amount, shareholders would have received by dividends a payback of 6.2 times the original input and book value would be 11.9 times the input.

CHAPTER III

THE ASSET STRUCTURE

Trust Company Disclosure

It is a happy fact that the published financial data for New York City Trust companies are abundant for the final quarter of the nineteenth century.

The main sources of published financial data are the Annual Reports of the New York State Superintendent of Banking. Each year and for each trust company, the Superintendent published two financial statements. One statement was supplied by the company. Companies reported to Albany twice a year (June 30 and December 31). From 1874-7 the Superintendent published only the June data and thereafter only the December data. The second statement originated with the annual state examiner's report.[1]

---

[1]The New York State Superintendent of Banking issues two reports each year: the Annual Report and the Annual Report Relative to Savings Banks. The Annual Report was usually published in January, to coincide with the opening of the legislative session. This Report carried a portion (normally the balance sheet) of the state examiner's report on each trust company. Trust companies were examined once a year. The distinctive feature of

The 1874 State legislation on Trust Companies authorized and directed the Superintendent to examine the companies and publish financial information thereon.[2] The first reporting date was June 30, 1874.

The Superintendent forwarded to each trust company a standard set of reporting forms. The forms included:

1. A detailed balance sheet.
2. A "supplementary" data form covering:
   a. Off-balance sheet debt guaranty liability.
   b. Gross income.
   c. Interest paid.
   d. Other expenses.
   e. Dividends paid.
   f. The amount of deposits under court order.
   g. The number of accounts and amount of deposits upon which interest was paid.
   h. The interest rate paid on deposits.
3. Schedule A, showing a list of bonds and mortgages held.

---

this listing was a detailed catalogue of each company's stock investment portfolio. The second report, the <u>Annual Report Relative to Savings Banks</u>, was published later in the legislative session, usually in late February or early March and included the year-end financial data submitted to Albany by the trust companies.

[2]New York State, <u>Laws, 1874</u>, Chapter 324, Sections 1 and 2.

4. Schedule B, showing stock investments held--with issue-by-issue coupon, cost basis, par value and market value.

5. Schedule C, showing collateralized loans, with the loan value and each collateral item identified.

6. Schedule D, showing the names of all financial institutions in which the trust company maintained deposits, the amount of the deposit and the interest rate paid thereon.

7. Schedule E, showing a detailed break-down of the "Other Asset" entry on the balance sheet.

Fortunately, the Superintendent reproduced a great deal of this information, including the detailed balance sheet, all the supplementary schedule, all of Schedule B and a summary of Schedule C.[3]

Not all companies willingly complied with the disclosure requirements. In 1881 the Mutual Trust Company,

---

[3]Unfortunately, the reports made on these forms have disappeared from the files of the New York State Banking Department. Only the abstracts printed in the Superintendent's Annual Reports remain. The set of forms upon which the foregoing analysis is based was apparently the duplicate copy of Central Trust Company for the December 31, 1875 reporting date. See: Central Trust Company, Semi-Annual Statements from July 1, 1876.

activating a dormant charter issued in 1868 to the Public Exchange (Company), refused to report to the New York State Banking Department. Superintendent A. B. Hepburn turned the matter over to the State Attorney General, who took the case to court. The court found in favor of the Superintendent of Banking and Mutual was compelled to report.[4]

The progressiveness of the regulatory agency, however, had its limits. Since the companies reported twice a year and the Superintendent only reproduced one of these reports, the income and expense figures on the supplementary schedule only covered six months. It was not until 1895 that the agency began to add to income statement figures from the two reports to give full twelve month data.

In addition to the Superintendent's Annual Reports, the trust companies often published financial data on their own initiative. The Mercantile Trust Company, engaged in the business of guaranteeing mortgage bonds (an off-balance sheet business), had printed as an advertisement in the Commercial and Financial Chronicle in 1876, the amount of the bonds so guaranteed, the value of the properties secur-

---

[4] A. B. Hepburn, Superintendent of Banking, New York State, Annual Report, December 8, 1882, Session 106, Assembly Document No. 5, pp. 9-10.

ing the bonds and the potential rental value of those properties.[5] From 1876 on, Central Trust printed for distribution twice a year the same detailed balance sheets as were sent to the Superintendent.

For the most part, however, self-initiated financial disclosure by the trust companies was disseminated by financial advertisements in such journals as the _Commercial and Financial Chronicle_ or _Poor's Railroad Manual_, which was oriented toward the banking customer and was selective--_e.g._, loans, deposits and capital.[6]

Since trust companies were not members of the New York Clearing House Association during the 1875-1900 period, their financial data were not included in the published weekly release of that Association.

---

[5] _Commercial and Financial Chronicle_, June 24, 1876, p. ii (Investors Supplement).

[6] In 1877, Central Trust paid the Evening Post $250 for six months of advertising (Central Trust Company, _Minutes of the Executive Committee_, January 9, 1877). Advertising costs like the common cold, is a complaint which time has not relieved: "The President referring to the expiration of contract which he had been authorized to make for advertising said that while he regretted to incur the expense attending renewals, it seemed necessary to follow the examples of other competing companies and keep the name of the Company before the public." (Central Trust Company, _Minutes of the Executive Committee_, March 4, 1879.)

The Asset Structure

Object and Basic Data. The object of this chapter is to examine structural and comparative characteristics of the major asset items--cash, mortgages, investments and loans. The next chapter will examine similar characteristics of the liability side of the balance sheet, and analyze the joint influence on earnings of the asset and liability items.

Table 3:1 reproduces the basic data upon which much of this chapter is built.

The trust companies held 9% of the banking assets in New York City in 1875 and 26% in 1900. The trust companies made an impressive penetration of the banking market. Moreover, as Table 3:2 indicates, the growth rate of trust companies was superior to other intermediaries in the 1875-1900 period, and in the sub-divisions of that period, with the exception of the State banks in the 1880-85 span. A compound annual growth rate of 9.6% over a twenty-five year period is a remarkable performance. To understand the reasons behind the rapid growth of the trust companies, attention must be focused on the individual balance sheet items.

Each of the major balance sheet asset items showed strong growth rates over the 1875-1900 period.

TABLE 3:1

New York City Financial Institutions
Aggregate Assets by Intermediary[7]
(000's)

Trust Companies:	Cash	Mortgages	Investments	Loans	Assets
1875	$ 4,554	$ 5,718	$ 21,304	$ 31,953	$ 67,032
1880	2,974	12,608	15,067	58,416	92,933
1885	19,500	9,039	35,067	96,027	163,659
1890	24,333	14,145	41,174	153,549	244,115
1895	43,835	17,030	63,743	170,046	322,060
1900	84,116	28,982	161,597	362,130	622,114

National Banks:	Cash	Mortgages	Investments	Loans	Assets
1875	$ 92,298	-	$ 81,031	$202,442	$ 399,758
1880	186,610	-	40,732	238,495	447,084
1885	189,725	-	38,815	236,890	479,249
1890	190,113	-	32,610	297,328	533,407
1895	151,004	-	99,251	363,848	632,501
1900	335,717	-	142,956	569,573	1,067,356

State Banks:	Cash	Mortgages	Investments	Loans	Assets
1875	$ 15,927	$ 90	$1,122	$ 43,556	$ 66,632
1880	23,539	47	765	41,567	71,349
1885	65,804	91	1,390	71,134	140,531
1890	41,554	165	3,490	88,599	148,775
1895	37,265	633	8,196	100,017	162,256
1900	89,292	751	8,604	131,249	251,031

Savings Banks:	Cash	Mortgages	Investments	Loans	Assets
1875	$ 13,600	$ 65,389	$115,326	-	$205,415
1880	10,557	44,550	150,021	-	220,630
1885	19,287	93,338	177,331	-	301,147
1890	20,608	146,713	188,897	-	371,993
1895	25,466	173,588	216,823	-	427,316
1900	36,727	242,437	278,222	-	570,517

Source: Data for National banks from Annual Reports of the Comptroller of the Currency. Data for other intermediaries from Annual Reports of the New York State Superintendent of Banking.

[7]Regulatory authorities reported aggregated data for New York City national banks, state banks and savings bnaks. Trust company data was aggregated by this writer from individual company statistics. The following table shows the exact source for each aggregation.

1. National Banks. U.S. Comptroller of the Currency, Annual Report.

	Date of Annual Report	Date of Balance Sheet	Page
1875	12/06/75	10/01/75	20-1
1880	12/06/80	10/01/80	158-9
1885	12/01/85	10/01/85	206-7
1890	12/01/90	10/02/90	254-9
1895	12/02/95	9/28/95	548-9
1900	12/03/00	9/05/00	722-3

2. State Banks. N.Y. State Superintendent of Banking, Annual Report.

	Date of Annual Report	Date of Balance Sheet	Page
1875	12/31/75	12/18/75	124
1880	11/29/81	12/11/80	107
1885	12/30/86	12/26/85	188
1890	1/12/92	12/20/90	263
1895	1/01/97	12/02/95	311
1900	12/26/01	12/04/00	214

3. Savings Banks. N.Y. State Superintendent of Banking, Annual Report Relative to Savings Banks.

	Date of Annual Report	Date of Balance Sheet	Page
1875	3/03/76	1/01/76	30-2
1880	2/23/81	1/01/81	9-11
1885	3/01/86	1/01/86	290-2
1890	2/28/91	1/01/91	268-70
1895	2/27/96	1/01/96	264-6
1900	2/26/01	1/01/01	332-4

4. Trust Companies. N.Y. State Superintendent of Banking, Annual Report (denoted by *) and Annual Report Relative to Savings Banks.

	Date of Annual Report	Date of Balance Sheet	Page
1875	12/31/75*	7/01/75	141-55
1880	2/23/81	12/31/80	279-88
1885	3/01/86	12/31/85	301-20
1890	2/28/91	12/31/90	335-68
1895	2/27/96	1/01/96	367-420
1900	2/26/01	1/01/01	440-529

TABLE 3:2

Compound Annual Growth Rates
of New York City Assets

	Trust Companies	National Banks	State Banks	Savings Banks
1875-80	6.8%	4.2%	1.4%	1.4%
1880-85	12.0	0.1	14.5	6.4
1885-90	8.3	2.2	1.1	4.3
1890-95	5.7	3.5	1.9	2.8
1895-00	15.5	11.0	9.1	6.0
1875-00	9.6	4.1	5.4	4.2

Source: Based on Table 3:1.

TABLE 3:3

Compound Annual Growth Rates
Major Asset Items of New
York City Trust Companies

	Cash	Investments	Mortgages	Loans	Assets
1875-80	-8.8%	-7.2%	17.1%	12.8%	6.8%
1880-85	46.0	18.2	-6.9	10.5	12.0
1885-90	4.5	3.3	9.4	9.8	8.3
1890-95	12.5	15.3	3.8	2.1	5.7
1895-00	13.9	14.0	11.2	16.3	15.5
1875-00	12.4	8.4	6.7	10.2	9.6

Source: Based on Table 3:1.

TABLE 3:4

Cash As A Percent of Assets
New York City

	1875	1880	1885	1890	1895	1900
National Banks	23.7%	39.1%	39.6%	35.6%	23.9%	31.5%
State Banks	23.9	33.0	39.7	27.9	23.0	35.5
Savings Banks	6.6	4.8	6.4	5.5	6.0	6.4
Trust Companies:	0.8	3.2	11.9	10.0	13.6	12.7
On Hand	0.2	0.0	5.1	2.4	3.0	1.1
On Deposit	0.6	3.2	6.8	7.6	10.6	11.6

Source: Based on Table 3:1.

Cash. Three elements of Table 3:4 are especially noteworthy: first, the percentage of assets held by trust companies in cash was considerably less than that held by commercial banks, but more on balance than that held by savings banks. Second, the percentage of cash-to-assets tended to increase as the century progressed. Thirdly, the trust companies held very little cash on hand, preferring instead to deposit it in a bank.

In the first observation, trust companies held significantly lower cash balances than commercial banks because: (1) no reserve requirements were set by law or regulation, and (2) the nature of the deposit structure was believed to be less volatile than that of the commercial banks.

National banks in New York City, under the National Bank Act of 1864 (Section 31) and the Redistribution Act of 1874 (Section 2), were required to maintain a minimum cash reserve equal to 25% of deposits. The ratio was in practice higher since: (1) the 25% was a minimum and a New York City national bank would want some operating leeway, and (2) items in process of collection, which were classified as cash in the printed reports, were not classified as cash in the reserve computation.

New York state banks were not required to maintain reserves against deposits until 1892, when a 15% minimum level was imposed by law for New York City banks.[8] Voluntary reserves, however, were kept, based either on mandatory levels of the New York Clearing House Association, if the bank were a member, or levels which individual experience dictated as prudent. The New York Clearing House,

---

[8]New York State, Laws, 1892, Chapter 37, Section 44. One half of the cash reserve could be kept on deposit with other New York Banks or Trust Companies, providing that the bank of deposit had capital of at least $200,000 and had been approved as a depository by the Superintendent of Banking. See also Margaret A. Schaffner, Trust Company Reserves, Comparative Legislative Bulletin No. 6, Wisconsin Free Library Commission, 1906, 18.

like the national banks, had a 25% reserve minimum.[9]

The absence of minimum reserve requirements allowed the trust companies to invest a substantially larger portion of their assets than the commercial banks, and certainly this would be a significant competitive advantage, both in maximizing existing capital and in attracting new capital to the industry.

This competitive advantage, however, must be placed in perspective. The absence of regulation alone would not have been enough to account for lower relative cash levels. The pressure of the financial community, especially the commercial banks through which the trust companies cleared, would have compelled higher cash levels--if the trust companies were otherwise structurally identical to commercial banks. But they were not. One important difference (in brief) was that the trust company deposit, like the savings bank deposit, was purchased.[10] This gave the trust company the ability to stabilize deposit levels by adjusting rates,

---

[9]Margaret G. Myers, The New York Money Market: Volume I, Origins and Development, Columbia University Press, New York, 1931, 250-4.

[10]The statement is one of degree. Clearing House banks were not supposed to pay interest on deposits, but a number did. See: Commercial and Financial Chronicle, August 2, 1884, 108.

thereby reducing deposit volatility.

While the trust companies carried lower cash ratios than the commercial banks, the cash ratios did tend to increase as the century moved on. One possible reason for this increase is pressure from the banking community. By the mid-1880's, members of the New York Clearing House expressed some concern that a weak link in the structure of New York banking was the fact that numerous non-member trust companies and banks used member banks for clearing purposes, but did not abide by reserve or reporting regulations of the Clearing House Association. This meant that in times of monetary crises, the member banks were actually supporting the credit of numerous non-member banks.

In 1891, the Clearing House apparently asked trust companies using member bank facilities to submit to examinations, because the trustees of Mercantile Trust, on January 22, 1891, agreed to allow the Clearing House "to make such examination of its condition as may be deemed necessary."[11] This voluntary compliance approach apparently had indifferent success. In 1899 the Clearing

---

[11]Mercantile Trust Company, Minutes of the Executive Committee, January 22, 1891.

House began to require that non-member trust companies clearing through member banks submit financial reports.[12] Unlike the member institutions, however, the trust company reports were not made public. In 1903 the Clearing House required that trust companies clearing through member banks maintain a cash-to-deposit ratio of ten percent.

Why did it take the Clearing House so long to act? Probably first because the trust companies were very good customers and, secondly, until the flurry of trust company formations in the mid 1890's there was not much question (in the commercial banker's mind) about the general credit quality of the trust companies. In point, in 1899 the Clearing House prohibited member banks from clearing checks of trust companies that had not been operating at least one year.

The trust companies, however, could not have been deaf to the discussions going on in the Clearing House. The trust companies had business relationships to protect also. In 1884, in the wake of the May financial panic, the Union Trust Company adopted a policy of carrying $3 million on hand, in cash, for the purpose of securing de-

[12] Commercial and Financial Chronicle, November 11, 1899, 990-1.

posits.[13] At the time, the $3 million represented about 15% of Union's deposits. While the Union action represented the most extreme case, it nevertheless points out the willingness of the trust companies to voluntarily bolster reserves.

Finally it has been noted that the trust companies carried a large portion of their cash balances in the form of deposits with commercial banks. Such deposits served three functions: (1) a source of funds for balancing check clearings, (2) as a reserve against deposit withdrawals and (3) as an investment.

In the first function, the commercial bank rendered a distinct service, especially if out-of-town collections were involved. For these services, the commercial bank would have, in theory at least, additional loanable funds in the form of the trust company deposits themselves.

In the third function, the deposits served as investments since the commercial banks often paid interest there-

---

[13]George W. Davidson, The Story of Central Hanover, unpublished manuscript, ca. 1932, 19. Davidson's rendition may be a little enthusiastic. The Minutes of the Union Trust Executive Committee (meeting June 5, 1884), said nothing about gold. The Committee also provided for a separate safe-vault to hold the cash reserve as distinct from tellers' balances) with only the President, First and Second Vice Presidents holding the combination.

on. An indication of how common this practice was is suggested by Schedule D of the previously mentioned reporting forms supplied to the trust companies by the Superintendent of Banking. Schedule D, which called for a break-down of deposits in banks (by name and amount) also had a separate column showing "at what rate of interest" the deposit was made. On December 31, 1875, Central Trust reported on deposits in a commercial bank (Mechanics National Bank) at 2% per annum.[14] In 1881 Mercantile Trust, after seeking bids for its deposits, placed a deposit with Fourth National Bank at 2½%. Since both of these rates are below prevailing call loan rates, it is apparent that the trust companies expected additional service from the commercial banks, which would be use of the Clearing House facilities.

Since at least a portion of the cash balances of the trust company were earning interest as deposits, cash itself became an invested asset of sorts, indicating another competitive advantage over the New York City commercial banks.

---

[14]As a general rule, the trustees of a trust company had to approve any depository for the company's funds--it was not at the sole discretion of the officers. In this case, the 2% rate was paid on daily balances over a minimum balance of $10,000. Central Trust Company, Minutes of the Executive Committee, October 5, 1875.

It was probably common, too, for a trust company to have deposits in more than one commercial bank. Between December, 1875 and August, 1876, Mercantile Trust had accounts in National Park Bank, Manhattan Company, and Chatham National Bank. The trust companies with a large corporate trust business, especially bond trusteeships, would probably in the normal course of business have deposit accounts with the bank of account of the issuer of the bond. The issuer of a bond could, for example, have the commercial bank debit his (the issuer's) deposit account and credit the trustee's (the trust company) account when a coupon payment came due.

The magnitude of trust company deposits with commercial banks increased quite markedly toward the end of the century.

While some of the trust company deposits may have been in non-member or out-of-town banks, the vast majority were probably with the larger member banks. With the trust companies accounting for 4.8% of the Clearing House member deposits in 1890 and rapidly rising to 9.2% in 1900, the trust companies were significant customers of the commercial banks. It is small wonder that the Clearing House banks were anxious to have the trust companies carry higher cash levels--it both strengthened the trust company reserves and supplied the commercial banks with a source of funds.

TABLE 3:5

Trust Company Deposits in Commercial Banks

Year	New York City Trust Company Deposits in Commercial Banks (000)	Clearing House Deposits (000)	Ratio
1875	$ 4,417	$245,895	1.8%
1880	2,935	272,466	1.1
1885	11,084	373,953	3.0
1890	18,506	386,819	4.8
1895	34,167	501,689	6.8
1900	76,754	838,404	9.2

Source: Data for trust companies derived from Annual Reports of the New York State Superintendent of Banking. Clearing House figures from weekly reports in Commercial and Financial Chronicle. Clearing House data for date nearest trust company statement date.

Mortgage. As Table 3:6 indicates, neither the national nor the state banks were investors in mortgages. The prevailing sentiment appears to have been that mortgages were not an acceptable line of business for commercial banks. National banks, of course, were largely excluded from participation in the mortgage market by Section 28 of the National Bank Act of 1864 and state banks by Chapter 649, Section 42, Laws of 1892.

TABLE 3:6

Mortgages as a Percent of Assets
New York City

	1875	1880	1885	1890	1895	1900
National Banks	0.0%	0.0%	0.0%	0.0%	0.0%	0.0%
State Banks	0.1	0.1	0.1	0.1	0.4	0.3
Savings Banks	31.8	20.2	31.0	39.4	40.6	42.4
Trust Companies	8.5	13.6	5.5	5.8	5.3	4.4

Source: Based on Table 3:1.

The major institutional holders of mortgages were Savings Banks and Life Insurance Companies.

Trust Companies were not primarily geared to the mortgage business--although there were significant exceptions. A few companies had a definite slant towards mortgages at one time or another during the 1875-1900 period: notably Jarvis-Conklin Mortgage Trust, Mercantile Trust, United States Mortgage Trust, Farmers Loan and Trust, and New York Life and Trust.

Although the evidence is thin, indications are that most of the mortgage business engaged in by the trust companies was for fairly large ticket items: in 1879, Central Trust took a $30,000 Duane Street mortgage--joining partnership with the one other mortgagor which the company had in its portfolio.[15] In 1886, Union Trust took a $300,000 mortgage on the Victoria Hotel, at 4%, three year maturity.[16] Prior to this event, Union had $15,000 of mortgages on its books.

Probably a portion of the trust companies' limited venture into mortgages was to accommodate good existing customers or to furnish liquidity to personal trust accounts, which often had real estate property as a principal asset.[17]

---

[15] Ibid., July 15, 1874.

[16] Union Trust Company, Minutes of the Executive Committee, January 14, 1886. With regard to the statutory prohibition against holding mortgages by national banks, one commentator observes: "When the new banking law of 1864 was framed, the suggestion was made that abuses would spring up, and that much injury might be done in our rapidly growing Western cities if the accumulated deposits of a bank were controlled by a clique of officers with powers to use them in monopolizing lands to the detriment of commerce." Commercial and Financial Chronicle, July 12, 1873, 40.

[17] Ibid., November 8, 1894. It was common in this regard, for the trust companies to supply liquidity to personal trust accounts (usually estates) by lending on property held by that account.

TABLE 3:7

Stocks as a Percent of Assets
New York City

	1875	1880	1885	1890	1895	1900
National Banks	20.8%	8.5%	8.1%	6.1%	15.7%	13.4%
State Banks	1.7	1.1	1.0	2.3	5.1	3.4
Savings Banks	56.1	68.0	58.9	50.8	50.7	48.8
Trust Companies	31.8	16.1	21.4	16.9	26.0	24.4

Source: Based on Table 3:1.

Stock Investments. "Stock Investments" refers to common and preferred stocks, U.S. Government bonds, political entity bonds and corporate bonds. Items of a hybrid nature, like a first mortgage railroad bond were classified as "Stock Investments" rather than "Mortgages."

The national banks had fairly explicit minimum constraints regarding the holding of U.S. Government bonds. Under Section 45 of the National Bank Act of 1864, associations designated as government depositories were compelled to pledge U.S. Government bonds with the Secretary of the Treasury to cover any federal deposits, and additionally, under Section 21, were required to maintain a U.S. Government bond level, pledged with the U.S. Treasury, of 111% of currency issued. In point of fact, because of cumbersome transportation and substitution problems, the associations kept bonds on deposit in Washington considerably in excess of their immediate requirements .

TABLE 3:8

National Bank Holding of Bonds
New York City

Year	Bonds/ Assets	=	Pledged Bonds for: Depository	+	Circulation	+	Excess Ratio
1875	20.6%		0.2%		6.3%		14.1%
1880	8.5		0.2		4.4		3.9
1885	8.1		0.2		2.6		5.3
1890	6.1		0.7		0.8		4.6
1895	15.7		0.2		2.7		12.8
1900	13.4		3.2		2.9		7.3

Source: Data derived from Annual Reports of the Comptroller of the Currency. See footnote 3:7.

In Table 3:8 the first column shows the ratio of Bonds (or Stock Investments) to Assets. The second and third columns separate the portion of the Bond-to-Asset ratio attributable to the statutory requirements on federal deposits and circulation. The last column shows the ratio of the remaining Bonds-to-Assets. With the exception of 1875, the last column represents almost entirely non-U.S. Government bonds.

The National associations in effect invested in U.S. Government bonds only to meet statutory requirements. This was a function mainly of the fact that the demand for U.S. Government bonds for statutory pledging purposes (including state banks and trust companies) was so great relative to the declining supply that the U.S. Government bonds normally sold at a premium.[18] Consequently, the associations were compelled to carry a portion of bond investments in issues with rather low comparative yields.

The savings banks held an unusually large portion of their assets in Stock Investments, over 50% for most of the period under examination. Focusing on 1885, Table 3:9 shows the distribution of Stock Investments held by New York City savings banks.

---

[18] On November 1, 1884, over 42% of the total U.S. Government interest bearing debt was held by national banks, state banks, savings banks and trust companies, compared with 37% in 1880. See Annual Reports of the Comptroller of the Currency, December 1, 1885 and November 27, 1880. The structural torque in the demand for U.S. Government bonds was intensified by the rise of the non-national bank segment of the financial community, which held 13% of the interest bearing U.S. debt in 1880 and 17% in 1884.

TABLE 3:9

Stock Investments: New York City Savings Banks: 1885

	Amount at Par (000)	Percent Distribution
U.S. Bonds	$ 85,852	58.4%
District Columbia 3-65 Bonds	1,110	0.8
New York State Bonds	3,651	2.5
Other State Bonds	12,239	8.4
Bonds of Cities in N.Y.	41,130	28.1
Bonds of Counties in N.Y.	2,380	1.6
Bonds of Towns in N.Y.	356	0.2
Bonds of Villages in N.Y.	56	0.0
Total	$146,774	100.0%

Source: Data derived from Annual Report on Savings Banks, 1886, New York Superintendent of Banking, p. 290.

Savings banks, as of 1885, held 58.4% of their bond assets in U.S. Government bonds and 41.6% in political entity bonds, most of which were issued by or within New York State. Savings banks, consequently were an extremely important source of funds for local political bodies. An interesting hypothesis could be tendered that in the eyes of the State Legislature, the primary asset function at this time of the savings banks was public financing, that savings bank legislation was colored to this end and that the mortgage emphasis only gradually came into prominence.

The trust companies held a fairly sizable portion of assets in Stock Investments during this period. Under the

New York State Act of 1874 (Chapter 324, Section 6) the trust companies were required to deposit with the Superintendent of Banking securities equal in value to 10% of paid-in capital. The securities could be issued by the U.S. Government, New York State or New York State political subdivisions. The Act did not define whether the securities were to be valued at cost, par, or market, but par came to be the accepted standard. The Act stated that the purpose of the deposit was as security for depositors and creditors.

Unlike the national banks, state banks or savings banks, the Trust Companies had virtually unlimited scope in investing. Using 1885 as a base for a cross-sectional analysis, the following table shows the distribution of the Stock Investment portfolio.

U.S. Government bonds constituted the majority by far of Stock Investments. State and Local bonds were rather scarce, but included issues from Massachusetts, New Hampshire, and Kentucky in addition to New York issues. Other bonds included script issued by Atlantic Mutual Insurance Company and bonds issued by Trinity Church (New York). Railroad bonds were a fairly sizable portion of the portfolio, with investments widely scattered among railway systems.

TABLE 3:10

Stock Investment Portfolio: 1885
New York City Trust Companies

	Amount at Market (000)	Percent Distribution
U.S. Government Bonds	$25,049	74.1%
State and Local Bonds	2,104	6.2
Railroad Bonds	5,972	17.7
Other Bonds	48	0.2
Total Bonds	$33,173	98.2%
Preferred Stock	0	0.0
Common Stock	622	1.8
Total Stock Investments	$33,795	100.0%

Source: Data derived from Annual Report 1886, of New York State Superintendent of Banking, pp. 301-20.

The maturity distribution of the above bond portfolio is shown in Table 3:11.

TABLE 3:11

Maturity Distribution Stock Investment Portfolio:
1885 New York City Trust Companies

Years	Amount at Market (000)	Percent Distribution
0 - 2	$ 2,026	6.1%
2 - 5	120	0.4
5 -10	5,501	16.6
10 and over	25,526	76.9
Total Bonds	$33,173	100.0%

Source: Data derived from Annual Report of Savings Banks, 1886, New York State Superintendent of Banking, pp. 301-20.

With over three-fourths of the bonds maturing in over ten years, the portfolio would appear to serve little by way of a liquidity function. But the figures may be deceiving.

First, since 1886, the receipts of the U.S. Government had exceeded expenditures. A portion of the surplus had been used to retire or refund the federal debt at lower interest rates and longer maturities. As a consequence, the maturities of the interest bearing U.S. Government debt were structurally imbalanced, with (in 1885) nearly 65% maturing in ten years or more and 85% in five years or more.[19] However, if an investor looked for liquidity in terms of the credit quality of the issuer rather than the maturity date, then quite conceivably the portfolio would be weighted towards U.S. Government bonds and with long maturities. In

---

[19] The U.S. Treasury Debt Statement of December 31, 1885 showed the following break-down of interest bearing debt:

Issue	Maturity	$ Amount*	Percent
3s	Optional	$ 194	15%
$4\frac{1}{2}$s	1891	250	20
4s	1907	738	59
Pacific	1895+	64	5
Other	1895+	14	1
	Total	$1,260	100%

* Thousands

See <u>Commercial and Financial Chronicle</u>, January 9, 1886, 49.

a trade-off, superior credit quality could over balance the risks of longer maturities. With mercantile failures, as reported by R. G. Dun and Company, increasing from 6,738 in 1882 to 10,968 in 1884 and the liabilities in such failures increasing from $101 million to $226 million, credit quality would have had occasion to be current in an investor's mind.[20]

Secondly, in a period of declining long term interest rates, representative of most of the 1875-1895 period, an investor would presume that his long term bonds would appreciate in value soon enough. The spread between cost and market would act as a buffer to absorb any discount which might arise if the holding had to be sold quickly. As a result, to an investor of 1885, a portfolio of longer maturities might not have posed as severe a liquidity problem as to an investor in a time of rising or fluctuating long term rates.

The functions of the trust company investment portfolio can be further illustrated by an actual case history. Table 3:12 shows the investment transaction by Central Trust Company in 1885. Purchase and sale activity is ac-

---

[20] Ibid., 37.

TABLE 3:12

Central Trust Company
Investment Account--1885
(000's)

Issue	Par Value Bought	Par Value Sold	Date
Louisville and Nashville, Car Trust	$ 56N		2/ 8
	22A		6/20
Louisville and Nashville, Purchase Money		$ 216E	5/ 3
Pittsburgh, Cleveland and Toledo, 6%, 1922		50R	10/10
Northern Pacific, Gen. Mortgage 6%		5R	4/16
		47R	4/17
		10R	7/ 8
		10R	7/11
		31R	7/13
		25R	7/14
		34R	7/15
		38R	7/16
N.Y., Lackawana and Western, 6% 1921		1R	4/11
		21R	4/16
		3R	4/17
		20R	5/ 9
		16R	5/11
		10R	5/18
		18R	5/13
		1R	5/15
		16E	6/ 6
Atlantic Mutual Insurance, Script	18N		5/ 6
	2A		5/ 7
	8A		10/ 1
	3A		10/ 2
	10A		10/24
West Shore, Guarantee Mortgages	91N		12/26
U.S. Government, 4 1/2%	50N		7/ 3
U.S. Government, Currency 6%		150R	7/ 1
		1R	7/ 8
		50R	7/ 8
		6R	7/ 8
		100R	7/14
		250R	7/20
		100R	10/28
		100R	11/14
U.S. Government, 4%		300R	1/28
		200R	1/30
	50A		5/16
	100A		5/18
	325A		5/19
	25A		5/21
	200A		7/ 1
	50A		7/11
	50A		7/13
	100A		7/13
	50A		7/15
	150A		7/16
		425R	8/31
	400A		9/ 3
	100A		11/ 9
	100A		11/11
Total	$1,960	$2,254	

N = New issue to portfolio.
A = Addition to existing holdings of an issue.
R = Reducation of existing holding of an issue
E = Elimination of issue from portfolio

Source: Central Trust Company, General Ledger-1885.

cumulated by issue.

Several points merit comment:

First, the par value of the investment portfolio at year end 1885 changed only slightly from the level prevailing at the end of 1884. But changes in stock levels are deceiving, the flow of activity is a more important indicator of the liquidity of a portfolio. Taking total sales (or credits to the portfolio) of $2,254,000 and dividing through by the stock level ($3,231,000) at the beginning of 1885, the portfolio shows a turnover ratio of 70%, indicating a fairly active use of the investment account.

Secondly, the activity was also wide-spread among issues. Three issues were eliminated during the year (one issue, Louisville and Nashville--Purchase Money, by redemption), five were added to the list (one issue, West Shore, Guarantee Morgage, resulting from a defaulted secured call loan), two existing holdings were either increased or decreased, and three holdings (not listed in the table) were undisturbed during the year.

Thirdly, the roster of activity indicates that railroad bonds were much less liquid than U.S. Government bonds. The activity in the U.S. Government, 4% for example, suggests a good two-way market, with the ability to move sizable amounts of money in a short time. By contrast, the sale activity in the Northern Pacific, 6%, and the N.Y. Lackawana and Western, 6%, indicates that the selling broker had to move slowly to avoid rupturing the market.

Fourthly, the predominantly buy activity in the U.S. Government, 4%, and the sell activity in the U.S. Government, Currency 6%, in July and November points to an interesting problem in investment strategy faced by bankers and brokers during this period. The 6% issue priced at about 135, was replaced by a 4% issue, priced at about 122. On a current yield basis, a 4.44% issue was being sold for a 3.28% issue. The reasoning behind Central's action appears to be that the 6%s were in the process of redemption by the U.S. Government. This meant that all the commercial banks, trust companies, savings banks, and insurance companies holding 6's for statutory purposes would be forced into the 4% market (the largest remaining U.S. Government issue) for replacement bonds. In the process, the price of the 4%s would be bid up. This in fact, did happen and by the end of 1886, the 4%s appreciated to 129.

Central Trust utilized the investment in another way on occasion--the lending of bonds under repurchase agreement. On March 4, 1879, the Executive Committee approved the loan, on collateral, to Kuhn, Loeb and Company, of \$100,000 4½% U.S. Government Bonds and \$200,000 10-40s, at an interest rate of 2% and returnable on demand.

Loans

TABLE 3:13

Loans as a Percent of Assets
Trust Companies--New York City

	1875	1880	1885	1890	1895	1900
National Banks	51.9%	49.9%	49.4%	55.7%	57.5%	53.3%
State Banks	65.3	58.2	50.6	59.6	61.6	52.3
Savings Banks	31.8	20.2	31.0	39.4	40.6	42.4
Trust Companies	47.7	62.9	58.7	62.9	52.8	54.7

Source: Based on Table 3:1.

Background. As Table 3:13 indicates, the commercial banks and trust companies had a loan-to-asset ratio in the 50-60% range over most of the 1875-1900 period. In terms of net assets (assets net of uncollected cash items) the range was probably closer to 55-65%.

Legal Framework. The national banks, under Section 29 of the National Bank Act of 1864, had a lending limit to any one customer of 10% of capital. The inital Congressional intent of this provision was to prohibit a monopolization of bank lending capacity by a few borrowers--which conceivably could have happened since Congress was at the same time limiting the privilege of issuing currency to a fixed amount ($300 million) and Congress viewed currency issue rather than deposit creation as the primary credit entry to the lending function.

In 1886, the Comptroller of the Currency, noting that the limits to currency issue were now removed, recommended to Congress: (1) the 10% limit on loans be extended to include surplus and (2) that the proposed limit could be exceeded on loans collateralized by security of high quality.[21]

The editors of the Commercial and Financial Chronicle endorsed the Comptroller's suggestion, observing that violations of the existing limit were wide-spread and:

> if the Comptroller of the Currency were to attempt to enforce it to-day he would probably have to shut up a very considerable percentage of the banks in our leading commercial centers.[22]

---

[21] Ibid., December 11, 1886, 708-9. On the November 12, 1900 examination data, 44 national banks in New York City reported 38,102 loans outstanding, of which 707 (or 1.9%) were in excess of statutory limits. See Comptroller of the Currency, Annual Report, 1900, xxiv.

[22] Commercial and Financial Chronicle, November 5, 1887, 589.

The credit demands of American business, the size of the individual company's borrowing need was, by 1887, vastly greater than in 1864, but still the original 1864 limit remained on the books until June 22, 1906.[23]

Although the limit was apparently violated (the Comptroller even noted this), the fact that (1) it existed at all must have had some inhibiting influence on lending policy and (2) the agitation in the 1880's for a liberalization of the limit suggest that the national banks were actually laboring under a competitive disadvantage.

In 1885, only two of the ten largest national banks that were members of the New York Clearing House, had lending limits of up to $500,000. One had a limit of $320,000, five of $200,000 and two of $150,000. In contrast, by the 1880's there were at least six trust companies that had the capacity to make loans in the $500,000 range or above--Central, Union, New York Life, Mercantile and U.S. Trust. Central Trust, for example, which under the national banking system would have had a lending limit of $100,000, made many call loans in 1885 in the $500,000 range, with a few even reaching the $1,000,000 level.[24]

---

[23]U.S. Congress, 59th Congress, Session 1, HR 8975.

[24]Central Trust Company, General Ledger--1885.

The ability to lend large sums, especially to railroads and stock brokers, must have placed the trust companies in an advantageous position to secure a large portion of a rapidly increasing market; and the relative advantage would increase as the century moved on.

The trust companies, unlike the national banks, labored under no statutory limitation on the amount that could be lent to any one customer. New York State did, however, impose statutory constraints on the total amount of loans (or deposits) which a trust company could have in relation to its capital. The 1874 Act relative to Moneyed Corporations (Chapter 324, Section 9) and the 1882 General Banking Act (Chapter 409, Section 227) limited the amount of loans a trust company could make to the ratio of ten times the sum of capital and surplus. In practice this limit was never even remotely approached by the trust companies. During the 1875-1900 period the trust companies in aggregate had loan-to-equity ratios ranging from 2-4 times, with only a few individual companies straying much beyond a 5 times ratio.

In 1882, the trust companies and state commercial bankers alike had a brief and bewildering scare with regard to loan and deposit limitations. In the 1882 recodification of the New York State Banking Law (Chapter

409, Subchapter 8) the Legislature decreed that no "moneyed corporation" could make loans or accept deposits in excess of three times capital stock (Section 179:8). Section 214 further defined "moneyed corporations" to mean:

> every corporation having banking powers, or having the power to make loans upon pledges or deposits, or authorized by law to make insurance.

Section 215 further stipulated that the provisions of this chapter (presumably Subchapter 8) applied to every corporation created or renewed or extended after January 1, 1828.

Had the provisions of Chapter 409 been enforced, the results would have been disastrous for a large portion of the trust companies and state banks, because the loan-to-capital and deposit-to-capital ratios were even then in excess of 3-to-1. A reduction in assets would have actually ensued.

Exactly what the Legislature was trying to do is not now clear, nor was it so at the time. Within a few months of the passage of Chapter 409, the New York Court of Appeals (Levitt v. Blatchford, 17 <u>N.Y.</u>) determined that Section 179:8 did not apply to existing corporations. Although it is difficult to reconcile the Court's decision with the letter of the law, the decision at least nullified a potentially serious constraint on the operations of the trust companies and state banks. The Legislature apparently agreed because the law was not brought up for refinement in subsequent sessions.

Loan Collateral. The state financial reporting format for trust companies divided loans into those made on collateral and those made on personal security.

TABLE 3:14

Loans: New York City Trust Companies

	Percent Made on Collateral	Percent Made on Personal Security	Total
1875	59.0%	41.0%	100.0%
1880	83.3	16.7	100.0
1885	88.8	11.2	100.0
1890	94.4	5.6	100.0
1895	83.1	16.9	100.0
1900	91.5	8.5	100.0

Source: Annual Reports of the New York State Superintendent of Banking. See Footnote 3:7.

Between 1875 and 1890, the trust companies moved sharply away from lending on personal security--or the character of the borrower (especially bills discounted).

The movement toward lending on collateral is probably a reflection of several trends: a tendency to make increasingly large loans, the growth of the New York call loan market and a greater availability of bond issues which were of collateralable quality. The sharp reversal of this trend in 1895 is most likely due to the financial crises of 1893 and 1895, the fall of the market value of collateral securities beneath margin and the ad hoc substitution of the personal recognizance of borrowers. Behind this influence, however, was another factor--the proliferation in the 1890's, especially after 1895, of numerous small trust companies which had a much higher portion of their loans in bills discounted than the larger trust companies.

One of the developments with the increase in collateralized loans was the rise of the professional call loan broker, with a list of bank and trust company customers to whom he supplied loans. In 1899, the Commercial and Financial Chronicle noted that the call loan brokers:

> are expected to be in attendance at the Stock Exchange during certain hours of the day for the purpose of loaning their employer's money on call.[25]

---

[25]Commercial and Financial Chronicle, August 26, 1899, 412.

The ability of banks and trust companies to put money out quickly and the availability of money to stock brokers was doubtless a lubricant for the New York financial market. The mechanism of collateralizing with securities made this quick transmission of funds possible, since the need for extensive credit scoring was thereby greatly reduced.

For several years, 1874-1881, publically reported data also indicated the value of collateral held for collateralized loans. In 1875 the collateral was valued at 121.2% for all New York City trust companies and in 1880, 123.6%. Some companies, notably Union Trust, and New York Life and Trust were more conservative in this regard, while others, especially U.S. Trust and Farmers Loan and Trust were more liberal.

In 1881, the trustees of Mercantile Trust passed a resolution requiring a 20% minimum margin (120%) on loans collateralized by non-dividend paying stocks. Moreover, to qualify as collateral, a security (stock or bond) had to be quoted on the New York Stock Exchange.[26] If this last requirement for eligibility was wide spread, then

---

[26] Mercantile Trust Company, Minutes of the Executive Committee, February 17 and 21, 1881.

it would have been a significant contributing force in the growth of the New York Stock Exchange, since ease of hypothecation would have been an important point for a large portion of security buyers.

Usury. Usury, or the taking of interest in excess of a statutory maximum rate was a recurring theme in New York State politics. Circulation and usury limits were probably the two most politically sensitive issues in banking in the last quarter of the nineteenth century.

Under Section 30 of the National Banking Act of 1864, the maximum interest rate national banks were permitted to charge was limited to the rate legislated on the state level for state banks.

In New York State, the Banking Act of 1838 set a maximum rate of 6%. In 1870 (Chapter 163, Section 1) the limit was raised to 7%. The 1870 Act, like the 1838 Act, also provided for a penalty of twice the amount of interest to be paid to the borrower for knowingly violating the usury law. In 1880, the maximum interest rate chargable was returned to 6% (Chapter 567, Section 1) where it remained throughout the century.

In practice, however, supply and demand determined the price of credit--not statute. Several avenues were open to bankers to circumvent statutory limits in times of tight money. For one, compensating balances as a percentage of loans. For another, the padding of collection commissions of bills of discount on the foreign exchange ledger (bills payable in other localities). The extent to which banks did use these techniques is not now known. In the area of call loans, however, the technique of circumvention was highly visible.

In New York City, call loans were customarily, but not exclusively made to stock brokers or underwriters and collateralized by quality stocks and bonds. The going rate on call loans were published weekly in the financial press. Much like the prime rate today, the call loan rate was an indicator of the cost of credit to the worthiest borrowers. Whenever the cost of credit exceeded the statutory limit (which was frequently), the quotation would read the statutory limit plus a per diem commission.[27] For example, in the week ending November 21, 1879, the call loan

---

[27] Call loan and prime paper rates were reprinted weekly in the Commercial and Financial Chronicle. The rates were influenced by the credit worthiness of the borrower, the quality of the collateral, and the secular supply and demand conditions for money. The rate was quite volatile, often depending much like the current Fed Funds market, on hourly conditions. A range in the rate in any one week of 200-300 basis points was common.

range was reported as 4-7%+1/8 p.d. In the week ending November 19, 1880 the range was 4-6%+1/6 p.d. The per diem charge was quite expensive to the borrower, since each 1/16 p.d. addition represented an effective 23% annual interest rate on top of the statutory maximum rate.

Everyone was aware of what was going on with the per diem charge. As early as 1873, Governor John Dix recommended that the usury laws be amended to apply only to cases where a rate had not been negotiated between borrower and lender.[28] Not until 1882, however, did the Legislature pass a liberalized usury law. By this law (Chapter 237, Section 1) all loans which: (a) were over $5,000, (b) were collateralized, and (c) had a negotiated rate in writing, were exempt from usury laws. The old system, said one commentator, was "absurd."[29] For the week ending November 24, 1882 the call loan range was reported as 4-30%.

Loan Characteristics. The use of year-end stock levels for the analysis of loan properties is useful,

---

[28] John Dix, Annual Message--January 7, 1873, New York State Assembly, Session 96, Assembly Document No. 2, 29.

[29] Commercial and Financial Chronicle, May 13, 1882, 512.

of course, but suffers from the lack of information on the flow of funds--which would have to come from general ledger accounts or subsidiary loan ledgers. Fortunately general ledgers are available for several banks.[30] In this section, loan transactions are analyzed for two trust companies--Central and Union, and two medium sized national banks--Phenix and Chatham.

The bookkeeping procedures, although varying among these banks, allow the analysis of the following loan accounts:

	Table	1885 Year-end $ (000)	1885 Year-end %
Central Trust:			
Bills Discounted	3:15:A	$ 1,999	14%
Call Loans	3:15:B	8,707	60
Time Loans	3:15:C	3,755	26
Total Loans	3:15:D	$14,461	100%
Union Trust:			
Total Loans	3:15:E	$20,564	100%

---

30 The General Ledgers examined represent some of the predecessor banks of Manufacturers Hanover Trust Company. Although Subsidiary Ledgers are not preserved, a great deal of the detail of daily operations still can be reconstructed from the General Ledgers. The nineteenth century accountant, while exhibiting the deadly perseverence that later became the hallmark of that profession, was universally endowed neither with good penmanship nor the capacity for unerring addition.

	Table	$ (000)	%
Phenix National:			
Temporary Loans	3:15:F	$ 1,719	69%
Notes Discounted	3:15:G	771	31
Total Loans	3:15:H	$ 2,490	100%
Chatham National:			
Loan Account	3:15:I	$ 968	26%
Bills Discounted	3:15:J	2,751	74
Total Loans	3:15:K	$ 3,719	100%

The nomenclature of the loan accounts obviously varied from bank to bank. Basically, the loan accounts could be regrouped into three divisions: bills discounted, call loans and time loans.

Bills discounted referred to rediscounted paper. Individual A owed individual B a debt, normally a trade debt, which was evidenced by a bill. Individual B would sell the bill to a bank at a discount, in order to secure working capital. The amount of the discount was influenced by: (1) the credit worthiness of individual A and, if applicable, the endorser of the bill, (2) the maturity date, which was usually less than four months and (3) prevailing market rates of interest. Bills were often payable in localities outside New York, in which case the bank would further reduce the proceeds of the bill to individual B by a collection fee--called "exchange." Banks which handled a substantial amount of out-of-town bills often would set up a special "foreign bills discounted" ledger. For a large portion of the commercial banking industry, discounting bills was the primary line of business. Of the banks and trust companies examined in this section, only Union did not discount bills.

Call loans were secured by various forms of collateral, especially warehouse receipts or negotiable stocks and bonds. The loans were payable on demand. The quality of the collateral influenced the interest rate.

Time loans were identical to call loans in most respects except in having a fixed maturity. Normally in any one lending institution, the average time loan would be smaller than the average call loan. Neither Chatham nor Phenix participated in time loans.

In the next set of tables, the transactions for each loan account, for each bank, are shown on a monthly basis. Again, the year 1885 is used for cross-sectional analysis. Several features of the tables are obvious: (1) the volume of loan transactions was substantially greater than the mere change in year-end stock levels would indicate (just how much greater is

TABLE 3:15:A

Central Trust
Bills Discounted
(000's)

1885	Loans Originated	Loans Repaid	Dollar Change	End of Month Balance
J	$ 981	$ 833	$ + 148	$ 2,180
F	1,228	652	+ 576	2,756
M	994	272	+ 722	3,478
A	510	359	+ 151	3,629
M	840	650	+ 190	3,819
J	744	785	- 41	3,778
J	730	689	+ 41	3,819
A	870	765	+ 105	3,924
S	467	784	- 317	3,607
O	571	666	- 95	3,512
N	456	1,248	- 792	2,720
D	132	853	- 721	1,999
1Q	3,203	1,757	+1,446	2,805*
2Q	2,094	1,794	+ 300	3,742*
3Q	2,067	2,238	- 171	3,783*
4Q	1,159	2,767	-1,608	2,745*
J-J	5,297	3,551	+1,746	3,274*
J-D	3,226	5,005	-1,779	3,264*
12 Mos.	8,523	8,556	- 33	3,269

* Monthly average

Source: Central Trust Company, General Ledger-1885.

TABLE 3:15:B

Central Trust
Call Loans
(000's)

1885	Loans Originated	Loans Repaid	Dollar Change	End of Month Balance
J	$ 1,826	$ 2,908	$ -1,082	$ 4,279
F	870	1,171	- 301	3,978
M	1,082	960	+ 122	4,100
A	536	250	+ 286	4,389
M	1,366	1,581	- 215	4,171
J	792	807	- 15	4,156
J	2,309	1,462	+ 847	5,003
A	4,281	2,691	+1,595	6,598
S	2,548	2,873	- 325	6,273
O	6,207	4,365	+1,842	8,115
N	6,639	6,714	- 75	8,040
D	6,099	5,432	+ 667	8,707
1Q	3,778	5,039	-1,261	4,119*
2Q	2,694	2,638	+ 56	4,237*
3Q	9,143	7,026	+2,117	5,958*
4Q	18,943	16,511	+2,432	8,287*
J-J	6,472	7,677	-1,205	4,178*
J-D	28,088	23,537	+4,551	7,122*
12 Mos.	34,560	31,214	+3,346	5,650*

*Monthly average

Source: Central Trust Company, General Ledger-1885.

TABLE 3:15:C

Central Trust
Time Loans
(000's)

1885	Loans Originated	Loans Repaid	Dollar Change	End of Month Balance
J	$ 1,028	$ 437	$ + 591	$ 6,023
F	466	718	- 252	5,771
M	670	507	+ 163	5,934
A	524	606	- 82	5,852
M	647	195	+ 452	6,304
J	908	374	+ 534	6,838
J	584	1,081	- 497	6,341
A	328	730	- 402	5,939
S	258	563	- 305	5,634
O	331	781	- 450	5,184
N	403	1,180	- 777	4,407
D	486	1,138	- 652	3,755
1Q	2,164	1,662	+ 502	5,909*
2Q	2,079	1,175	+ 904	6,331*
3Q	1,170	2,374	-1,204	5,971*
4Q	1,220	3,099	-1,879	4,448*
J-J	4,243	2,837	+1,406	6,120*
J-D	2,390	5,473	-3,083	5,209*
12 Mos.	6,633	8,310	-1,677	5,664*

*Monthly average

Source: Central Trust Company, General Ledger-1885.

TABLE 3:15:D

Central Trust
Total Loans
(000's)

1885	Loans Originated	Loans Repaid	Dollar Change	End of Month Balance
J	$ 3,835	$ 4,178	$ - 343	$12,482
F	2,565	2,541	+ 23	12,505
M	2,746	1,739	+1,007	13,867
M	2,853	2,426	+ 427	14,294
J	2,444	1,966	+ 478	14,772
J	3,623	3,232	+ 391	15,163
A	5,484	4,186	+1,298	16,461
S	3,273	4,220	- 947	15,514
O	7,109	5,812	+1,297	16,811
N	7,498	9,142	-1,664	15,167
D	6,717	7,423	- 706	14,461
1Q	9,145	8,458	+ 687	12,833*
2Q	6,867	5,607	+1,260	14,311*
3Q	12,380	11,638	+ 742	15,713*
4Q	21,324	22,377	-1,053	15,480*
J-J	16,012	14,065	+1,947	13,572*
J-D	33,704	34,015	- 311	15,597*
12 Mos.	49,716	48,080	+1,636	14,585*

*Monthly average

Source: Central Trust Company, General Ledger-1885.

TABLE 3:15:E

Union Trust
Total Loans
(000's)

1885	Loans Originated	Loans Repaid	Dollar Change	End of Month Balance
J	$ 5,786	$ 7,462	& -1,676	$14,738
F	5,084	5,240	- 156	14,582
M	4,355	5,374	-1,019	13,563
A	5,732	5,132	+ 600	14,163
M	4,984	6,341	-1,357	12,806
J	3,779	4,837	- 986	11,820
J	6,496	3,531	+ 494	12,314
A	5,090	4,837	+ 253	12,567
S	4,865	3,531	+1,334	13,901
O	19,659	17,353	+2,306	16,207
N	23,169	20,077	+3,092	19,299
D	30,272	29,007	+1,265	20,564
1Q	15,225	18,076	-2,851	14,294*
2Q	14,495	16,238	-1,743	12,929*
3Q	16,451	14,370	+2,081	12,927*
4Q	73,100	66,437	+6,663	18,690*
J-J	29,720	34,314	-4,594	13,611*
J-D	89,551	80,807	+8,744	15,808*
12 Mos.	119,270	115,121	+4,150	14,709*

*Monthly average

Source: Union Trust Company, General Ledger-1885.

TABLE 3:15:F

Phenix National
(000's)

1885	Loans Originated	Loans Repaid	Dollar Change	End of Month Balance
J	$ 1,419	$ 1,457	$ - 38	$ 1,361
F	1,874	1,553	+ 321	1,682
M	2,370	2,551	- 181	1,501
A	1,485	1,365	+ 120	1,621
M	1,830	1,834	- 4	1,617
J	1,784	1,632	+ 152	1,769
J	2,364	2,100	+ 264	2,033
A	2,427	2,194	+ 233	2,266
S	1,714	2,178	- 464	1,802
O	2,856	2,964	- 108	1,694
N	2,383	2,419	- 36	1,658
D	2,270	2,209	+ 61	1,719
1Q	5,663	5,561	+ 102	1,514*
2Q	5,099	4,831	+ 268	1,669*
3Q	6,505	6,472	+ 33	2,033*
4Q	7,592	7,592	- 83	1,690*
J-J	10,762	10,392	+ 370	1,591*
J-D	14,014	14,064	- 50	1,861*
12 Mos.	24,776	24,456	+ 320	1,726*

*Monthly average

Source: Phenix National Bank, General Ledger-1885.

TABLE 3:15:G

Phenix National
Notes Discounted
(000's)

1885	Loans Originated	Loans Repaid	Dollar Change	End of Month Balance
J	$ 142	$ 228	$ - 86	$ 703
F	181	321	- 140	563
M	186	180	+ 6	569
A	208	158	+ 50	619
M	165	212	+ 53	672
J	218	187	+ 31	703
J	199	212	- 13	690
A	189	190	- 1	689
S	313	215	+ 98	787
O	286	212	+ 74	861
N	262	350	- 88	773
D	272	274	- 2	771
1Q	509	729	- 220	611*
2Q	691	557	+ 134	664*
3Q	701	617	+ 84	772*
4Q	820	836	- 16	801*
J-J	1,200	1,286	- 86	637*
J-D	1,521	1,453	+ 68	761*
12 Mos.	2,721	2,739	- 18	699*

* Monthly Average

Source: Phenix National Bank, General Ledger-1885.

TABLE 3E:15:H

Phenix National
Total Loans
(000's)

1885	Loans Originated	Loans Repaid	Dollar Change	End of Month Balance
J	$ 1,561	$ 1,685	$ - 124	$ 2,064
F	2,055	1,874	+ 181	2,245
M	2,556	2,731	- 175	2,050
A	1,693	1,523	+ 170	2,240
M	2,093	2,046	+ 49	2,289
J	2,002	1,819	+ 183	2,472
J	2,563	2,312	+ 251	2,723
A	2,616	2,384	+ 232	2,955
S	2,027	2,393	- 366	2,589
O	3,142	3,176	- 34	2,555
N	2,645	2,769	- 124	2,431
D	2,542	2,483	+ 59	2,490
1Q	6,172	6,290	- 118	2,126*
2Q	5,790	5,388	+ 402	2,334*
3Q	7,206	7,089	+ 117	2,756*
4Q	8,329	8,428	- 99	2,492*
J-J	11,962	11,678	+ 284	2,230*
J-D	15,535	15,517	+ 18	2,624*
12 Mos.	27,497	27,195	+ 302	2,427*

*Monthly average

Source: Phenix National Bank, General Ledger-1885.

TABLE 3:15:I

Chatham National
Loan Account
(000')

1885	Loans Originated	Loans Repaid	Dollar Change	End of Month Balance
J	$ 217	$ 237	$ - 20	$ 839
F	266	178	+ 88	927
M	240	272	- 32	895
A	142	192	- 50	845
M	151	225	- 74	771
J	239	184	+ 75	846
J	297	243	+ 54	900
A	320	367	- 47	853
S	166	178	- 12	841
O	305	363	- 48	783
N	262	162	+ 100	883
D	422	348	+ 85	968
1Q	723	687	+ 36	887*
2Q	552	601	- 49	821*
3Q	783	788	- 5	864
4Q	1,000	873	+ 127	878*
J-J	1,275	1,288	- 13	854*
J-D	1,783	1,661	+ 122	871*
12 Mos.	3,058	2,949	+ 109	863*

*Monthly average

Source: Chatham National Bank, General Ledger-1885.

TABLE 3:15:J

Chatham National
Bills Discounted
(000's)

1885	Loans Originated	Loans Repaid	Dollar Change	End of Month Balance
J	$ 760	$ 896	$ - 136	$ 2,104
F	826	682	+ 144	2,248
M	783	622	+ 161	2,409
A	782	666	+ 116	2,525
M	958	983	- 25	2,500
J	626	672	- 46	2,454
J	980	929	+ 51	2,505
A	822	692	+ 130	2,635
S	942	759	+ 183	2,818
O	807	812	- 5	2,813
N	1,036	993	+ 43	2,856
D	909	1,014	- 105	2,751
1Q	2,369	2,200	+ 169	2,253*
2Q	2,366	2,321	+ 45	2,493*
3Q	2,744	2,380	+ 364	2,652*
4Q	2,752	2,819	- 67	2,806*
J-J	4,735	4,521	+ 214	2,373*
J-D	5,496	5,199	+ 297	2,729*
12 Mos.	10,231	9,720	+ 511	2,551*

*Monthly average

Source: Chatham National Bank, General Ledger-1885.

TABLE 3:15:K

Chatham National
Total Loans
(000's)

1885	Loans Originated	Loans Repaid	Dollar Change	End of Month Balance
J	$ 977	$ 1,133	$ - 156	$ 2,943
F	1,092	860	+ 232	3,175
M	1,023	894	+ 129	3,304
A	924	858	+ 66	3,370
M	1,109	1,208	- 99	3,271
J	885	856	+ 29	3,300
J	1,277	1,172	+ 105	3,405
A	1,142	1,059	+ 83	3,488
S	1,108	937	+ 171	3,659
O	1,112	1,175	- 63	3,596
N	1,298	1,155	+ 143	3,739
D	1,342	1,362	- 20	3,719
1Q	3,092	2,887	+ 205	3,141*
2Q	2,918	2,922	- 4	3,313*
3Q	3,527	3,168	+ 359	3,517*
4Q	3,752	3,692	+ 60	3,685*
J-J	6,010	5,809	+ 201	3,227*
J-D	7,279	6,860	+ 419	3,601*
12 Mos.	13,289	12,669	+ 620	3,414*

*Monthly average

Source: Chatham National Bank, General Ledger-1885.

important, because banking manages flows of funds, not just stock levels), (2) experience varied widely among the banks, and (3) experience varied considerably among homogeneous classes of loans. The data in Table 3:15: A-K can be manipulated to make these features more precise.

First, the quarterly experience in loans originated or repaid is measured as a percentage of loans originated or repaid for the entire year.

As Table 3:16 indicates, loan activity tended to be heavier in the second half of the year than in the first half, and tended to be heaviest of all in the fourth quarter. To some extent this reflected the normal seasonal pattern of financing relating to the autumn financing of agricultural production and harvesting. But to some extent it probably also reflected the fact that the economy became progressively stronger in a secular sense as 1885 unfolded.[31]

Among the trust companies participating in the stock market oriented call loan market, activity became noticeably stronger after June (in Central's case) following the

---

[31] Commercial and Financial Chronicle, January 9, 1886, 37-9.

TABLE 3:16

1885--Seasonal Distribution of Loan Transactions*

	Central Trust				Union Trust
Loan Origination:	Call	Time	Bills Discounted	Total Loans	Total Loans
1Q	11%	33%	38%	18%	13%
2Q	8	31	24	14	12
3Q	26	18	24	25	14
4Q	55	18	14	43	61
Year	100%	100%	100%	100%	100%
Loan Repayment:					
1Q	17%	20%	20%	17%	16%
2Q	8	14	21	12	14
3Q	22	29	26	11	13
4Q	53	37	33	22	57
Year	100%	100%	100%	100%	100%

	Phenix National			Chatham National		
	Temporary Loans	Notes Discounted	Total Loans	Loans	Bills Discounted	Total Loans
Loan Origination:						
1Q	22%	19%	23%	24%	23%	23%
2Q	21	25	21	18	23	22
3Q	27	26	26	25	27	27
4Q	30	30	30	33	27	28
Year	100%	100%	100%	100%	100%	100%
Loan Repayment:						
1Q	22%	27%	23%	23%	23%	23%
2Q	20	20	20	21	23	23
3Q	27	22	26	26	24	25
4Q	31	31	31	30	30	29
Year	100%	100%	100%	100%	100%	100%

*Seasonal Distribution equals loans originated or repaid in any one quarter as a percent of loans originated or repaid during the entire year.

Source: Based on Table 3:15:A-K.

buoyant market effects of the rate negotiations between the New York Central, Pennsylvania and West Shore railroad companies. Union, a rather conservative institution at the time, held back on the call loan market until October, when management apparently felt the possibility of a Fall money crisis was past. Repayment activity, as Table 3:16 also indicates, in the call loan area fairly closely paralleled loan origination activity. One of the attributes of the call loan market was that lenders could enter and leave the market on discretion.

Companies lending in the call loan market were quite sensitive to financial crises. Insight into just how sensitive is furnished by the number of loans made on a monthly basis by Union Trust Company. Table 3:17 compares two years market by financial crises, 1884 (beginning in May) and 1893 (beginning in July) with two normal adjacent years, 1883 and 1892.

In times of financial crises, the trust company would pull back from the call loan market out of concern about the solvency of the stock broker and the marketability of the collateral; the stock broker also would tend to pull back under the influence of higher interest rates, and the unattractive prospects of carrying inventory in a declining market.

TABLE 3:17

Number of Loans Made:
Union Trust Company

Month	1883	1884	1892	1893
J (4 weeks)	291	175	128	134
F (4)	244	193	225	262
M (5)	164	255	310	182
A (4)	180	190	254	121
M (4)	397	223	269	125
J (5)	516	145	217	134
J (4)	206	43	113	52
A (4)	116	33	302	60
S (5)	273	96	363	41
O (4)	181	80	188	18
N (4)	160	85	161	67
D (5)	223	149	208	67
Total (52)	2,951	1,667	2,738	1,264

Source: Union Trsut Company, Minutes of Executive Committee, 1883, 1884, 1893, 1894.

In the bills discounted class of loans there is a noticeable tendency for the repayment activity to be heavier in the fourth quarter than origination activity and for origination activity to be heavier in the third quarter than repayment activity. Bills discounted were mainly trade or mercantile based paper. Quite possibly, in the third quarter, especially in the interior of the country, funds were scarce, trade bills were forwarded (by brokers specializing in this) to New York to be discounted. When funds flowed back to the interior, as a result of the harvests, the bills discounted would be maturing, just in time to boost fourth quarter repayment activity. If this suggestion is correct, then the customary strain arising from the outflow of correspondent deposits from New York to the interior in the early Fall would be mitigated to some extent by increased repayments of bills discounted held by New York banks. The degree of mitigation would depend, among other things, on the size and dates of harvests in the various parts of the country.

Unlike the commercial banks, where bills discounted was an essential and primary line of business, Central Trust apparently regarded bills discounted as secondary or supplementary to the call loan line of business. This much is suggested by the Loan Origination activity in bills discounted as the year moved on and the demand for call loan money became stronger.

The data on loan repayments serves as a reminder that the loan portfolio is also an integral source of liquidity for a bank. Different classes of loans had different repayment, or turnover, or liquidity properties.

As Table 3:18 illustrates, the average bill discounted tended to mature in three to four months, the average call loan in a slightly more liquid two months and average time loans in about eight months. The high liquidity ratio for

TABLE 3:18

Loan Portfolio Liquidity Ratios: 1885

	Liquidity Ratio
Central Trust:	
Bills Discounted	4.2X
Call Loans	5.8
Time Loans	1.6
Total Loans	3.7
Union Trust:	
Total Loans	7.0
Phenix National:	
Temporary Loans	17.5
Notes Discounted	3.5
Total Loans	12.4
Chatham National:	
Loan Account	3.4
Bills Discounted	4.3
Total Loans	4.0

Source: Based on Tables 3:15 A-K. The Liquidity Ratio equals loan repayments for the year, divided by loan account balance at December 31, 1884.

Phenix National's Temporary Loan account seems to be related to a special line of business concentration, possibly the financing of commodities or merchandise in transit or repurchase financing with professional loan brokers. Phenix's close relationship with Atlantic Mutual Insurance, which did considerable ocean cargo and hull insurance, suggests the first possibility. The bank's substantial certified check business suggests the second possibility.

Exactly what would be the aggregate liqudity ratio of a bank or trust company would depend at any one point in time on seasonal characteristics, management's assessment of the secular tone of the financial market, and the types of customers the lender serviced.

In any event, the above data suggests that the aggregate loan maturities of both banks and trust companies were basically short. But there were important exceptions in the trust company field--those companies engaged in lending on Western mortgages.

Western Mortgages--A Case Study. The Fire Proof Warehousing Company was chartered in 1868. The primary objective of the company, as the title suggests, was the construction of a fireproof structure and the storage of merchandise therein. The charter provided, among other things, that each room in the warehouse would be equipped "with an electric fire alarm, which, when acted upon by a degree of heat above the temperature of the atmosphere, will cause the ringing of a bell upon the building,..."[32]

---

[32]N.Y. State, Laws, 1868, Chapter 806, Section 1. Subse-

The charter also allowed several powers incidental to the warehouse business, including insuring, cooperage, repacking, lighterage and advancing money on stored merchandise.

In 1869 and 1870 the charter was amended, in both instances refining and broadening the lending function. In 1870, the company's name was changed to Mercantile Loan and Warehouse Company.

In 1873, the charter was again amended, this time changing the name to Mercantile Trust Company and increasing corporate powers to include real estate and mortgage activities.

The company began operations around 1871. Initially business focused on the New York mercantile market. Loans were made on a secured basis and characteristically in the $20,000-40,000 range. Mercantile's singular distinction, however, rested in the fact that Equitable Life Assurance Society, the second largest life insurance company in New York City, owned 5,505 of the company's 10,000 shares, or over 55%. No other New York City trust company

---

quent amendments of consequence to the Act chartering Mercantile Trust: Laws, 1869, Chapter 185; Laws, 1870, Chapter 212, Laws, 1873, Chapter 845; and Laws, 1880, Chapter 425.

is known to have had a direct tie approaching this magnitude with another financial intermediary.[33] In 1876, several of Mercantile's directors were also trustees of Equitable, and the Executive Committee, the center of the company's power structure was dominated by Henry B. Hyde and James W. Alexander, the number one and two men respectively of Equitable.[34]

This case study concentrates on the 1875-6 period, when Mercantile engaged almost exclusively in lending on Western mortgages. Although lending on Western mortgages was not a dominant theme in the trust company movement, it was nevertheless important. Three other companies identified with the movement were prominent lenders on Western lands--Jarvis-Conklin Mortgage Trust, United States Mortgage Company and Equitable Trust Company (no relation to Equitable Life Assurance). Several other prominent companies which were not identified with the trust movement were also important lenders on Western lands, including the

---

[33]Atlantic Mutual Insurance Company, however, owned over half of the shares of Phenix National Bank.

[34]R. Carlyle Buley wrote: "Although Hyde was a small stockholder, he gave orders in Mercantile Trust, which was a tenant in the Equitable Building, much the same as he did in his own company." The Equitable Life Assurance Society of the United States, Appleton-Century-Crofts, New York, 1959, 44.

New England Mortgage and Security Company and many brokers specialized in retailing of Western mortgages.

Early in December, 1874, Mercantile first became interested in lending money on Western lands.[35] A special committee of three, all members of the powerful Executive Committee, was appointed to investigate the matter. By mid-December, the committee reported favorably and Mercantile elected to go into the mortgage business. In a very short time mortgages would be, as the company advertised, the "only business."

Two individuals were primarily responsible for the company's entrance into Western mortgages: Colonel John J. McCook, a lawyer with the firm of Alexander and Green, and General Louis Fitzgerald. Neither individual had been closely associated with Mercantile prior to this time.

McCook was hired as the company's solicitor with primary responsibilities for reselling mortgages or bonds backed by mortgages. McCook was to be compensated at a rate of $2,000 for each $1,000,000 of bonds sold.

---

[35]The basic data for this section was derived from: Mercantile Trust Company, Minutes of the Executive Committee: February 18, 1874-June 4, 1875; Minutes of the Executive Committee (Bond Department): January 5, 1875-December 12, 1876, and Minutes of the Executive Committee: December 19, 1876-October 2, 1884.

General Louis Fitzgerald, an experienced mortgage man, was hired as a Vice President to run the Bond Department. Fitzgerald's contract ran for five years and carried a salary of $6,000 per annum, plus $1,000 for each $1,000,000 of bonds sold.

Early in January, 1875, both McCook and Fitzgerald were elected to the Board of Directors. Fitzgerald directed the organizational efforts, the most exacting of which was creating the system for originating loans. Late in January, Fitzgerald and McCook swung through the Western states (Kentucky, Indiana, Iowa, Missouri, and Illinois) appointing a General Manager for each state.

The General Manager was the key position in the company's field system. The Manager's overall responsibilities included developing a force of lawyers, agents and appraisers, and monitoring the quality of loans offered to the company. The Executive Committee, while fully aware of the theoretical attractiveness of Western loans, was nevertheless quite uneasy about the prospect of poor or fraudulent loans being fed to the company. By the 1870's, mortgage fever had been the end of more than one American banker. The Executive Committee saw the General Manager as the critical filter for credit quality.

When Fitzgerald and McCook started their Western

swing, they had already reviewed a list of potential General Managers. The list came from the files of Equitable Life Assurance. Each name

> ...had already been approved by the Committee by reason of their experience and success in making loans for another Company and their long tried faithfulness, trustworthiness and conservatism as Agents of the Equitable Life Assurance Society.[36]

While Fitzgerald and McCook were making the appointments in person and evaluating local conditions, President Henry B. Hyde, still uncertain, instituted on his own initiative inquiries on the personal character of the prospective General Agents. The responses were favorable and by February 5, 1875, the Executive Committee offically confirmed the first appointments of the field force.

The field organization for originating loans grew rapidly in the Spring of 1875. General Agents were added in all of the initial states plus Kansas, Iowa, and Minnesota. By September, 1875, or twenty months after entering the Western mortgage business, Mercantile Trust had seven hundred and forty men in the field, working through one hundred and fifty-three agents.

---

[36]Mercantile Trust Company, Minutes of the Executive Committee (Bond Department): January 5, 1875-December 12, 1876-October 2, 1884.

General Agents in the field received a commission from the company, probably on the order of 1% of the principal value of the mortgage, although the possibility that some agents negotiated a supplemental fee (a finder's fee) with a borrower cannot be ruled out.

On February 4, 1875, the first batch of loans received from the West was reviewed by the Executive Committee. The credit scoring techniques were well-thought out, highly standardized and largely inflexible.

Loan applications were submitted to the Executive Committee by the agents on standardized forms supplied by the Committee. Information on the forms indicated the location of the property, the appraised value of the land, the appraised value of buildings on the land, estimated annual rental, the amount of the loan requested, a maturity date, and an interest rate. By the Spring of 1875, each loan application had to be accompanied by a map (printed at the Company's expense) showing the location of the property and a floor plan of the building(s). The maps were checked against a master library of town and county maps kept in the New York office.

Loans generated by the field organization were forwarded to New York for approval (or rejection). Mercantile's Executive Committee, meeting once or twice a week, processed the loans according to well-defined rules: maturity--5 year maximum, interest rate--9½% sometimes in Chicago but usually 10%, the principal loan could not exceed 33% of the appraised value of farm lands or 50% of the appraised value of improved city property, and the potential rental value had a minimum 10 year pay back period. Rarely were these rules relaxed.

Loan volume boomed. In February, 1875, the first month of operation, forty-four loans were processed, representing $330,500 in aggregate and a $7,511 average loan value. In March, 1875, sixty-eight loans were processed, with an aggregate value of $322,000 and an average value of $4,735. Of the one hundred and twelve loans processed in February and March, eight-five were accepted. Vice President Fitzgerald was busy, he requested and received a clerk--annual salary, $800.

By November, 1875, three hundred and thirty-five loans had been made, aggregating $1,071,500 with an average loan value of $3,199. By June, 1876, the company had made $1,670,500 in loans. The rate of loan submission was strong, but substantially below the heady pace of the early months.

In spite of the structural safeguards built in to insure effective credit scoring, the Executive Committee remained uneasy about the quality of loans. A new line of business, wide geographical distances and strangers borrowing money, all combined, prompted the Executive Committee to follow a cautious and restless course. In November, 1875, the Committee hired a special traveling agent to scrutinize proposed as well as existing loans and to monitor the "character and position of those through whose instrumentality loans were made."[37]

Once Mercantile placed a mortgage on the books three options were open: (1) the loans could be resold, (2) they could be retained by the company for investment, or (3) they could be resold with a company guaranty. The first option was not practical because it would be quite difficult for the purchaser in a secondary market to service the mortgage. The second and third options, however, were realistic, and the company used both extensively. By June 13, 1876, Mercantile had made mortgage loans of $1.7 million, with 44% still held by the company and 56% sold with the company's guarantee. The latter, of course, were off balance sheet items. How did the company manage each option?

---

[37]Ibid., meeting of November 5, 1875.

If the company retained the mortgages, the sources of supporting funds could theoretically come from: (1) deposits, (2) debenture notes, or (3) stockholders equity. The earnings on this segment of the business would be the spread between interest income and expenses, less a certain allocation of administrative expenses. First year earnings also would be penalized by commissions to originating agents.

Mercantile did not look to deposits as a source of funds. In fact, as long as Western mortgages were the main line of business, the company was out of the deposit market altogether. On July 1, 1874, the company reported $638,000 in deposits, on July 1, 1875, $49,000 and nothing for deposits in 1876, 1877, or 1879.

The reasons for this were two-fold: first, among New York City trust companies, deposits were basically a money market item, bid for competitively like call loan money was lent. Moreover, deposit flows could be seasonally erratic. Deposits consequently lacked the stability needed to support a long-term asset structure.

Secondly, it was difficult to be in the New York deposit market without being in the New York loan market. The two markets were closely related in terms of business connections. The spheres of customers in the loan and deposit markets overlapped. Certainly the administrative and operational structure which would support the deposit business would be virtually the same as that for the loan business. A bank was either in or out of both markets.

Debenture notes were considered a legitimate source of funds, although they were not utilized until late in the period (1878) of the company's interest in Western mortgages--a time when the company's organization for resale of the mortgages was deteriorating. Even then the debentures were probably intended to act as a bullet instrument, maturing in three years or about the same time as a large portion of the characteristic five-year mortgages put on the books in 1875 and 1876. Equitable Trust, the other major firm dealing in Western mortgages at the time, however, made a more extensive use of the debenture option as a source of funds.[38]

Stockholders equity, the third potential source of funds, was actually sufficient at any time to cover retained mortgages and a United States Government bond

---

[38] Equitable's Mortgage Bonds outstanding exceeded \$14.1 million at one point (December 31, 1881), while Mercantile's barely exceeded \$0.5 million (December 31, 1880). The Bonds of both companies were quoted monthly in the Commercial and Financial Chronicle in 1871. See also: Commercial and Financial Chronicle, September 2, 1876, 226.

liquidity buffer. Paid-in capital was $1.6 million on July 1, 1875, with $115 thousand in retained earnings. Paid-in capital increased to $2.0 million late in 1875.

The company's policy toward stockholders equity affords an interesting insight into capital theory of the 1870's. The charters of the trust companies provided two capital constraints: first a minimum paid-in capital necessary to commence business, and secondly, a maximum allowable capital limit. In Mercantile's case, the first was $200,000 subscribed, with $50,000 paid-in, and the second was $5 million. Par value was $100, giving a potential range of outstanding shares of 20-50,000.

In May, 1875, when the company had $2 million of paid-in capital (20,000 shares outstanding), the Executive Committee established the following long term policy: if net earnings allowed, a 7% dividend would be paid annually on par value, any net earnings in excess of the dividend would be transferred to a reserve fund from which the Directors would periodically issue stock dividends until the 50,000 allowable shares were outstanding. Once the allowable limit was reached, all net earnings would be distributed as dividends. Moreover, the authorized but unissued shares were not to be distributed in any manner but the above.

The policy was never implemented. Dividends of varying rates were paid, no stock dividends were issued through the rest of the century and net earnings were simply accumulated in retained earnings.

In actuality, the basic design of Mercantile Trust was not to retain the mortgages, but to exercise the third alternative--to resell the mortgages with a company guaranty. Moreover, the company's initial intention was to resell the mortgages (represented by a "mortgage bond") in Europe, not New York City.

The formation of a distribution system to resell the mortgages did not evolve as smoothly as the formation of the mortgage origination system. For the better part of 1875 and 1876, the Executive Committee was badgered with reappraisals of old distribution policies and false starts with new ones.

The beginning went smoothly enough. In early January, 1875, Vice President Fitzgerald was authorized to order 20,000 pamphlets, entitled <u>Safe Sure</u>, which explained the nature of the company's mortgage business and the meaning of the company's guarantee on the mortgage bond. <u>Safe Sure</u>, printed at a cost of 2.5 cents each, was intended for distribution to potential buyers of the mortgage bonds and represented an early version of the contemporary prospectus.[39]

Early in February, 1875, the Executive Committee took two significant steps--both illustrating the importance of Europe in the company's distribution philosophy. First a directorship was offered to Robert MacKenzie of Dundee, Scotland. An overseas director was quite unusual in New York banking cirlces. Second, Colonel McCook was sent to "Europe" (the company's terminology, McCook actually only went to England) to negotiate with underwriters for the sale of up to $5 million of mortgage bonds.

McCook left early in March with a statement of the company's condition as of March 1, 1875 in his pocket. Negotiations with potential underwriters went slowly, and it was not until early May, 1875, that the Executive Committee received McCook's request to approve McCullock and Company of London as the company's agent in Great Britain. McCook was still in England. There is some indication that MacKenzie and the McCullock firm were associated.

---

[39]Mercantile Trust Company, Minutes of the Executive Committee: February 10, 1874-June 4, 1875, meeting of January 21, 1875. Unfortunately no copies survive.

At this time (May, 1875) the Executive Committee also discussed the possibility of setting up sub-boards (advisory boards) in London and Manchester, but nothing came of this.

In early May, 1875, the Executive Committee also took up, somewhat belatedly it would seem, the form of the company's guaranty of the mortgage bonds.

Additional significant developments in May included: first, setting the commission to any underwriter (firm or individual) at 1% of the face value of a mortgage bond sold, providing that if the underwriter sold $200,000 of bonds in any one year, an additional 1% would be paid on the whole amount. Secondly, an arrangement with Williams and Deacon and Company of London to be joint agents in Great Britain with McCullocks. Apparently relations with McCullocks were not entirely satisfactory. And thirdly, the Executive Committee provided that the dollar amount of mortgage bonds guaranteed by the company could not exceed ten times the paid up capital and surplus. The constraint was probably designed to ease the way of the agents selling the bonds. The constraint was never even remotely tested. At this time the company had about $1.7 million in capital and surplus, giving a guaranty constraint of $17 million, but the company probably never guaranteed at any one time more than \$2 million of bonds.

Throughout April, May, and June, McCook remained in England. Some progress was made in the marketing of bonds and Baring Brothers and Company of London were brought in as agents to strengthen the sales effort.

Another indication that arrangements in Great Britain were not flowing as smoothly as desired, in late June, 1875, the Executive Committee instructed Vice President Fitzgerald to prepare a plan for the sale of the bonds in the Eastern States.

Late in July, 1875, McCook returned to the United States, bearing reports of his progress and Mr. MacKenzie's resignation as a director.

Sales of the bonds seemed to be satisfactory, but well below the company's anticipations. By November, 1875, at least \$365,000 of bonds had been sold and by June, 1876, \$936,500.

The distribution of bonds, however, continued to have problems. In November, 1875, in order to stimulate the London underwriters, the commission on bond sales was increased to 2½%.

Moreover, McCook reported that the fact that the company was also in the Safe Deposit business hindered the sale of bonds in Europe, because the safe deposit business "was construed by foreign capitalists as an additional obligation of the company."[40]

In the wake of McCook's report, the directors of Mercantile Trust hurriedly chartered Mercantile Safe Deposit Company. All of the safe deposit business was sold to the new company. The decision to take this step is an indication of Mercantile's firm commitment to the business of originating and guaranteeing mortgage paper. The safe deposit business was no incidental factor in Mercantile's operation. Officials of the State of New York, reporting to the Superintendent of Banking on the results of a February 8, 1875 examination stated:

> The safe deposit business of the company is increasing rapidly. It now pays all the expenses of the company.[41]

Within a year of this report, Mercantile Trust was out of the safe deposit business.

---

[40] Mercantile Trust Company, Minutes of the Executive Committee (Bond Department): January 5, 1875-December 12, 1876, meeting of October 5, 1875.

[41] D. C. Ellis (Superintendent of Banking) Annual Report Relative to Savings Banks, April 29, 1875, New York State Legislature, Session 98, Assembly Document No. 108, 332-3. Also: Session 99, Assembly Document No. 97, 342.

The foreign distribution system continued to give the company trouble. The directors, growing restive, instructed the President in January, 1876, to prepare a list of foreign bankers doing business in New York

> that they /the directors/ might judge intelligently as to the necessary steps to be taken to establish the most favorable business relations for the Company.[42]

In March, 1876, McCook went again to London, returning in April with recommendations that Mercantile abandon agency relationships with London firms, setting up instead its own London office. Which the company did, with a Mr. Ashmore in charge. The London firms never even remotely reached the company's sales objectives.

At the same time, efforts were finally coming to fruition to establish a distribution system in the Eastern States. A Mr. McMahon was hired in April, 1876, to canvass "Bank officers and others" in the East with a view of encouraging them to become agents for the sale of Mercantile's bonds.

The commission arrangements with the domestic agents were fairly liberal, suggesting that the company was having

---

[42] Mercantile Trust Company, Minutes of the Executive Committee (Bond Department): January 5, 1875-December 12, 1876, meeting of January 18, 1876.

some difficulty in setting up an agency system. Arrangements with Neher and Calder, a Troy, New York firm, provided for a 2% commission, advertising expenses and a ½% over-ride commission on all other bonds sold in Troy. Arrangements with a Mr. Camp of West Winsted, Connecticut called for a 2% commission plus traveling expenses.

C. H. Dillingham, hired to set up agencies in New England, received a guarantee of $400 per month for six months, plus an over-ride commission of ¼% on all bonds sold over a hurdle of $480,000.

In August, 1876, the company felt the demand for the bonds was good enough to raise the price to 102. The coupon remained at 7%, the same as always. The company was actually bringing the effective yield of its bonds in line with the decline in general bond yields over the previous twelve months.

Between January, 1875 and August, 1876, the minutes of the Executive Committee were peppered with adjustments to the distribution system. While the company focused on the distribution problem, another and equally severe problem crept in quite undetected in the procedures for originating mortgages.

In August, 1876, the directors instructed Henry Hurlbut,

Chairman of the Executive Committee, to undertake a special review of the organization problem. A month later Hurlbut reported.

There was indeed a problem--the Executive Committee was not approving loans submitted by the field organization, as the following table suggests.

TABLE 3:19

Summary of Mortgage Loan Activity
February, 1875-August, 1876

	Loan Amount	
Submitted by Field Force	$6,814,000	
In Process	1,868,500	
Processed	$4,945,500	
Rejected by Exec. Comm.	3,145,400	Est.
Accepted	$1,800,000	Est.
Retained	800,000	Est.
Sold with Guaranty	$1,000,000	Est.

Source: Mercantile Trust Company, Minutes of the Executive Committee (Bond Department), September 12, 1876.

Approximately 64% of the loan volume submitted by the field force was rejected by the Executive Committee. The $1.8 million accepted was barely a tenth of the company's capacity. Little wonder that Hurlbut could state:

> ...the great distance of the Home office from the Agencies and the want of personal knowledge of the Agents by the Committee gradually had the effect of weakening their confidence in their repre-

> sentatives and united to the continued feeling of depression as to the future prospects of the Company, created upon the part of the Committee greater and greater distrust, till it became so doubtful if applications would pass at all, or if passed, if for enough to satisfy applicants, that one by one, gradually but surely, this extensive organization for loaning, has slipped away from us and we are today without enough applications to absorb the funds at hand.[43]

One benefit did follow from the Executive Committee's cautious policy: of the 478 loans made during this period, not one went sour.

The company's response to the problem of faltering loan originations was to decentralize lending authority in such a manner, that loans which met basic and explicit standards would be virtually automatically approved by the Executive Committee. It was thereby hoped that agents would be encouraged again to start mortgages flowing to New York.

The damage, however, had been done. Mercantile's venture into Western lands was on the wane. By 1880 the Company was virtually out of the mortgage guaranty business and back into the deposit and commercial loan business.

---

[43] *Ibid.*, meeting of September 12, 1876.

CHAPTER IV

THE LIABILITY STRUCTURE

Object and Basic Data

The previous Chapter examined the growth, structural and comparative characteristics of major asset items. The object of Chapter IV is to do the same for the major credit balance items--deposits and capital. The Chapter also examines profitability of trust companies and commercial banks.

1885 will again serve as a point for cross-sectional analysis.

Table 4:1 reproduces the basic data upon which much of this Chapter is built. As in the case of the major asset items, the trust companies showed a deep penetration of the liabilities market in the 1875-1900 period. The trust companies, which held 8.9% of New York City's deposits in 1875, held 24.6% by 1900. Even more impressive, trust companies held 10.3% of New York City's banking capital (i.e., total equity) in 1875 and 33.2%, or a third, in 1900. A notable entrepreneurial performance.

TABLE 4:1

New York City Financial Institutions
Aggregated Liabilities by Intermediary
(000's)

	Deposits	Circulation	Surplus & Capital
Trust Companies:			
1875	$ 48,302	--	$ 16,581
1880	61,963	--	20,185
1885	129,323	--	29,945
1890	183,052	--	50,368
1895	251,318	--	61,176
1900	525,764	--	116,142

	Deposits	Circulation	Surplus & Capital
National Banks:			
1875	$268,045	$ 18,400	$102,958
1880	379,621	18,642	79,231
1885	390,849	9,948	78,013
1890	428,634	3,622	100,958
1895	506,718	14,341	110,528
1900	884,408	29,367	137,153

	Deposits	Circulation	Surplus & Capital
State Banks:			
1875	$ 44,542	$ 38	$ 21,600
1880	53,863	17	17,136
1885	117,945	3	21,585
1890	117,158	3	30,415
1895	130,623	--	31,163
1900	213,089	--	32,377

	Deposits	Circulation	Surplus & Capital
Savings Banks:			
1875	$184,188	--	$ 20,687
1880	193,235	--	27,357
1885	255,946	--	45,199
1890	319,113	--	50,481
1895	378,085	--	49,229
1900	506,263	--	64,069

Source: Data for National banks from Annual Reports of the Comptroller of the Currency. Data for other intermediaries from Annual Reports of the New York State Superintendent of Banking. See Footnote 3:7.

Table 4:2 restructures the data in Table 4:1, to show the comparative compound annual growth rates in deposits and capital over the 1875-1900 span and subdivisions.

TABLE 4:2

Compound Annual Growth Rates
of New York City Deposits and Capital

	Deposits			
	Trust Companies	National Banks	State Banks	Savings Banks
1875-80	5.1%	7.2%	3.9%	0.8%
1880-85	15.8	0.6	16.9	5.8
1885-90	7.2	1.9	- 0.1	4.5
1890-95	6.6	3.4	2.2	3.5
1895-00	15.9	11.0	10.8	6.1
1875-00	10.0	4.9	6.6	4.1

	Capital			
	Trust Companies	National Banks	State Banks	Savings Banks
1875-80	4.0%	- 5.4%	- 4.8%	5.8%
1880-85	8.2	- 0.3	4.7	10.6
1885-90	11.0	- 5.3	7.1	2.2
1890-95	3.9	1.8	0.5	- 0.5
1895-00	13.6	4.4	0.8	5.4
1875-00	8.1	1.2	1.6	4.6

Source: Based on Table 4:1.

The trust companies showed a superior growth rate in deposits and capital over the 25 year 1875-1900 period, and also in each subdivision with the exception of national bank deposits in 1875-80 and savings bank capital in 1875-80. The specific reasons for the superior performance of the trust companies are examined in the following paragraphs.

Deposits

TABLE 4:3

Deposits as a Percent of Liabilities
New York City

	1875	1880	1885	1890	1895	1900
Trust Companies	72.1%	66.7%	79.0%	75.0%	78.0%	79.4%
National Banks	68.8	79.5	81.6	80.4	80.1	82.9
State Banks	66.8	75.5	83.9	78.8	80.6	86.9
Savings Banks	89.7	87.6	85.0	85.8	88.5	88.7

Source: Based on Table 4:1. Liabilities, of course, equal to Assets shown in Table 3:1.

The rather high deposit-to-liability ratio shown by the savings banks reflects first that these companies were mutuals, not stock, and hence never had the sizable initial input of capital to the liability side, as characterized the publicly held companies. Secondly, the deposit structure of the savings bank basically served the accumulation and safety needs of the customer, not a transaction need as is the case of commercial banks. Consequently, the volatility of the savings bank deposit tended to be low, allowing a higher deposit-to-capital ratio.

In most of the years cited in Table 4:3, the national

and state banks had slightly higher deposit-to-liability ratios than the trust companies. The deposit figures upon which these ratios are based, however, include items in the process of collection, or deposited checks drawn on other banks which have yet to clear. Since the commercial banks were heavily involved in the clearing function, and the trust companies were not, it is probable that a larger portion of the commercial banks' deposits were in uncollected items. The effect of this is to slightly inflate the deposit-to-liability ratio of commercial banks relative to that of the trust companies.

The deposit data for the trust companies, as reported by the Superintendent of Banking, distinguished between demand deposits and trust deposits. Unfortunately the Superintendent nowhere defined the terms, leaving individual trust companies to allocate their deposits between the two classes according to their own judgement--and that judgement varied widely. Virtually all the trust companies seemed to be of one mind in placing receivership deposits in the trust category. Receivership deposits were collected in the process of recovering the assets of companies in bankruptcy, and for which the trust company had been appointed receiver. In several trust companies, the trust deposit category correlates positively with known periods of financial and mercantile distress.

Other classes of deposits which may have been allocated to the trust category by some trust companies are deposits generated by personal trust accounts, certificates of deposit and certified checks. One company, however, U.S. Trust, one of the largest and most prestigious of the trust companies, throughout the entire 1875-1900 period classified all its deposits in the trust category, even though the external evidence suggests that U.S. Trust's deposits were structurally no different from other large trust companies--which classified most of their deposits in the demand category. The reason why U.S. Trust followed the procedure it did was apparently due to the provision in the charter which authorized the company to "receive moneys in trust."[1] No other provision was made in the charter for receiving deposits.

The trust companies paid interest on the majority of their deposits--demand, certificate of deposits and those generated by personal trust accounts. The minimum rate payable on personal trust account deposits was often specified by the charter. The 1853 charter of U.S. Trust and

---

[1] New York State, Laws, 1853, Chapter 204, Section 2.

the 1871 charter of American Mortgage and Trust Company, for examples, set a minimum rate of 3.0% on trust deposits over one hundred dollars.

Interest was paid on demand deposits as well as certificates of deposit. As the name of the category implies, demand deposits could be withdrawn on demand. Certificates of deposit had a fixed maturity--with 3-6 months a characteristic range. At any point in time, the interest rate bid for demand deposits normally would be lower than that for certificates of deposit.

Table 4.4 shows the percentage of deposits upon which trust companies actually paid interest over the 1875-1900 period.

TABLE 4:4

Interest Bearing Deposits
New York City Trust Companies

	Aggregate Deposits (000)	Interest Bearing Deposits (000)	Percent
1875	$ 48,302	$ 46,249	95.7%
1880	61,963	58,370	94.2
1885	129,323	114,361	88.4
1890	183,053	166,460	90.0
1895	251,318	233,630	93.0
1900	525,764	488,550	92.9

Source: Annual Reports of the New York State Superintendent of Banking. See footnote 3:7.

As Table 4:4 illustrates, the trust companies paid interest on the vast majority of deposits. Those deposit classifications upon which interest was not paid were mainly: items in process of collection, coupon accounts, and receivership accounts. In 1885, the drop in the ratio of interest bearing deposits-to-total deposits is traceable to the rise in receivership accounts flowing from the adverse economic conditions in 1884.

Coupon accounts were a deposit category associated with a trust company's corporate trust functions. As a trustee under indenture for a bond or other debt, a trust company would receive from the issuing company a deposit to pay the coupon at the appropriate time. While there could be several techniques for paying coupons, the usual process was for the coupon holder to present his claim on the due date at the trust company, at which time he would be paid cash or issued a check (payable through a Clearing House member bank). The coupon accounts would be largest in January and July, the heaviest due date months. As the 1875-1900 period moved on, the amount of long term debt increased rapidly in the nation and the corporate trust business of the New York trust companies increased correspondingly. Exactly how large a percentage of deposits the non-interest bearing coupon account was is difficult to estimate for the aggregate figures. For Central Trust, however, the figure was quite substantial.

TABLE 4:5

Coupon Account/Total Deposits
Central Trust Company

Year-end	Coupon Account Deposits (000)	Total Deposits (000)	Percent
1880	$ 331	$ 4,701	7.0%
1885	636	16,545	3.8
1890	1,966	19,228	10.2
1895	2,264	28,806	7.6
1900	3,161	40,792	7.7
Compound Annual Growth Rate:			
1880-00	11.9%	11.4%	

Source: Central Trust Company, General Ledgers: A, B, C.

Central Trust had far and away the largest book of corporate trust business of any trust company. Accordingly, the industry average coupon account-to-total deposit percentage was undoubtedly considerably less, perhaps only one-fifth of the Central Trust ratio.

The size of the average interest bearing deposit in the trust companies was considerably larger than that in the savings banks. It is apparent from Table 4:6, that the trust companies and the savings banks were bidding in entirely different deposit markets. The savings banks were

TABLE 4:6

Average Account Size of Interest Bearing Deposits
New York City

Year-end	Aggregate Trust Companies	Aggregate Savings Banks
1875	$ 6,675	$348
1880	8,342	371
1885	9,833	378
1890	11,183	388
1895	11,829	408
1900	15,089	457

Source: New York State Superintendent of Banking, Annual Reports. See footnote 3:7.

directed at the small, individual saver, while the trust companies focused on the corporate money market. Apart from commercial paper, there was very little choice for the corporate treasurer seeking a productive haven for funds.[2] The trust companies, offering a capital-safe highly liquid and remunerative depository, stepped into this deficient spot in the money market.

Both trust companies and savings banks were expected

[2]Commercial and Financial Chronicle, August 2, 1884, 108. An interesting indirect confirmation of this hypothesis is found in the minority report to the New York Clearing House resolution. Arguing against the resolution, the minority report noted that the payment of interest was the means of attracting large deposits, which were useful "to banks and communities."

to pay interest on deposits. The financial community universally recognized that the issuance of interest bearing deposits was normal and structurally justified by these intermediaries. The same cannot be said of the commercial banks.

In 1853, 1873 and 1884, the New York Clearing House passed resolutions prohibiting the paying of interest on deposits. Most of the commercial banks seem to have abided by these resolutions. But a troublesome minority did not--the fact that such resolutions had to be passed more than once suggests as much. The fact too, that the resolutions were passed at the time of the founding of the Clearing House (1853) and in the wake of two financial panics (1873, 1884) suggests that the greater part of the banking community considered the payment of interest on deposits as incompatible with sound commercial banking and as a contributing factor to financial panics. The editor of the Commercial and Financial Chronicle, arguing in support of the 1884 Clearing House resolution to prohibit the paying of interest on deposits, stated:

> The public can see no reason why institutions /i.e., commercial banks/ that keep their vaults filled with dynamite /i.e., interest bearing

deposits/ should be allowed with Clearing House limits.[3]

Although there was no law prohibiting national banks from paying interest on deposits, in 1870 Comptroller of the Currency Highland R. Hurlburd, and in 1873 his successor John Jay Knox, cited the peril to the banking system of such practices. Both Comptrollers regarded the practice as "evil." Yet each was reluctant to encourage Congressional legislation to prohibit the practice, since such legislation would only constrain the national banks, leaving the state banks with a competitive advantage in the quest for deposits.[4]

To some degree, civil statute was in direct opposition to what the Comptroller and authorities in the Clearing House felt was sound policy. In 1882, the State Legislature passed the massive Law Relating to New York City (Chapter 410). Title 3, Section 165 of this Act, relating to the duties of the New York City Chamberlain, provided that no bank or trust company could be designated as a depository for city money unless:

---

[3] Commercial and Financial Chronicle, July 12, 1884, 31.

[4] Comptroller of the Currency, Annual Reports, November 7, 1870 and November 28, 1873, reprinted in the Commercial and Financial Chronicle, December 10, 1870, 746, and December 6, 1873, 768-9.

> ...its officers shall agree to pay into the city treasury interest on the daily balances at a rate to be fixed by the mayor and chamberlain, and said comptroller of the city of New York, by a majority vote, which rate shall not be less than two and one-half percent.

Since the city had to have deposits somewhere and there was also a $2,000,000 maximum limit on deposits in any one bank or trust company, it is evident that some depositories would be paying interest in spite of the objections of the banking authorities.

As the century moved on, the pointed opposition of the Comptroller's office to the payment of interest mellowed. In 1890, the Comptroller, while specifically side-stepping the question of whether or not interest should be paid on deposits to normal, local customers, lashed out against the bidding for deposits on the open market. The Comptroller felt that money so borrowed was very likely to flee the bank at an unpredictable time, leaving the bank in a serious liquidity crisis. The Comptroller, aiming his criticism at big-money deposits, specifically decried the practice of acquiring deposits through a broker and/or from geographical locations outside of a bank's native trade area.

The Comptroller proposed to limit such deposits by reclassifying them as borrowed money, thereby bringing them under Section 36 of the National Bank Act of 1864, which prohibited a bank from borrowing more than 100% of its paid-in capital.[5]

Unfortunately income statements are not available for most commercial banks in the 1875-1900 period, either on an aggregate or individual basis. As a consequence it is extremely difficult to determine which commercial banks did pay interest on deposits, on how much of their deposits, and when the practice was most prevalent.

The problem, however, can be approached indirectly. There is little doubt that the unusual growth of the trust companies in the 1875-1900 period was in a great measure due to the growth in deposits stemming from the payment of interest. Without a transaction function, the trust companies had little to lure depositors except the interest payment feature. It would follow then, that those commercial banks which also showed unusually high growth rates in deposits would also be paying interest. Returning to Table 4:2, showing the compound annual growth rates in deposits, the state banks showed a growth rate comparable with trust companies in the 1880-85 period and both state and national banks showed a well above average

---

[5]Comptroller of the Currency, Annual Report, December 1, 1890, 10-14.

growth rate in the 1895-1900 period.

The records of Hanover National Bank tend to verify the connection between the payment of interest and the growth of deposits. In Chart 4:1, Hanover's annual interest payment is correlated with the Bank's year-end net deposit levels from 1879-1900. The correlation is rather close. Especially noteworthy is the sharp rise in interest paid and deposit levels in the 1895-1900 period. The break in the upward trend of interest paid in 1884, 1890, 1893 and 1895 and 1899 correlates with down periods in the business cycle and suggest that the payment of interest was also sensitive to business conditions, whatever the long term policy of management might be.[6] The magnitude of the break in interest paid in 1885 and its continuation into 1886 (a year of rising interest rates) implies that the 1884 resolution of the Clearing House to prohibit the payment of interest on deposits was received with some temporary support from Hanover. The level of Hanover's interest payments in 1885 and 1886, as Chart 4:1 indicates, was the lowest of

---

[6] G. H. Moore, ed., Business Cycle Indicators, Volume 1, National Bureau of Economic Research, Princeton University Press, Princeton, N. J., 1961, 670.

CHART 4:1

Interest Payments and Deposit Levels
Hanover National Bank: 1879-1900

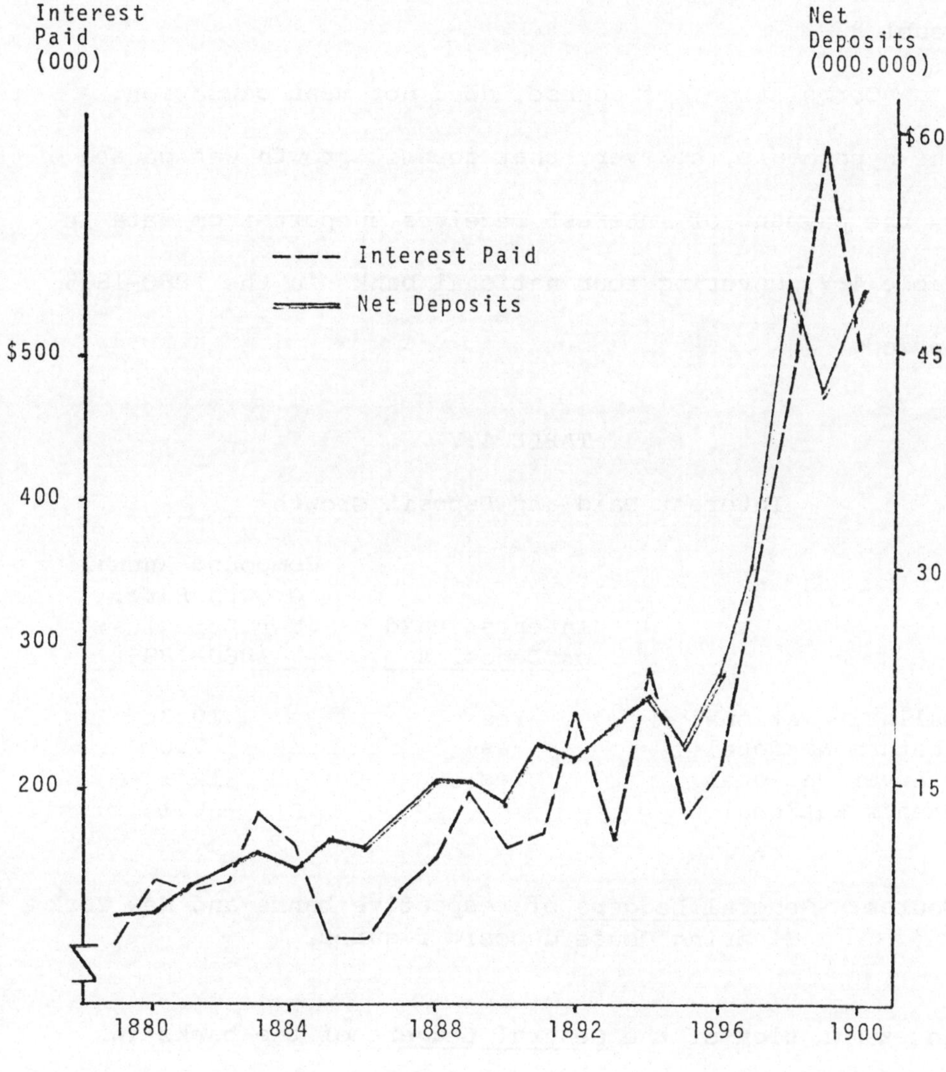

Source: Hanover National Bank, General Ledgers.

any years in the 1880-1900 span. But economic pressures were apparently not to be denied by resolutions. Between 1886 and 1889, the level of interest paid nearly doubled.

Correlation, of course, does not mean causation. The hypothesis, however, that deposit growth was caused by the payment of interest receives support from data in Table 4:7, covering four national banks in the 1880-1885 period.

TABLE 4:7

Interest Paid and Deposit Growth

	Interest Paid on Deposits	Compound Annual Growth Rate: Net Deposits: 1880-1885
Gallatin National	Yes	10.3%
Chatham National	Yes	7.0
Hanover National	Yes	12.1
Phenix National	No	- 6.1

Source: General Ledgers of respective banks and New York Clearing House deposit figures.

An examination of the General Ledgers of the banks in Table 4:7 reveals that the three that did pay interest had positive growth rates in net deposits in the 1880-1885 period, and the one that did not, had a negative growth rate. Each of the banks that did pay interest was doing so largely on correspondent bank balances. The magnitude of the growth rate in deposits actually ranks exactly with the relative size of the correspondent bank balances in each case. The one bank that did not pay interest had only a minor correspondent network, confined mostly to collection. As will become evident in the subsequent paragraphs dealing with certified checks, the poor deposit growth performance can not be charged exclusively to the failure to pay interest on deposits.

One additional element of evidence further suggests that deposit growth was tied to the payment of interest. Table 4:2 indicates that in the 1875-1880 period the savings banks showed a comparatively low growth rate in deposits; low compared to the experience of savings banks in subsequent periods and low relative to the other intermediaries in the 1875-80 period. This rather poor showing appears to be traceable to the passage in 1877 by the Legislature of a law (Chapter 256) which lowered the maximum rate of interest payable by savings banks from 6% to 5%. The result of this Law, observed State Superintendent of Banking, Henry L. Lamb,

> ...was to cause the withdrawal of a large amount of the capitalist accounts from savings banks,

> and the falling off of deposits is also attended by a decline in the average deposit.[7]

The year-end assets of the New York City savings banks actually declined from $200 million in 1876, to $196 million in 1877 and $185 million in 1878. The logical beneficiaries of the switch in bank deposits would be the trust companies.

When state and national banks did pay interest on deposits, their growth rates were much closer to those of the trust companies. The ability of the trust companies to attract deposits over the entire 1875-1900 period without direct or indirect censure or reflection on their financial soundness must be regarded as a prime contributing factor to their superior growth rate. In effect, the trust companies were virtually alone over most of the 1875-1900 period in offering a safe, liquid, remunerative haven for corporate funds. The failure of commercial banks to develop techniques, instruments and regulatory endorsement to meet the emerging demands of corporate treasurers allowed the trust companies to preempt the market and to become very quickly muscular competitors.

---

[7] Henry L. Lamb, Superintendent of Banking, New York, Annual Report Relative to Savings Banks, March 20, 1878, 101 Session, Assembly Document No. 89, 10.

Moreover, the ability to pay interest on deposits gave the trust companies immense flexibility in managing the day-to-day money position. For example, in 1885, Union Trust, in response to a burgeoning demand for funds in the call loan market, put $750,000 of certificates of deposit on the books in one day (November 25) and $1,000,000 additional two days later (November 27). These two transactions alone, increased the existing deposit base by over 8%. That funds of this magnitude could be added to the deposit structure, witnesses first to the money management attitude of the trust companies, secondly to the availability of funds for such deposits and thirdly contrasts sharply with the commercial banks, who were virtually at the mercy of the seasonal and transactional demands of the mercantile community.

Although it is surely a question of degree and individual management attitudes, the ability of the trust companies to pay interest on deposits seems to have given them a much greater capacity for self-determination than was enjoyed by the commercial banks.

In Chapter III, the general ledgers of two trust companies (Central and Union) and two commercial banks (Phenix and Chatham) were examined with a view to exploring the characteristics of the respective loan portfolio. In this section of Chapter IV, the same objective is pursued in regard to deposits.

The bookkeeping procedures, while varying among the banks, allow an analysis of the following deposit accounts:

		1885 Year-end	
	Table	$ (000)	%
Central Trust:			
Pass Book Account	4:8:A	$ 7,514	45%
Certificates of Deposit	4:8:B	8,377	51
Coupon Account	4:8:C	637	4
Total Deposits	4:8:D	$16,528	100%
Union Trust:			
Ledger Deposits	4:8:E	$21,250	88%
Certificates of Deposit	4:8:F	2,816	12
Certified Checks	4:8:G	32	0
Total Deposits	4:8:H	$24,098	100%
Phenix National:			
Ledger Deposits	4:8:I	$ 2,656	80%
Foreign Ledger	4:8:J	229	7
Certified Checks	4:8:K	416	13
Total Deposits	4:8:L	$ 3,301	100%
Chatham National:			
Ledger Deposits	4:8:M	$ 4,515	96%
Certified Checks	4:8:N	186	4
Total Deposits	4:8:O	$ 4,701	100%

The entry entitled "Pass Book Account" under Central Trust, was actually equal to the entry "Ledger Deposits" in the other companies. The term "Pass Book" referred to the book held by a depositor and in which debits and credits were entered and initialed by the teller. The Pass Book, was in effect the depositor's record of his trans-

TABLE 4:8:A

Central Trust
Pass Book Account
(000's)

1885	Monies Deposited	Deposits Withdrawn	Dollar Change	End of Month Balance
J	$ 3,659	$ 4,133	$ - 474	$ 5,309
F	1,379	1,584	- 205	5,104
M	2,473	1,588	+ 885	5,989
A	2,912	2,548	+ 364	6,353
M	2,782	2,331	+ 451	6,804
J	942	1,310	- 368	6,436
J	1,395	1,451	- 56	6,380
A	1,266	1,221	+ 45	6,425
S	2,028	1,900	+ 128	6,553
O	4,035	2,655	+1,380	7,933
N	4,957	6,149	-1,192	6,741
D	3,545	2,772	+ 773	7,514
1Q	7,511	7,305	+ 206	5,467*
2Q	6,636	6,189	+ 447	6,531*
3Q	4,689	4,572	+ 117	6,453*
4Q	12,537	11,576	+ 961	7,396*
J-J	14,147	13,494	+ 653	5,999*
J-D	17,226	16,148	+1,078	6,462*
12 Mos.	31,373	29,642	+1,731	6,462*

*Monthly Average

Source: Central Trust Company, General Ledger-1885.

TABLE 4:8:B

Central Trust
Certificates of Deposit
(000's)

1885	Monies Deposited	Deposits Withdrawn	Dollar Change	End of Month Balance
J	$ 2,064	$ 2,597	$ - 533	$ 8,873
F	1,495	1,181	+ 314	9,187
M	1,390	1,429	- 39	9,148
A	2,064	1,735	+ 329	9.477
M	1,056	760	+ 296	9,773
J	1,099	1,358	- 259	9,514
J	1,313	842	+ 471	9,985
A	1,920	914	+1,006	10,991
S	443	1,947	-1,504	9,487
O	1,770	2,126	- 356	9,131
N	2,649	2,586	+ 63	9,194
D	1,970	2,787	- 817	8,377
1Q	4,949	5,207	- 258	9,069*
2Q	4,219	3,853	+ 366	9,588*
3Q	3,676	3,703	- 27	10,154*
4Q	6,389	7,499	-1,110	8,900*
J-J	9,168	9,060	+ 108	9,329*
J-D	10,065	11,202	-1,137	9,527*
12 Mos.	19,233	20,262	-1,029	9,428*

*Monthly Average

Source: Central Trust Company, General Ledger-1885.

TABLE 4:8:C

Central Trust
Coupon Account
(ooo's)

1885	Monies Deposited	Deposits Withdrawn	Dollar Change	End of Month Balance
J	$ 1,242	$ 1,588	$ - 346	$ 68
F	420	405	+ 15	83
M	636	260	+ 376	459
A	427	785	- 358	101
M	340	370	- 30	71
J	824	242	+ 582	653
J	458	970	- 512	141
A	416	360	+ 56	197
S	508	295	+ 213	410
O	550	670	- 120	290
N	748	780	- 32	258
D	709	330	+ 379	637
1Q	2,298	2,253	+ 45	203*
2Q	1,591	1,397	+ 194	275*
3Q	1,382	1,625	- 243	249*
4Q	2,007	1,780	+ 227	395*
J-J	3,889	3,650	+ 239	239*
J-D	3,389	3,405	- 16	322*
12 Mos.	7,278	7,055	+ 223	281*

*Monthly Average

Source: Central Trust Company, General Ledger-1885.

TABLE 4:8:D

Central Trust
Total Deposits
(000's)

1885	Monies Deposted	Deposits Withdrawn	Dollar Change	End of Month Balance
J	$ 6,965	$ 8,318	$ -1,353	$14,250
F	3,294	3,170	+ 124	14,374
M	4,499	3,277	+1,222	15,596
A	5,403	5,068	+ 335	15,931
M	4,178	3,461	+ 717	16,648
J	2,865	2,910	- 45	16,603
J	3,166	3,263	- 97	16,506
A	3,602	2,495	+1,107	17,613
S	2,979	4,142	-1,163	16,450
O	6,355	5,451	+ 904	17,354
N	8,354	9,515	-1,161	16,193
D	6,224	5,889	+ 335	16,528
1Q	14,758	14,765	- 7	14,740*
2Q	12,446	11,439	+1,007	16,394*
3Q	9,747	9,900	- 153	16,856*
4Q	20,933	20,855	+ 78	16,692*
J-J	27,204	26,204	+1,000	15,567*
J-D	30,680	30,755	- 75	16,744*
12 Mos.	57,884	56,959	+ 925	16,171*

*Monthly Average

Source: Central Trust Company, General Ledger-1885.

TABLE 4:8:E

Union Trust
Total Individual Ledger Deposits
(000's)

1885	Monies Deposited	Deposits Withdrawn	Dollar Change	End of Month Balance
J	$10,103	$10,697	& - 594	$15,019
F	6,034	5,635	+ 399	15,418
M	7,287	6,591	+ 696	16,114
A	20,274	15,249	+5,125	21,139
M	9,015	13,468	-4,453	16,686
J	10,992	9,452	+1,540	18,226
J	9,267	10,948	-1,681	16,545
A	6,385	6,076	+ 309	16,854
S	6,178	6,493	- 315	16,539
O	11,248	9,659	+1,589	18,128
N	9,629	9,086	+ 543	18,671
D	17,287	14,708	+2,579	21,250
1Q	23,424	22,923	+ 501	15,517*
2Q	40,281	38,169	+2,112	18,683*
3Q	21,830	23,517	-1,687	16,646*
4Q	38,164	33,453	+4,711	19,350*
J-J	63,705	61,092	+2,613	17,100*
J-D	59,994	56,970	+3,024	17,998*
12 Mos.	123,699	118,062	+5,637	17,549*

* Monthly Average

Source: Union Trust Company, General Ledger-1885.

TABLE 4:8:F

Union Trust Company
Certificates of Deposit
(000's)

1885	Monies Deposited	Deposits Withdrawn	Dollar Change	End of Month Balance
J	$ 1,526	$ 1,085	$ + 441	$ 5,014
F	133	1,058	- 925	4,089
M	379	1,483	-1,104	2,985
A	515	517	- 2	2,983
M	168	457	- 289	2,694
J	96	344	- 248	2,446
J	350	531	- 181	2,265
A	144	202	- 58	2,207
S	452	463	- 11	2,196
O	775	339	+ 436	2,632
N	2,390	830	+1,221	3,853
D	553	1,590	-1,037	2,816
1Q	2,038	3,626	-1,588	4,029*
2Q	779	1,318	- 539	2,707*
3Q	946	1,196	- 250	2,222*
4Q	3,718	3,098	+ 620	3,100*
J-J	2,817	4,944	-2,127	3,368*
J-D	4,664	4,294	+ 370	2,661*
12 Mos.	7,481	9,238	-1,757	3,015*

*Monthly Average

Source: Union Trust Company, General Ledger-1885.

TABLE 4:8:G

Union Trust Company
Certified Checks
(000's)

1885	Monies Deposited	Deposits Withdrawn	Dollar Change	End of Month Balance
J	$ 1,196	$ 1,206	$ - 10	$ 19
F	1,039	1,036	+ 3	21
M	1,739	1,726	+ 13	34
A	1,724	1,724	0	34
M	1,312	1,310	+ 2	36
J	1,204	1,178	+ 26	62
J	1,422	1,426	- 4	58
A	894	917	- 23	35
S	1,004	1,018	- 14	21
O	1,688	1,684	+ 4	25
N	1,724	1,693	+ 31	56
D	3,707	3,731	- 24	32
1Q	3,974	3,968	+ 6	25*
2Q	4,240	4,212	+ 28	44*
3Q	3,320	3,361	- 41	38*
4Q	7,119	7,108	+ 11	38*
J-J	8,214	8,180	+ 34	34*
J-D	10,439	10,469	- 30	38*
12 Mos.	18,653	18,649	+ 4	36*

* Monthly Average

Source: Union Trust Company, General Ledger-1885.

TABLE 4:8:H

Union Trust Company**
Total Deposits
(000's)

1885	Monies Deposited	Deposits Withdrawn	Dollar Change	End of Month Balance
J	$11,629	$11,792	$ - 163	$20,052
F	6,167	6,691	- 524	19,528
M	13,833	14,228	- 395	19,133
A	20,789	15,766	+5,023	24,156
M	9,183	13,923	-4,740	19,416
J	11,088	9,770	+1,318	20,734
J	9,617	11,483	-1,866	18,868
A	6,529	6,301	+ 228	19,096
S	6,630	6,970	- 340	18,756
O	12,023	9,994	+2,029	20,785
N	12,019	10,224	+1,795	22,580
D	17,840	16,322	+1,518	24,098
1Q	31,629	32,711	-1,082	19,571*
2Q	41,060	39,459	+1,601	21,435*
3Q	22,776	24,754	-1,978	18,907*
4Q	41,882	36,540	+5,342	22,487*
J-J	72,689	72,170	+ 519	20,503*
J-D	64,658	61,294	+3,364	41,394*
12 Mos.	137,347	133,464	+3,883	30,948*

* Monthly Average

* Adjusted to eliminate double debit of Certified Checks.

Source: Union Trust Company, General Ledger-1885.

TABLE 4:8:I

Phenix National
Ledger Deposits
(000's)

1885	Monies Deposited	Deposits Withdrawn	Dollar Change	End of Month Balance
J	$11,105	$10,835	$ + 270	$ 2,653
F	12,894	13,273	- 379	2,274
M	9,898	10,204	- 306	1,968
A	9,415	9,380	+ 35	2,003
M	13,683	13,791	- 108	1,895
J	11,316	10,950	+ 366	2,261
J	11,285	11,120	+ 165	2,426
A	11,324	11,624	- 300	2,126
S	9,420	9,526	- 106	2,020
O	16,536	16,103	+ 433	2,453
N	11,449	11,738	- 289	2,164
D	12,356	11,864	+ 492	2,656
1Q	33,897	34,312	- 415	2,298*
2Q	34,414	34,121	+ 293	2,053*
3Q	32,029	32,270	- 241	2,191*
4Q	40,341	39,705	+ 636	2,424*
J-J	68,311	68,433	- 122	2,176
J-D	72,370	71,975	+ 395	2,308*
12 Mos.	140,408	140,408	+ 273	2,242*

* Monthly Average

Source: Phenix National Bank, General Ledger-1885.

TABLE 4:8:J

Phenix National Bank
(000's)

1885	Monies Deposited	Deposits Withdrawn	Dollar Change	End of Month Balance
J	$ 6,396	$ 6,122	$ + 274	$ 478
F	4,563	4,710	- 147	331
M	5,560	5,477	+ 83	414
A	6,130	6,149	- 19	395
M	5,283	5,128	+ 155	550
J	6,378	6,057	+ 321	871
J	6,653	6,878	- 225	646
A	4,746	4,565	+ 181	827
S	5,496	5,739	- 243	584
O	8,588	8,750	- 162	422
N	6,855	6,833	+ 22	444
D	7,669	7,884	- 215	229
1Q	16,519	16,309	+ 210	408*
2Q	17,791	17,334	+ 457	605*
3Q	16,895	17,182	- 287	686*
4Q	23,112	23,467	- 355	365*
J-J	34,310	33,643	+ 667	507*
J-D	40,007	40,649	- 642	525*
12 Mos.	74,317	74,292	+ 25	516*

* Monthly Average

Source: Phenix National Bank, General Ledger-1885.

TABLE 4:8:K

Phenix National Bank
Certified Checks
(000's)

1885	Monies Deposited	Deposits Withdrawn	Dollar Change	End of Month Balance
J	$ 3,593	$ 3,582	$ + 11	$ 211
F	6,595	6,630	- 35	176
M	4,462	4,396	+ 66	242
A	3,492	3,531	- 39	203
M	6,726	6,716	+ 10	213
J	4,322	4,247	+ 75	288
J	5,271	5,286	- 15	273
A	4,521	4,730	- 209	64
S	3,582	3,455	+ 127	191
O	8,549	8,598	- 49	142
N	5,340	5,221	+ 119	261
D	5,197	5,042	+ 155	416
1Q	14,650	14,608	+ 42	210*
2Q	14,640	14,494	+ 46	235*
3Q	13,374	13,471	- 97	176*
4Q	18,086	18,861	+ 225	273*
J-J	29,290	29,101	+ 88	222*
J-D	32,460	32,332	+ 128	225*
12 Mos.	61,750	61,434	+ 216	223*

* Monthly Average

Source: Phenix National Bank, General Ledger-1885.

TABLE: 4:8:L

Phenix National Bank
Total Deposits**
(000's)

1885	Monies Deposited	Deposits Withdrawn	Dollar Change	End of Month Balance
J	$17,501	$16,946	$ + 555	$ 3,342
F	17,457	18,018	- 561	2,781
M	15,458	15,615	- 157	2,624
A	15,545	15,568	- 23	2,601
M	18,966	18,909	+ 57	2,658
J	17,694	16,932	+ 762	3,420
J	17,938	18,013	- 75	3,345
A	16,070	16,398	- 328	3,017
S	14,916	15.138	- 222	2,795
O	25,124	24,902	+ 222	3,017
N	18,304	18,452	- 148	2,869
D	20,025	19,593	+ 432	3,301
1Q	50,416	50,579	- 163	2,916*
2Q	52,205	51,409	+ 796	2,893*
3Q	48,924	49,549	- 625	3,053*
4Q	63,453	62,947	+ 506	3,062*
J-J	102,621	101,988	+ 633	2,905*
J-D	112,377	112,496	- 119	3,057*
12 Mos.	214,998	214,484	+ 514	2,981*

* Monthly Average

** Adjusted to eliminate duplicate debits from certified checks.

Source: Phenix National Bank, General Ledger-1885.

TABLE 4:8:M

Chatham National Bank
Ledger Deposits
(000's)

1885	Monies Deposited	Deposits Withdrawn	Dollar Change	End of Month Balance
J	$12,880	$12,724	$ + 156	$ 4,101
F	11,139	11,128	+ 11	4,112
M	11,296	11,402	- 106	4,006
A	11,882	11,537	+ 345	4,351
M	11,628	12,085	- 457	3,894
J	11,820	11,658	+ 162	4,056
J	12,176	12,034	+ 142	4,198
A	10,686	11,041	- 355	3,843
S	11,582	11,550	+ 32	3,875
O	13,920	13,367	+ 553	4,428
N	12,987	12,955	+ 32	4,460
D	14,467	14,412	+ 55	4,515
1Q	35,315	35,254	+ 61	4,073*
2Q	35,330	35,280	+ 50	4,100*
3Q	34,444	34,625	- 181	3,972*
4Q	41,374	40,734	+ 640	4,668*
J-J	70,645	70,534	+ 111	4,087*
J-D	75,818	75,359	+ 459	4,320*
12 Mos.	146,463	145,893	+ 570	4,204*

*Monthly Average

Source: Chatham National Bank, General Ledger-1885.

TABLE 4:8:N

Chatham National Bank
Certified Checks
(000's)

1885	Monies Deposited	Deposits Withdrawn	Dollar Change	End of Month Balance
J	$ 2,817	$ 2,855	$ - 38	$ 129
F	2,974	2,930	+ 44	173
M	2,660	2,693	- 33	140
A	2,656	2,653	+ 3	143
M	2,732	2,634	+ 98	241
J	2,898	2,968	- 70	171
J	2,810	2,850	- 40	131
A	2,304	2,338	- 34	97
S	2,363	2,271	+ 92	189
O	2,750	2,811	- 61	128
N	2,592	2,551	+ 41	169
D	3,554	3,537	+ 17	186
1Q	8,451	8,479	- 27	147*
2Q	8,286	8,255	+ 31	185*
3Q	7,477	7,459	+ 18	139*
4Q	8,896	8,899	- 3	161*
J-J	16,737	16,733	+ 4	166*
J-D	16,373	16,358	+ 15	150*
12 Mos.	33,110	33,091	+ 19	158*

* Monthly Average

Source: Chatham National Bank, General Ledger-1885.

TABLE 4:8:0

Chatham National Bank
Total Deposits
(000's)

1885	Monies Deposited	Deposits Withdrawn	Dollar Change	End of Month Balance
J	$15,697	$15,579	$ + 118	$ 4,230
F	14,113	14,058	+ 55	4,285
M	13,956	14,095	- 139	4,146
A	14,538	14,190	+ 348	4,494
M	14,360	14,719	- 359	4,135
J	14,718	14,626	+ 92	4,227
J	14,986	14,884	+ 102	4,329
A	12,990	13,379	- 289	3,940
S	13,945	13,821	+ 124	4,064
O	16,670	16,178	+ 492	4,556
N	15,579	15,506	+ 73	4,629
D	18,021	17,949	+ 72	4,701
1Q	43,766	43,732	+ 34	4,220*
2Q	43,616	43,535	+ 81	4,285*
3Q	41,921	42,084	- 163	4,111*
4Q	50,270	49,633	+ 637	4,829*
J-J	87,382	87,267	+ 115	4,253*
J-D	92,191	91,717	+ 474	4,470*
12 Mos.	179,573	178,984	+ 589	4,362*

* Monthly Average

Source: Chatham National Bank, General Ledger-1885.

actions.[8]

The entry "Foreign Ledger" under Phenix National referred to correspondent bank and individual deposits from outside of the "City." Since foreign deposits were a separate line of business, usually with a separate department and set of clerks, and a unique clearing mechanism, banks with a correspondent business normally set up separate subsidiary ledgers for such business and often carried the summary balances to the general ledger quite distinct from other deposit categories.

Like the experience of the loan portfolio observed in Chapter III, the debit and credit transactions in the deposit portfolio were large relative to stock levels, experience varied considerably from bank to bank and among the various categories of deposits.

In Table 4:9, the debit (withdrawal) and credit (deposit) transactions are summarized to show seasonal distributions. In general, paralleling experience in the loan portfolio, deposit transactions were heaviest in the fourth quarter, reflecting the normal post-harvest activity in financial settlements and, in this case, the secular up-trend in the economy as 1885 moved on.

---

[8]S. S. Packard, Bank Bookkeeping, New York, 1897, 9-10.

TABLE 4:9

1885--Seasonal Distribution of Deposit Transactions*

	Central Trust				Union Trust			
Deposits	Pass Book	C.D.s	Coupon Acct.	Total	Ledger	C.D.s	Cert. Checks	Total
1Q	24%	26%	32%	25%	20%	27%	21%	23%
2Q	21	22	21	22	32	11	23	30
3Q	15	19	19	17	18	13	18	17
4Q	40	33	28	36	30	49	38	30
Yr.	100%	100%	100%	100%	100%	100%	100%	100%
Withdrawals								
1Q	25%	26%	32%	26%	19%	39%	21%	25%
2Q	21	19	20	20	33	15	23	29
3Q	15	18	23	17	20	13	18	19
4Q	39	37	25	37	28	33	38	27
Yr.	100%	100%	100%	100%	100%	100%	100%	100%

	Phenix National				Chatham National		
Deposits	Ledger	Foreign	Cert. Checks	Total	Ledger	Cert. Checks	Total
1Q	24%	22%	23%	23%	24%	26%	25%
2Q	25	24	23	25	24	25	24
3Q	21	23	22	23	23	22	22
4Q	29	31	32	29	29	27	29
Yr.	100%	100%	100%	100%	100%	100%	100%
Withdrawals							
1Q	24%	22%	24%	24%	24%	26%	25%
2Q	24	23	23	24	24	25	24
3Q	23	23	22	23	24	23	24
4Q	29	32	31	29	28	26	27
Yr.	100%	100%	100%	100%	100%	100%	100%

*Seasonal distribution equals deposits debited or credited in a quarter as a percent of deposits debited or credited over entire year.

Source: Based on Tables 4:8:A-O.

In the area of Certificates of Deposit, the portfolio management technique of Central Trust contrasts noticeably with that of Union Trust. As Tables 4:8:B, 4:8:F and 4:9 illustrate, Central's acquisition of C.D. funds was heavier than Union's in the second and third quarter. Central thereby acquired a sizeable volume of time funds when such funds were available and rates were low. When the call loan market began to pick up in June, Central had the funds in hand to meet the demand. Union, by contrast reacting slowly to the call loan market, did not become a big buyer of C.D. money until the fourth quarter. The average maturity of the trust company C.D., as Table 4:11 indicates, was around six months.

The Chatham National Bank also issued Certificates of Deposit. Unfortunately the condition of this particular section of Chatham's General Ledger is wanting in clarity and it has not been possible to reconstruct a transactions table of the debits and credits for 1885. The General Ledger does allow a rough estimate of the size of Chatham's C.D. Account--probably around $80 thousand or less than 2% of total deposits. Chatham's General Ledger, however, also allows a reconstruction of the size distribution of C.D.s issued by the Bank.

TABLE 4:10

Chatham National Bank
Distribution of Certificates of Deposit:
by Size: 1885

Size of C.D. Issued	Number of C.D.s Issued: Jan.-June	July-December	Full Year	Percent Distribution
$ 00.00 - $ 10.00	3	3	6	1.5%
10.01 - 15.00	10	6	16	4.0
20.01 - 50.00	48	42	90	22.1
50.01 - 100.00	43	44	87	21.5
100.01 - 250.00	28	36	64	15.8
250.01 - 500.00	27	26	64	13.1
500.01 - 1,000.00	7	34	41	10.1
1,000.01 - 2,000.00	9	18	27	6.7
2,000.01 - over	10	11	21	5.2
	185	220	405	100.0%

Source: Chatham National Bank, General Ledger, 1885.

The striking feature of Table 4:10 is the very small size of the C.D.s issued by Chatham, almost like saving account activity. The bank issued C.D.s for amounts of less than $10.00. The few C.D.s issued for over $2,000.01 were mostly just barely over, with one issued for $10,000.00. All of this contrasts sharply with the practice of Central and Union, who normally issued C.D.s in the $100,000-$500,000 range.

In Central's Coupon Account, withdrawals were heaviest in January and July, corresponding with the due dates of coupons on bonds under indenture. The deposits into this account, in anticipation of due dates, normally started in December and June. The extraordinarily heavy traffic in this account in January suggests that a sizable portion of the corporate debt was still on a once-a-year coupon payment date. Compensation for acting as a bond trustee was in two forms: first, a fee charged by the trust company for accepting the trusteeship (the fee was not amortized over the life of the bond) and secondly, the interest free undistributed balances in the coupon account. In Central's case in 1885, these balances were 1.7% of average deposits, which, assuming a 4.79% gross earning yield (Central's average yield on loans in 1885), contributed about 1.4% of loan income and 1.0% of gross income.

Union Trust also had a sizable corporate trust business and doubtless had some subsidiary ledger or off-ledger tickler scheme to monitor the payment activity of bonds under indenture. Unfortunately, however, unlike Central, Union consolidated these accounts before taking the totals to the General Ledger. Union's coupon deposit account is consequently blended in with Ledger Deposits and not susceptible to separate analysis.

The National Banking Act did not convey at this time corporate trust powers to national banks. But national banks might still have Coupon Accounts in their deposit structure, because bonds could be made payable at a national bank; in effect making the national bank a paying agent. Among the national banks in New York City during the 1880's frequently mentioned as paying agents were: National Bank of Commerce, National City Bank, National Park Bank, Mechanics National Bank, Metropolitan National Bank and Importers and Traders National Bank.

The Certified Check accounts represent checks which have been stamped or otherwise verified by the bank or trust company to indicate to the recipient of the check

TABLE 4:11

Deposit Turnover: 1885

	Turnover Ratio
Central Trust:	
Pass Book Account	5.1 X
Certificates of Deposit	2.1
Coupon Account	17.0
Total Deposits	3.7
Union Trust:	
Ledger Deposits	7.6
Certificates of Deposit	2.0
Certified Checks	643.0
Total Deposits	6.6
Phenix National:	
Ledger Deposits	58.9
Foreign Ledger	364.2
Certified Checks	307.2
Total Deposits	77.0
Chatham National:	
Ledger Deposits	37.0
Certified Checks	198.1
Total Deposits	43.5

Source: Based on Tables 4:8:A-O. Turnover ratio equals withdrawals for year divided by deposit base of December 31, 1884.

that the funds for payment of the check are available, that the bank has earmarked funds for the check so certified and that the check will not be refused on grounds of insufficient funds.[9]

[9] U.S. Supreme Court, "Merchants Bank v. State Bank," 10 Wallace, 604 and N.Y. Court of Appeals, "Henry Clews et al., Respondents, Bank of New York, National

The need for certified checks arises because the clearing of checks is not instantaneous. The individual accepting the check runs a risk that funds will not be available to honor the check when he presents it for payment. The time lag might be caused by the necessity for a check to clear through a geographically distant bank or it might be caused by an institutional factor, like a clearing house only processing for same-day payment a check received before 10:00 a.m. Certification eliminates this risk for the recipient of the check.[10]

The transactions in the Certified Check account are quite high in relation to the balances in the account, as indicated in Table 4:11. This much is understandable since certification was actually one step in the payment process.

The certified check, however, for all of its economic usefulness, was actually a contentious issue in the early 1880's between the national banks and the Comptroller of the Currency--the resolution of which strengthened the competitive position of the trust companies relative to the national banks.

Banking Association, Appelant," June 20, 1882, 89 N.Y. Reports, 419.

[10] Commercial and Financial Chronicle, January 1, 1876, 3.

The debate arose over the process of "over-certification." Over-certification was associated mainly with the stock brokerage business and consisted of a bank certifying a check when the maker of the check did not actually have funds on deposit to cover the check at the time the check was certified. Obviously any bank engaged in over-certification expected the funds to be available by the time the check returned for payment. The accounting entry in over-certifying would be:

Uncollected funds	(Customer A)	$ XXX	
Certified Check	(Customer A)		$ XXX

When the funds arrived:

Cash Ledger		$ XXX	
Uncollected funds	(Customer A)		$ XXX

And when the certified check was presented for payment:

Certified Check	(Customer A)	$ XXX	
Cash Ledger			$ XXX

The process of over-certification, then, resulted in swelling the float for a period of time.

The certified check was necessary in the stock brokerage business because one-day settlements were the normal practice. The broker would buy a bond, the seller would deliver the bond the same day and receive in return good funds--or a certified check. If the broker were buying for his own inventory or for a margin account customer (and these probably represented the majority of transactions), he would then go to a bank or trust company, probably using the bond purchased as collateral for a loan to support the inventory (his or the margin account customer's).[11]

Over-certification does not seem to have resulted in any undue losses to the banking community. From a national bank's position the problem was that over-certification was illegal. On March 3, 1869, Congress passed an Act to prohibit the certification of checks when sufficient funds were not on deposit. Nevertheless, the law was not enforced, apparently because over-certification was not a frequent or sizable practice for many years. In the early 1880's, however, among certain New York City national banks, over-certification increased at an alarming rate.

That the compound annual growth rate in deposits of national banks in the 1875-80 period was slightly superior to that of the trust companies (see Table 4:2) is probably attributable to the rise in the practice of over-certification of checks.

---

[11] _Ibid_., November 1, 1879, 445.

TABLE 4:12

Certified Checks Outstanding New York City National Banks

	Total Number of Banks	Certified Checks (000)	Number of Banks*	Certified Checks (000)
October 1, 1875	48	$ 28,049	9	$ 17,835
October 2, 1876	44	38,725	9	20,723
October 1, 1877	47	29,200	9	17,576
October 1, 1878	46	40,296	9	26,148
October 2, 1879	46	58,828	9	42,875
October 1, 1880	45	61,791	9	43,396
October 1, 1881	48	97,522	9	71,635
October 3, 1882	50	$137,317	9	$105,482

*A subset of total banks.

Source: Comptroller of the Currency, Annual Report, December 2, 1882.

The data in Table 4:12 was developed by John Jay Knox, Comptroller of the Currency. As the volume of certification rose, the Comptroller became alarmed. The nine banks singled out (the banks were not identified by name) by the Comptroller represented the major abusers of the over-certification process.

On the Comptroller's urging, Congress passed an Act on July 12, 1882 which put teeth in the Act of March 3, 1869, providing maximum fines of $5,000 and five years imprisonment for any national bank officer who over-certified a check. The Act of 1882 moreover not only prohibited the direct over-certification of a check, but also resorting to "any device, or receive any ficticious obligation, direct or collaterial, in order to evade the provisions [of the Act of 1869]."[12]

---

[12]An argument could be made to the effect that the Comptroller objected to over-certification not because of the inherent credit risk, but because a certified check had most of the economic attributes of circulation--except no U.S. bonds had to be pledged and no circulation tax was assessed on certified checks. That certified checks had been used as a money proxy and that Congress and the regulators were aware of the practice is suggested by Section 110 of the Ways and Means Act (June 30, 1864) wherein a tax was imposed on state bank circulation and certified checks were specifically included in the definition of circulation.

In U.S. Supreme Court, "Mercants Bank v. State Bank," December, 1870 (10 Wallace, 604), Justice Swayne, de-

The New York City national banks took the passage of the Act of 1882 with ill grace, as did the Wall Street investment community. The editors of the Commercial and Financial Chronicle thought the prohibition against over-certification might induce a wholesale conversion of national bank charters into state charters.[13]

Over-certification was obviously one important element in the business activity of several national banks in New York City. On passage of the July 12, 1882 Act, these banks immediately took evasive action, claiming that the certified checks were really acceptances, which the banks felt they were entitled to issue under Paragraphs 3 and 7 of Section 5,136 of the Revised Statutes, which authorized the "making of contracts" and the endowment of powers "incidental to the business of banking." The issuance of certified checks among the 9 designated banks even increased from \$45.5 million on July 1, 1881, to

---

livering the Court's opinion, said:

> The object of certifying a check, as regards both parties, is to enable the holder to use it as money. The transferee takes it with the same readiness and sense of security that he would take the notes of the bank. It is avail-also to him for all the purposes of money. 648

[13] Commercial and Financial Chronicle, July 15, 1882, 62; July 22, 1882; July 29, 1882, 115-6.

$105.5 million on October 3, 1882.

The national banks apparently took their cue from an 1874 decision on the West Virginia Supreme Court (7 West Virginia, 544) which held that the March 3, 1869 Act did not prohibit a national bank from making a conditional acceptance of a check, providing the maker of the check had funds on deposit by the time the check was presented for payment.

Comptroller Knox, in turn, understandably received the evasive actions of the banks with equal ill grace, asking in early Fall 1882, Attorney General Benjamin Brewster for an opinion on the following points:

1. Could a national bank accept a check if the funds were not actually on deposit? Brewster replied that they could not.
2. If a national bank can accept checks without having good funds on deposit, is the acceptance limited for any one customer to one-tenth of paid-in-capital, as suggested by the Section 29 of the National Bank Act of 1864. The Attorney General replied in the negative, since Section 29 only referred to moneys borrowed by the bank.
3. If a national bank can accept checks without

having good funds on deposit, is the total amount of such acceptances limited to the amount of paid-in capital, as suggested by Section 36 of the National Bank Act of 1864. Brewster replied that it was so limited. This point, while academic in light of Brewster's answer to the first question, was nevertheless rather important because if Brewster's answer to the first question had been affirmative, his answer to the third question would put a limit of the total amount of over-certifications which could take place--probably a limit well below the amount of certified checks outstanding on October 3, 1882, which were over 9 times paid-in capital of the 9 banks singled out by the Comptroller.[14]

The effect of the Comptroller's actions in 1882 on the certified check operations of Phenix National Bank (probably one of the 9 culprits singled out by the Comptroller) is shown in Table 4:13. In Table 4:13 the credit

---

[14] Comptroller of the Currency, Annual Report, December 2, 1882, reprinted in Commercial and Financial Chronicle, December 9, 1882, 670-1.

TABLE 4:13

Phenix National Bank
Deposit Transactions in Certified Checks

	1880	1881	1882	1883	1884
J	$ 138,089	$ 200,300	$ 186,937	$ 72,378	$ 69,718
F	121,647	203,171	170,906	77,596	57,768
M	147,657	171,237	174,983	74,991	52,196
A	130,826	133,165	137,167	70,370	49,977
M	150,254	212,738	101,505	51,088	44,842
J	120,250	169,397	120,057	55,006	5,039
J	104,609	170,151	118,253	51,771	7,406
A	83,301	141,230	124,034	58,692	4,519
S	96,822	146,332	157,176	66,412	3,685
O	115,386	187,301	146,355	90,006	5,664
N	168,956	147,631	139,776	56,405	4,012
D	211,898	201,919	90,698	69,240	4,894
Twelve Mos. Total:	$1,589,695	$2,084,572	$1,667,847	$793,955	$309,720

Source: Phenix National Bank, General Ledger, 1880-5.

transactions to the certified check account are shown monthly for 1880-1884. Transactions for 1885 are shown in Table 4:8:K.

As Table 4:13 illustrates, the Comptroller's actions had a dramatic effect. Phenix, a bank with $3.5 million net deposits in 1880, was doing transactions in the certified check business of $1.6 million in 1880, $2.1 million in 1881, and $1.7 million in 1882. The pattern here is revealing. In July 1882, when the Act imposing penalties for over-certification was passed, the tempo of the certified check business did not break at all. The Opinion of the Attorney General, however, pronouncing "acceptances" of checks without sufficient funds to be illegal was probably communicated to Phenix and other national banks in mid-November, 1882. In December, the certification process abruptly fell off. Judging from the ratio of total deposit transactions in 1883 to 1882, it could be ventured that roughly 50% of Phenix's certified checks prior to the Comptroller's action represented over-certifications.

The financial crisis which hit in May 1884, further reduced Phenix's certified check business. That the break should be so sharp between May and June, 1884, suggests strongly that Phenix was doing a substantial business with the Wall Street community, as opposed to Chatham, which was mainly oriented to the mercantile and correspondent bank communities.

The Comptroller's actions in 1882 with regard to over-certification was probably sound banking policy, but in terms of relative strengths of competing financial intermediaries, these actions worked strongly against the interest of the national banks: for by these actions the Comptroller denied the national banks the right to extend a service which the investment community regarded as essential. This tended to weaken the ties between the national banks and the investment community, and to increase the reliance of the investment community on services rendered by trust companies.

It is impossible to quantify the benefit the trust companies received and the disutility the national banks suffered from the Comptroller's 1882 actions, but, judging from the outraged reaction of the national banks to the Act of July 12, 1882, the effect was substantial.

Comparative Liquidity

In Tables 3:18 and 4:11, the turnover or liquidity ratios of Central Trust, Union Trust, Phenix National and Chatham National were calculated. The turnover ratios represented the total debit (in the case of deposits) or credit (in the case of loans) transactions for the year, divided by the balance in the respective accounts at the beginning of the year. In Table 4:14 the total loan and deposit turnover ratios for each trust company and bank are paralleled.

TABLE 4:14

Loan and Deposit Turnover: 1885

	Total Loans	Total Deposits
Central Trust	3.7 X	3.7 X
Union Trust	7.0	6.6
Phenix National	12.4	77.0
Chatham National	4.0	43.5

Source: See Tables 3:18 and 4:11.

On a net basis (deposits net of uncollected items) the ratio of loans outstanding-to-deposits was roughly one-to-one for these four institutions. Table 4:14 shows that the turnover rates in the loans and deposits of the trust companies were in very good balance. The managements of the trust companies were able to match the principal maturity flows of the two sides of the balance sheet--this involved discretionary action on both the asset and liability sides.

By contrast, the commercial banks had widely disparate turnover rates between the asset and liability sides. The transactions needs of the depositor governed the turnover characteristics of the commercial bank deposit structure. There was little the commercial banker could do to manage the turnover rate, since the reason in most cases for having a deposit account in a commercial bank was the convenience of the clearing facilities. Given, then, the exogenous volatility of the liability side, the commercial banker would have to respond with something he could control--a larger reserve buffer of cash reserves (See Table 3:4).

Involvement in the transaction function was apparently quite expensive. In 1885, Central supported $322 in average deposit dollars for every one dollar of salary, Union $543, but Chatham only $97 and Phenix only $96.[15]

The capital-to-liability ratios of savings banks were much lower than those of the commercial banks or trust companies, although the gap narrowed considerably between 1874 and 1900. In the normal course of events, savings banks would be expected to have lower capital ratios, since: (1) as mutual companies the initial input of capital probably

---

[15] Based on respective General Ledgers.

would be considerably less than that of a publicly held corporation; (2) the legislation (which was quite tight by 1877) over the functions of a savings bank engendered a low risk operation which could tolerate lower capital ratios.

TABLE 4:15

Capital as a Percent of Liabilities
New York City

	1875	1880	1885	1890	1895	1900
Trust Companies	24.7%	21.7%	18.2%	20.6%	19.0%	17.5%
National Banks	26.0	16.6	16.2	18.9	17.5	12.8
State Banks	32.4	24.0	15.4	20.4	19.2	12.9
Savings Banks	10.0	12.3	15.0	13.6	11.5	11.2

Source: Based on Table 4:1. Liabilities, of course, equal to Assets shown in Table 3:1. Capital includes paid-in, surplus and undivided profits.

The commercial banks, as Table 4:15 indicates, had higher capital-to-liabilities ratios in 1875 than the trust companies, but lower ratios by 1885. This was due in part to the fact that (see Table 4:2) the commercial banks showed very low growth rates in capital in the 1875-1900 period and the trust companies rather high growth rates.

The reasons for the superior growth rate in trust company capital are four-fold:

1. The trust companies attracted new capital, the commercial banks did not (reflecting the superior profitability of the trust companies).
2. High rates of taxation encouraged an exodus of capital from commercial banks.
3. The trust companies were more profitable, thus generating greater earnings to retain.
4. Trust companies had lower pay-out ratios on dividends.

These four inter-related points are examined in the following paragraphs:

New Capital. In 1875, the total number of trust companies in New York City was 9. By 1900, the number had risen to 31. Over the same period the number of national banks declined from 48 to 44, a net change of minus 4. The financial entrepreneur apparently felt the trust company vehicle was a more advantageous spot for investments.

Table 4:16 shows the net change in the capital accounts between 1875 and 1900 for the trust companies and commercial banks and disaggregates the change into that portion due to new capital investment and that due to growth in retained earnings.

As Table 4:16 indicates, all of the net new capital investment in the New York City financial intermediaries in the 1875-1900 period went into the trust companies. The reason for this, of course, was the higher profitability of the trust companies, which will be discussed subsequently.

TABLE 4:16

Change in Capital Accounts: 1875-1900
New York City
(000s)

		Trust Companies	National Banks	State Banks
Capital Accounts:	1900	$116,142	$137,153	$32,377
	1875	16,581	102,958	21,600
Net Change		$ 99,561	$ 36,195	$10,777
Due to: New Capital Investment		25,419	- 5,700	- 662
Growth in Retained Earnings		74,142	41,895	11,439

Source: Based on Table 4:1. See footnote 3:7.

Taxation. No aspect of banking operations was more heavily litigated in the 1864-1900 period than taxation. Much of the tax law was fairly explicit, but much too was a gray area. Legislative bodies changed tax laws, courts changed interpretations and taxing authorities applied the law with varying degrees of zeal.[16]

[16] A synopsis of important litigation relating to banking in the 1864-1900 period is found in the Comptroller of the Currency, Annual Report, December 3, 1900, 210-30.

In New York City, national banks, state banks and trust companies were each subject to taxes imposed by three political jurisdictions:

1. The City of New York.

2. The U.S. Government

3. The State of New York

Taxes imposed by the City of New York were restricted to a tax on the real estate owned by the bank or trust company and to taxes incidental to real estate ownership--such as a water tax. The bank or trust company, accordingly would factor a tax item into the equation when deciding whether to buy or rent an office building. The amount of the tax depended on the rate of taxation (which was set by the State Legislature each year) and the assessed valuation of the property. Of the three jurisdictions of taxation, the New York City tax on real estate was often the largest item--assuming a company owned its office building.[17] The only serious controversies con-

---

[17] In 1900, for example, Central Trust paid:

Authority	Rate	Tax
U.S. Government	2 % on Capital	$ 21,008
N.Y. State	2½% on Dividend	12,500
N.Y. City	2.01921% on Real Estate	114,380

See: General Ledger, 1900.

cerning this form of taxation were on whether or not the assessment was equitable, and these controversies occurred throughout the 1875-1900 period. The principle of real estate taxation by local authority was not itself challenged.[18]

Taxation by the U.S. Government fell into three statutory groups:

1. National banks were taxed under Section 41 of the National Bank Act of 1864. This Section provided for a tax on circulation of a yearly rate of 1%, on deposits at a yearly rate of ½ of 1% and on capital (less the amount invested in U.S. Government bonds) also at a yearly rate of ½ of 1%.[19] Taxes on deposits and capital were abolished by

---

[18] National Bank Act, 1864, Section 41.

[19] The abolition of the tax on capital had, in theory at least, a perverse effect on national bank circulation. Since under the Act of 1864, capital was taxed at an annual rate of ½ of 1% and the value of capital taxed was net of holdings of U.S. bonds, a bank had an incentive to hold U.S. bonds. With the passage of the March 3, 1883 Act, this incentive disappeared. Since circulation was based on holdings of U.S. bonds, circulation would, other things being equal, tend to contract as the bonds contracted. In actuality, the bonds held for circulation had started to decline for the national bank system in 1882, but the Act of March 3, 1883 may have accelerated the trend.

legislation passed March 3, 1883; while taxes on circulation continued beyond that.

2. State banks and trust companies were taxed under Section 110 of the Ways and Means Act of June 30, 1864. This Section provided for a federal tax on deposits and capital (less investments in U.S. Bonds) at a yearly rate of ½ of 1%, and on circulation at a yearly rate ranging from 1% to 2%, depending on the ratio of circulation to capital. The tax on circulation was subsequently (March, 1865) raised to 10%.

   The June 30, 1864 tax law remained effective, as regards state banks and trust companies, until repealed on March 3, 1883 (47 Congress, Chapter 121) by Congress.

3. Capital of national banks, state banks and trust companies remained un-taxed by the U.S. Government from 1883 until 1898, when Congress passed an Act to Meet War Expenditures (55 Congress, Chapter 448, Section 2). This Section provided for an annual tax on capital and surplus at a yearly rate of $50 for the first $25,000, and $2 for every additional $1,000.

Based on U.S. taxation alone, the national banks were on a parity with state banks and trust companies, except that national banks still had to pay tax on circulation. Quantitatively this meant the national banks still had to pay roughly a third of their historic tax bill to the federal government.

Taxation by New York State was also the product of several statutes, only here the basic polarity was between the national and state banks on one hand and the trust companies on the other. The reason for this particular polarity was that Section 41 of the National Bank Act of 1864, while allowing national banks to be taxed by the states, also provided that the rate of taxation imposed by the states had to be the same as that imposed by the state on banks organized under state charters.

The purpose of this provision was to prevent the states from placing the national banks at a competitive tax disadvantage.[20]

1. Under New York Laws of 1857 (Chapter 456, Section 3) all stock corporations were taxable on the sum of capital and any surplus in excess of 10% of

---

[20] U.S. District Court, "Mercantile Bank v. New York, 121, U.S., 138.

capital, less the assessed value of real estate owned. The rate of taxation, expressed in terms of so many mills per dollar of property, was determined by legislation passed each year. In 1875, for example, the rate was 5.125 mills, with 1.250 mills for the support of schools, 1.375 for general purposes, 2.000 for bounty debt and 0.500 for the new capitol.[21]

2. In 1866, a separate Law (Chapter 761), specially singling out national and state banks, was designed to place the two groups on a non-discriminating footing. The Law provided that the shareholders were to be taxed (not the bank), that the bank was to collect the taxes, and that the basis of taxation was to be the "value of their shares" less a proportionate amount of the assessed real estate in which the capital of the bank was invested. The failure of the Law to specify exactly how to determine the "value of their shares" later would become an issue of considerable contention.

---

[21] Lucius Robinson, Annual Report of the Comptroller of of the State of New York, January 4, 1876, Session 99, Assembly Document No. 3, 47.

One interesting aspect of this Law was that it did not provide for the deduction from the "value of their shares" of the proportionate amount of U.S. Government bonds held by the bank. The banks objected that this was an indirect taxation of U.S. bonds, in violation of the U.S. Constitution. The U.S. Supreme Court, however, upheld the legality of the New York law.[22]

The tax rate, again, was determined each year by legislation.

3. In 1881, the State Legislature passed a Law (Chapter 477) providing that hereafter the shareholders of national and state banks would be taxed on deposits and capital and surplus (less a proportionate amount of the assessed real estate owned by the bank) at an annual rate of ½ of 1%. This tax remained on the books throughout the century.

4. In 1881, another Law was passed (Chapter 361) providing that trust companies would be taxed at a rate of one and one-half mills per dollar of par value capital stock, unless dividends were paid

---

[22] U.S. Supreme Court, "VanAllen v. The Assessors," 3 Wallace, 573.

in the amount of 6% or greater on the par value, in which case the tax rate would be one-quarter mill for each one percentum of dividends paid.

Based on state taxation alone, the national and state banks were at a parity with the trust companies until 1881 and at a disadvantage thereafter.

The combined effect of federal and state taxation can be determined by a hypothetical model of three financial institutions. The model holds the financial parameters of each institution equal and assumes one institution is taxed as a national bank, one as a state bank and one as a trust company. The model will derive taxes as assessed in the years 1875, 1885, and 1900, which cover the three major combinations of tax laws.

The tax level of the national bank in each case would have been higher by the federal tax imposed on circulation. The national bank was not required to have circulation, and this model assumed that it did not, but in fact virtually all national banks did have circulation outstanding.

Table 4:17 indicates that in the 1875-1881 period, all three types of institutions were on a tax parity, whether the tax was imposed by federal or state authority.

In the 1882-1900 period, the state tax law favored the

TABLE 4:17

Effect of Taxation on Hypothetical Banks

Assumptions for All Banks in All Years

Deposits	$8,000,000
Capital	1,000,000
Surplus	700,000
U.S. Bonds	500,000
Circulation	none
Real Estate	none
Dividends	80,000

	National Bank	State Bank	Trust Company
1875 Taxation			
Federal Taxation:			
Deposits	$40,000	$40,000	$40,000
Capital	6,000	6,000	6,000
Subtotal	$46,000	$46,000	$46,000
State Taxation:			
Deposits	$ 4,100	$ 4,100	$ 4,100
Capital	820	820	820
Dividends	–	–	–
Subtotal	$ 4,920	$ 4,920	$ 4,920
Total Taxation:	$50,920	$50,920	$50,920
1885 Taxation			
Federal Taxation:			
Deposits	$ –	$ –	$ –
Capital	–	–	–
Subtotal	–	–	–
State Taxation:			
Deposits	$40,000	$40,000	$ –
Capital	8,500	8,500	–
Dividends	–	–	2,000
Subtotal	$48,500	$48,500	$ 2,000
Total Taxation:	$48,500	$48,500	$ 2,000
1900 Taxation			
Federal Taxation			
Deposits	$ –	$ –	$ –
Capital	3,400	3,400	3,400
Subtotal	$ 3,400	$ 3,400	$ 3,400
State Taxation:			
Deposits	$40,000	$40,000	$ –
Capital	8,500	8,500	–
Dividends	–	–	2,000
Subtotal	$48,500	$48,500	$ 2,000
Total Taxation:	$51,900	$51,900	$ 5,400

trust companies, by a very substantial margin. That the State Legislature consciously did this cannot be doubted. The 1881 Law (Chapter 361) under which the trust companies were taxed, was based on a near identical Law (Chapter 542) passed in 1880. Only the 1880 Law specifically excluded banks from its provisions. The 1881 Law specifically provided that trust companies were not excluded. Moreover in the General Banking Law of 1882 (Chapter 409) the 1881 (Chapter 361) tax base for trust companies was reaffirmed by the Legislature.

Over the 20 years of taxation, from 1881-1900, the favored position of the trust companies would have been an important incremental factor in the growth rate of capital.

But quite apart from the adverse effects of discriminatory taxation, the capital position of the commercial banks even suffered considerably in the 1875-80 period (see Table 4:2), when there was no discriminatory taxation.

The burden of taxation was widely protested by the banks themselves in the 1870's. Moreover, the collectors of taxes (county treasurers were the agents of the state) objected to the cumbersome procedures they had to go through to collect bank taxes.[23] And scarcely a year went by from 1870-1881 that the Governor or Superintendent of Banking did not prod the Legislature to alleviate the burden of bank taxation. The remarks of Superintendent Ellis in 1874 were representative:

> If the law /on bank taxation/ were literally executed, the burden would be almost too heavy to be borne in many of the cities of the State. But in the majority of the cases, the palpable inequality of the law is partially corrected by the illegal, but nevertheless only just action of the assessors, who assess bank capital at a percentage of the actual sum paid in.[24]

In part the trouble arose because about 1875 the State assessors of the capital of banks elected to value bank shares at the market price or, more commonly since market transactions were often limited, at the sum capital and surplus. The normal manner in the past had been to assess bank shares at the proportionate amount of par

---

[23] See Report of the Commissioners, May 1, 1871, New York City, Department of Taxes and Assessments, 7, 11-12. Under state law, County Treasurers (or their equivalent) were the collectors of state taxes. After deducting a prescribed amount (for example, for county poor houses) the Treasurer forwarded the balance to the state. The state did not always take joy in this arrangement. See: John Dix, Governor's Annual Message, January 6, 1874, New York State, Session 97, Assembly Document No. 2, 16-17.

[24] D. C. Ellis, Superintendent of Banking, New York, Annual Report, December 31, 1875, Session 98, Assembly Document No. 5, 8.

capital only. The perilous fiscal position of the state in the early 1870s, however, apparently prompted the assessors to be more zealous in their valuation. The Law of 1866 (Chapter 761) only stipulated that the bank shareholders would be assessed on the "value of their shares," whatever value that might be.

The Gallatin National Bank challenged the more liberalized mode of assessment in the State Supreme Court. The Court upheld the assessors. Gallatin appealed the finding to the State Court of Appeals, but again the assessors were upheld.[25]

The Gallatin position was widely supported by the banking community. In April, 1876, the New York Clearing House issued a toughly worded resolution with two key themes: (1) the new mode of bank taxation is more stringent than that applied to other "species of property," and (2) that the new mode of taxation will drive capital out of banking.[26]

The flight of capital out of the New York City commer-

---

[25] New York State Court of Appeals, "The People ex. rel. The Gallatin National Bank et al., Appelants, v. The Commisioner of Taxes and Assessments, Respondents," December 19, 1876, 22 Sickels, 516-21.

[26] Commercial and Financial Chronicle, April 22, 1876, 386.

cial banks became a major problem between 1875 and 1880. Reductions in capital were permitted for national banks under Section 13 of the National Bank Act of 1864, and for state banks and trust companies under Laws of 1875, Chapter 50.

In 1878 the editors of the Commercial and Financial Chronicle observed (in an article entitled "Save the Banks"):

> But inasmuch as we are firmly persuaded both that the banking interest is unduly taxed, and that the public are really and deeply concerned in recognizing and remedying the cause of complaint, we desire again to point out wherein that concern exists. Capital invested in banks is taxed, and while the law is unchanged it cannot resist; but one thing it can do, to wit: run away.[27]

The Commercial and Financial Chronicle, as Table 4:18 illustrates, was speaking from a well buttressed position.

The burden of taxation, then, was a contributing factor to the flight of capital from the commercial banking industry.

Profitability

The superior growth rate in trust company capital was also aided by a relatively higher profitability, measured in terms of rates of return on total capital.

---

[27] Ibid., August 10, 1878, 133.

TABLE 4:18

Reduction in Capital: 1876-8
New York City Clearing House Banks

Year	No. of Banks Reducing Capital	Former Capital (000)	Reduced Capital (000)	Decrease (000)
1876	5	$ 6,800	$ 3,700	$4,100
1877	8	24,600	15,600	9,000
1878	7	11,000	8,190	2,810

Source: Commercial and Financial Chronicle, August 10, 1878, 133.

TABLE 4:19

Rate of Return Ratios

	Net Earnings		Rate of Return*	
	National Banks (000)	Trust Companies (000)	National Banks	Trust Companies
1875	$ 6,717	$ 1,798	6.5%	10.8%
1880	8,142	1,638	10.3	9.5
1885	5,030	2,506	6.5	9.2
1890	8,225	6,184	8.1	12.6
1895	4,788	6,601	4.3	10.8
1900	16,107	12,797	11.7	11.0
Average			7.9	10.7

*On capital and surplus

Source: For national banks, Annual Reports of the Comptroller of the Currency; for trust companies, Annual Reports Relative to Savings Banks, New York State Superintendent of Banking. See footnote 3:7.

On balance the rate of return on total capital was superior for the trust companies. In most years, the spread in the rates of return would be even more in the trust companies' favor if average rather than year-end capital data had been used in the denominator of the equation. In 1880, the national bank's superior performance was due in some measure to the withdrawal, previously noted, of capital from the industry. In 1900, the rate of return of the trust companies managed to stay very close to the national banks, even though of the 31 reporting companies, 14 were less than 3 years old.

The data in Table 4:19 suggest that the national banks were much more sensitive to economic cycles than the trust companies. The three years in which the national banks did relatively well, 1880, 1890, and 1900 were all predominately years of economic expansion. In the same vein, the three wherein the national banks did not do well, 1875, 1885 and 1895, were all years of economic contraction.[28]

If, as appears, the commercial banks did not do well in times of economic distress, then indeed 1875-1900 was a most hazardous period of operations, because 49% of the

---

[28]G. H. Moore, <u>op. cit</u>., 121.

months in this period were contractionary.[29]

One factor which worked quite heavily against the earnings of the commercial banks was loss items. Loss items included loan losses, defaulted investments and amortization of premiums on investments. Unfortunately data of this detail in comparative income statements is rather limited. However, from available data, the loss items of the national banks were considerably higher than those of the trust companies.

TABLE 4:20

Loss Item Ratios
National Banks: New York City

Year	Loss Items/ Total Capital	Loss Items/ Net Earnings
1875	5.8E%	89.3E%
1880	2.6	25.2
1885	4.1	63.7
1890	3.6	43.7
1895	3.0	70.0
1900	2.4	21.1

Source: Comptroller of Currency, Annual Reports. See footnote 3:7.

Since net earnings in each year were after the effect of loss items, it is apparent that losses stood large in

[29] Ibid.

relation to earnings and also as a substantial portion of capital. Although comparable figures are not available for trust companies, a survey of the General Ledger profit and loss accounts of Central, Union, Atlantic and Metropolitan Trust companies reveals only occasional and generally quite small loss items. For Central and Union, there probably was, on average, less than one loan loss each per year.

The different type of loans made by the two classes of institutions probably accounts for the superior loss experience of the trust companies. For commercial paper or discounted notes (the characteristic loans of the commercial bank) there was very little recourse beyond the name of the borrower. In the case of loans collateralized by high quality securities (the characteristic loan of the trust company) management had recourse to collaterial whose value was usually independent of the name of the borrower.[30]

Moreover, the commercial banks on average had a larger portion of smaller businesses as customers than did the trust companies, and the smaller businessmen would be more likely to default on a loan than the larger customer.

---

[30] Commercial and Financial Chronicle, August 5, 1882, 151.

Dividends

Another element contributing to a faster growth rate in trust company capital was a higher retention of earnings.

TABLE 4:21

Dividend Payout Ratio
New York City

	Dividends		Payout Ratio	
	National Banks (000)	Trust Companies (000)	National Banks	Trust Companies
1875	$6,414	$ 850	95.5%	47.3%
1880	4,767	970	58.5	59.2
1885	4,067	1,390	80.8	35.3
1890	4,574	2,138	55.6	34.6
1895	4,660	3,280	97.3	49.7
1900	5,265	4,805	37.7	37.5
Average			70.1	47.3

Source: For national banks, Annual Reports of the Comptroller of the Currency; for trust companies, Annual Reports Relative to Savings Banks, New York State Superintendent of Banking. See footnote 3:7.

While the data in Table 4:21 covers only six years, the evidence still seems sufficient to conclude that on balance the trust companies had a lower payout ratio.

The earnings of the national banks, judging from the very high payout ratios of 1875, 1885 and 1895 were much more sensitive to economic cycles than those of the trust companies. Dividends, on the other hand, did not move up or down with the trend of earnings. Managements seem to have thought of dividend policy not in terms of a payout ratio, but in terms of a percentage of paid-in capital. This was, in fact, how dividends were expressed (e.g., 5% on par). This mode of conceptualizing dividend policy may have stemmed from the fact that the securities market in the 1875-1900 period was overwhelmingly dominated by the bond market, although this became less so as the century drew to a close. For the majority of the nineteenth century investors, however, investment choices were measured in terms of yield of income alternatives.

That the absolute dollar dividend paid in 1900 by the national banks in New York City was actually lower than that paid twenty-five years earlier, while the dividend paid by the trust companies increased over five times, in and of itself attests to the superior profitability of the trust companies.[31]

---

[31] The question arises whether or not shareholders were slow to collect dividends and if so did a company have a workable float balance from this source. As an example, on July 10, 1885, Union Trust's Dividend No. 42, of $25,000, became payable. By the end of the day only $13,617.50 remained uncollected; by the end of the second day $8,640.00; by the end of the fifth day $3,820.00 The last outstanding amount ($70.00) for the 42 dividend payment

was collected 144 days after it became payable. On an annualized basis, Union had a float of $488.01 from Dividend No. 42. The earnings from this amount, of course, would be very small.

CHAPTER V

THE END OF THE CENTURY: SIGNS OF MATURITY

Object of the Chapter

In the years between 1870 and 1900 New York City trust companies grew at a steady and, by comparison with commercial banks, rapid pace. By the end of the nineteenth century the trust companies were a distinct and muscular financial intermediary.

Beginning in the 1890's, however, certain developments began to take place which would eventually guide the trust company movement into the mainstream of the commercial banking system. This was, in retrospect, a significant development because it brought an immense amount of entrepreneurial vitality back into the commercial banking (especially the state) system, as well as the very sizable block of business which the trust companies had captured. By contrast, the trust company movement could have gone another way; it could have become an even more distinct financial intermediary from the commercial banking system (or systems). In which case the structure of the American financial system would probably be radically different than it is today.

The object of this Chapter is to examine what were these developments in the 1890's which guided the trust company movement into the mainstream of the commercial banking system. Three principal developments will be examined: (1) the excessive formation of trust companies in the 1898-1899 period and the reaction thereto, (2) the assimilation of trust companies into the American Bankers' Association, and (3) the extent of interlocking directors.

The Formation of Trust Companies: 1898-1899

Approximately fifty New York City based trust companies were chartered in the 1870-1900 period. Thirty-one became operative and of these ten were chartered in the brief two year span from 1898 to 1899.

While each of these ten trust companies became operational almost immediately upon receiving its charter, at least eight additional companies (Industrial Trust Company of America, Mutual Trust, Federal Trust, Century Trust, Harlem Trust, Sterling Trust, Empire Trust, and Astor Trust) were in advanced stages of organization.

What prompted this sudden rush of trust company forma-

TABLE 5:1

New Trust Companies: 1898-1899
New York City

Company	Date Chartered
Bankers Trust[1]	1899
City Trust	1899
Fifth Avenue Trust	1898
International Banking	1899
Merchants Trust	1899
Morton Trust	1899
N.Y. Realty, Bond, Exchange[2]	1898
Produce Exchange Trust[3]	1898
Standard Trust	1898
Trust Company of America	1899

Source: Superintendent of Banking, New York Annual Report, 1900.

tion?

First, since the trust company legislation of 1887 (Laws 1887, Chapter 546), entry into the industry had been very easy. Regulatory barriers were low. Apart from a minimum paid-in capital requirement of $500,000, chartering was largely a matter of filing papers with the Superintendent of Banking in Albany and a minor amount of legal

[1]Merged with Atlantic Trust (1900). The Bankers Trust presently operating in New York City was chartered in 1903.

[2]Name changed (1899) to Central Realty, Bond and Trust Company.

[3]Name changed (1900) to Bowling Green Trust Company.

busy-work.

Stated in another way, the spate of trust company formations in 1898 and 1899 was not due to a sudden relaxation of regulatory standards.

Second, the business environment and money market conditions were jointly noticeably more favorable from mid-1897 to late 1899 than in most of the 1891 to mid-1897 period. The period from 1891 to mid-1897 was pitted by three recessions, international balance of payment deficits and, seriously for Wall Street, the lingering threat of a triumph of pro-silver monetary forces. Reflecting the strain on business conditions in this period, the check clearings through the New York Clearing House Association, as Table 5:2 illustrates, were actually lower in the years from 1891-7, than they were in 1890. In fact, no trust companies were formed in New York City during the seven years ending 1897. But in the next two years, with relatively favorable economic conditions, ten were chartered. As in the 1870-3 period, trust company formations were influenced by general economic conditions.[4]

---

[4]The correlation between economic conditions and trust company formations was recognized by the regulatory authorities. See: Frederick D. Kilburn (Superintendent of Banking, New York), "Control and Supervision of Trust Companies," Annals of the American Academy of Political Science, July, 1904, 42.

TABLE 5:2

New York City Check Clearings

Year	Amount (billions)
1890	$ 37.5
1891	33.7
1892	36.7
1893	31.3
1894	24.2
1895	29.8
1896	28.9
1897	33.7
1898	42.0
1899	60.8
1900	52.6

Source: Commercial and Financial Chronicle, January 12, 1901, 64.

Third, in the mid-1890's, trust companies began to receive wide public acclaim as "growth companies." Beginning around 1894, the Commercial and Financial Chronicle carried semi-annual features on trust companies. The articles keyed on the aggregate statistics compiled by the State Superintendent of Banking and stressed the growth angle. The descriptive phrases used by the Chronicle were most laudatory: "...a most important body of financial institutions..." "...they have had a wonderful growth..." "The trust companies are very profitable concerns and net handsome returns even in dull times...," "One of the most interesting phenomena of the times...," "...marvelous growth and expansion..."[5]

Another writer was even more enthusiastic:

> ...you will easily believe me when I say that for earning capacity no financial institution has ever been invented that could compete with the trust companies.[6]

The encomniums directed towards the trust companies were grounded in fact, as the authors saw them at that time. The superior growth of assets translated into superior gain for all those associated with the companies. For the officers of the trust company, salaries were higher. In 1875, the salary of the President of Central Trust was $10,000 per year, in 1885, $15,000, and in 1899, $50,000 plus a $50,000 bonus. The employees of Central (since 1887) received an annual profit-sharing distribution of 10% of net profits.[7] For the investor in trust company

---

[5] Commercial and Financial Chronicle, August 17, 1895, 260; February 29, 1896, 390; August 6, 1898, 251; February 18, 1899, 302. See also: Bankers Magazine, April, 1889, 725; March, 1900, 353.

[6] Guy Morrison Walker, Trust Companies: A Study of the Nature of their Business and the Source of Their Great Earning Power, Boston Press of Boston, 1903, 16.

[7] Central Trust Company of New York, Trustee's Minutes, November 30, 1875; December 23, 1884; December 20, 1887; December 19, 1899.

stocks, dividends also increased at a rapid rate.[8] Moreover, the performance of trust company stocks in the market place was noticeably superior to those of commercial banks, as Table 5:3 indicates.[9] Over the 1880-1900 period, the Trust Company Stock Index increased at a compound annual rate of 9.2%, compared with 3.5% for the Commercial Bank Stock Index.

The United States Investor, speaking of the stock performance of trust companies from 1895-1899, said:

> Is it any wonder that such an appreciation in trust company shares has convinced capitalists that there is money in the business,...[10]

---

[8]See Table 4:21.

[9]Both indices are based on the year-end market values of six companies, all of which were important institutions in their industry and which appear to have had relatively good liquidity. The companies included in the Trust Company Stock Index were: Central, Farmers, Mercantile, N.Y. Life, Union and U.S. Trust. Those included in the Commercial Bank Index were: American, American Exchange, Central, Commerce, Fourth, and Manhattan.

[10]United States Investor, November 4, 1899, 1507. The Investor showed a table with annual readings for each of the four years for thirteen trust companies. The Investor, following an ancient penchant of its trade, lifted the table from the New York Times of October 15, 1899, 22. The Times, for its part, expressed admiration for the performance of trust company stocks; particularly since "...the stocks of these companies are in no sense speculative; that they are, as a rule, about as strictly investment stocks as can be found."

TABLE 5:3

Stock Market Indicies For
Trust Companies And Commercial Banks
New York City
(1880 = 100)

Year-end	Trust Companies	Commercial Banks
1880	100	100
1881	114	105
1882	131	107
1883	143	110
1884	146	99
1885	148	106
1886	170	118
1887	183	118
1888	213	123
1889	167	137
1890	302	133
1891	287	131
1892	287	142
1893	274	127
1894	291	132
1895	326	156
1896	353	155
1897	391	168
1898	460	169
1899	589	191
1900	580	199

Source: Based on quotations in Commercial and Financial Chronicle.

Additionally, the trust companies had a contra-cyclical dimension which the commercial banks did not have. The ability of the trust companies to show consistent growth in a period spotted with three recessions must have been an appealing characteristic to financial

TABLE 5:4

Annual Growth Rates In Assets
New York City

Year	Trust Companies	National Banks
1890	+ 5.5%	- 6.4%
1891	+ 4.4	+ 4.6
1892	+ 9.6	+ 7.9
1893	+ 2.7	- 9.9
1894	+ 5.5	+27.5
1895	+ 6.4	- 8.5
1896	+ 0.7	-11.8
1897	+22.4	+31.5

Source: Same as Table 3:1.

entrepreneurs. As indicated in Chapter IV, this contracyclical characteristic was traceable to the trust company practice of paying interest on deposits.[11]

---

[11] For exactly the same reason trust company earnings would be less cyclical than those of commercial banks. Since, among the trust companies, the ratio of interest sensitive liabilities-to-interest sensitive assets approached a value of 1, the income effect of a change in interest rates on one side of the balance sheet would roughly be paralleled by a counter effect on the other side. The net interest rate spread and net interest income, accordingly, would tend to be consistent over the cycle, assuming no volume changes. The commercial banks, however, with a very low ratio of interest senstive liabilities-to-interest sensitive assets, would suffer a decline (increase) in gross income as interest rates declined (increased) and this would be transmitted directly to net income since there would be no significant offsetting movement in interest expense. If, as Table 5:4

The formation of trust companies, in fact, was so hectic in 1899, the United States Investor called it a "mania."[12] The press abounded with rumors of companies in the process of formation, having the most special connections with the most prominent financiers and the promise of an early oversubscription of the stock. The atmosphere was feverish, expectant, not unlike the enthusiasm for gold in 1848.

When the Produce Exchange was in the formative stage, one newspaper stated authoritatively that "the interest of Standard Oil Company in /Produce/ will not be small." Six days later it turned out that the "Standard" of the rumor was Standard National Bank, a hapless little entity limping toward liquidation.[13]

When the proposed Astor Trust Company was in the formative stages it was rumored that John Jacob Astor himself was interested in the company and might be active in its management and someone had already offered to buy 10,000

---

suggests, commercial bank asset volume was also sensitive to the cycle, then commercial bank earnings would be doubly impacted by the cycle--by rates and by volume. See: Table 4:19.

[12] United States Investor, December 30, 1899, 1781.

[13] New York Times, November 28, 1897, 13; and December 4, 1897, 3.

shares although no stock as yet had been offered.[14]

The combination, then, of three forces (ease of entry, favorable economic conditions after a sustained period of uncertainty, and an emerging and broadly heralded recognition of trust company potential) led to the proliferation of trust company formations in 1898-9.

The significance of the spate of company formations in 1898-9 for the trust company movement was two-fold: first, for the first time a large number of marginally qualified entrepreneurs entered the trust company movement, and second, the formations also indicated that major financial capitalists were using the trust company as the central instrument, or at least as an important instrument, in their dealings. Both of these developments would eventually give rise directly, or otherwise create an environment whereby, the structural advantages enjoyed by trust companies were reduced. Both of these developments merit further examination.

The Marginal Entrepreneurs. Apparently some individuals felt that the structural advantages enjoyed by

---

[14] United States Investor, August 26, 1899, 1126.

trust companies were so great that mere entry into the industry would meet with success, regardless of economic conditions and the level of entrepreneurial ability. In this they were wrong.

By the end of 1900, two of the trust companies formed in 1898-9 had run into difficulty.

One of these companies, Bankers Trust, was sound financially, even though the first year of operation (1899) was unprofitable. In 1900 Bankers merged into the conservative Atlantic Trust Company, which was controlled by the Atlantic Mutual Insurance Company.

The interesting feature about Bankers was the overwhelming control by stock brokers. Of the twenty-one directors, at least thirteen were stock brokers, and most of these were members of the New York Stock Exchange. Included in that number was George W. Ely who resigned as Secretary to the Exchange to become President of Bankers and Ransom H. Thomas, who was a Vice President of the Exchange.[15]

The possibility exists that the brokers intended to

---

[15] Commercial and Financial Chronicle, September 2, 1899, 473.

use Bankers Trust as an underwriting vehicle, or maybe simply to get the market price of the stock above book value (or what was paid-in in the intial subscription) and then sell out or merge.

If this is so, then it is also possible that the financial panic of December, 1899 and the combined effects in 1900 of lower underwritings, lower stock prices and lower trading volume could have weakened the capital position of the brokers to the extent that they wanted to recover the capital invested in Bankers, regardless of their original plans.

The terms of the merger suggest that something like this did happen. By terms of the merger, the Bankers' shareholder received two-thirds of his original subscription price in cash, representing a distribution from Bankers capital just prior to the merger and the balance in stock of Atlantic Trust. For every share of Bankers stock ($200 subscription price), a Bankers shareholder received $133 plus one-third share of Atlantic.

Bankers could work a deal like this because Atlantic was over-capitalized by industry standards. Atlantic, by taking 100% of Bankers business and only 33% of Bankers capital was actually improving on its under-leveraged position.

Furthermore, eight of the Bankers directors went on the twenty-four man Atlantic board, but not one of these eight men were brokers.

The other company which ran into difficulty was Produce Exchange Trust Company. Interestingly, Produce Exchange acquired its initial block of business by exchanging its stock for the stock of Standard National Bank.[16] Of the seventeen directors, at least nine were members of the New York Produce Exchange.[17] The Company's operations were suspended in December, 1899, coincident with the financial panic of that time. Since September, rumors had been abroad that the company was in financial difficulty. Following the company's suspension, the receiver discovered that virtually all of the loans outstanding were syndicate loans, involving underwriting deals with indefinite

---

[16] New York Times, December 4, 1897, 3. In a variation on this theme, the stockholders of the First National Bank in Brooklyn were given the option in 1899 of taking their dividend in cash or stock of the new Williamsburg Trust Company. The dividend was an extra, amounting to 150% of First National's par. The deal actually proposed the conversion of the capital into a trust operation. See Commercial and Financial Chronicle, March 11, 1899, 454.

[17] Letter from Frank Brainard to New York Superintendent of Banking, F. D. Kilburn, January 27, 1898, Bowling Green Trust Company, New York State Banking Department, Albany, N.Y. Archive Number 117981.

maturities.[18] Produce Exchange resumed business in 1900, but with a change in management and a new name--Bowling Green Trust.

The troubles of Bankers and Produce Exchange confirmed the suspicion held by some of the more knowledgeable bankers in New York, that too many trust companies had been formed in 1898-9; that their managements were of an untested character. Prior to this time most of the trust companies were well-anchored in the existing commercial banking-Clearing House structure. The directorates between the two intermediaries were closely interlocked, and, to some extent, the officers of the trust companies were drawn from commercial bank sources. But with the 1898-9 formations, a new set of sponsors came into the trust company picture; promoters from the stock exchange, the produce exchange and industry.

All of this made the New York banking community nervous. In November, 1899, the Clearing House took steps to protect itself. Hereafter, no trust company could clear its checks through the facilities of the Clearing House Association until that company had been in operation at least

[18] Commercial and Financial Chronicle, December 23, 1899, 1277.

one year. Moreover, before a trust company could clear, it had to submit to an examination by a Clearing House committee and thereafter had to furnish weekly financial statements to the Association.[19]

The ultimate object of the Clearing House's action was to see that the trust companies maintained adequate reserves. Although the subject of trust company reserves had emerged several times during the 1890's within Clearing House circles, the significance of the 1899 action is that it marked the first time that the commercial banking community made a determined effort to put a reign on one of the structural advantages enjoyed by the trust companies. Speaking of the Clearing House's new rules regarding trust companies, the New York Times editorialized:

> They are the first official recognition, or at least, the first effectual recognition, of the fact that certain trust companies, in increasing amount, are doing a purely banking business, and of the principle that if they enter on this course they should be subjected to the conditions that have gradually been accepted as essential by the banks.[20]

---

[19] *Ibid.*, November 11, 1899, 990-1. Two of the three members of the Clearing House Sub-committee which drafted this policy were directors of old line trust companies--H. W. Cannon and F. D. Tappen.

[20] *New York Times*, November 10, 1899, 7. In addition to the "reserve" aspect of the Clearing House's new policy, there is another, more subtle, overtone. The smaller and medium sized national banks in the city were not doing especially

The Clearing House's 1899 action also prompted some discussion of the State Legislature passing mandatory reserve requirements on trust companies.[21]

Not until 1903 did the Clearing House actually place a 10% reserve requirement on trust companies clearing through member banks. And legislation was not passed in New York until 1906 setting a minimum 15% statutory re-

---

well. The largest and most powerful national banks, however, were doing quite well. One reason for this was they had sizable correspondent bank balances. Correspondent balances accounted for about 40% of the deposits in 1900 among the N.Y.C. national banks. About half of the deposit growth in the last five years came from correspondent balances. In March, 1899 the Clearing House passed a resolution stating that any trust companies or other non-member banks clearing through the Association's facilities had to maintain standard rates on the collection of out-of-town checks. In September, 1899, Produce Exchange Trust stated that it no longer would use the Association's facilities but would collect out-of-town checks free of charge. Other trust companies were rumored to be prepared to do the same thing. Had this movement become wide-spread, it would have gone right to the jugular vein of the correspondent balances--the one area where the national banks had a competitive edge over the trust companies. It is possible that the Clearing House's November action was a warning from the big national banks to the big trust companies to stay away from their correspondent systems. See: Commercial and Financial Chronicle, March 11, 1899, 455; September 2, 1899, 473. New York Times, September 9, 1899, 6; January 3, 1900, 10.

[21] Commercial and Financial Chronicle, November 18, 1899, 1038. Also: New York Times, March 12, 1900, 10.

serve limit.[22] But the proliferation of trust companies in the 1898-9 period actually triggered the movement which resulted in the imposition of these reserve regulations.

The Commercial and Financial Chronicle commented on the Bankers and Produce Exchange troubles as follows:

> ...a check has been given to the formation and creation of new companies....At the same time it is doubtless true that the experience in this instance has in a measure served to induce an attitude of reserve on the part of the public towards all institutions of this class which have no long record of successful management behind them,...[23]

The Major Financial Capitalists. The second important development to emerge from the formation of trust companies in 1898 and 1899 was the aggressive use of the trust company vehicle in the operations of the major financial capitalists.

The latter part of the 1890's was characterized by a

---

[22] New York State, Laws, 1906, Chapter 337. Also: Theodore Gilman, "Trust Company Reserves," Bankers Magazine, April 1904, 518-23. And: Letter from A. S. Fissell, A. B. Hepburn, Stephen Baun, Andrew Mills, Edward W. Sheldon and E. S. Marsten to Governor Charles E. Hughes, December 16, 1907, Manuscript, Reference: N. Y. Public Library THI/+, p.v. 15, No. 6.

[23] Commercial and Financial Chronicle, February 17, 1900, 302. Also: United States Investor, December 30, 1899, 1781.

wave of mergers and consolidations; representing the putting together of large industrial groups, called "trusts" by the popular press. The editors of the Commercial and Financial Chronicle said in retrospect of 1898:

> ...the year is distinguished as no other year for the number and magnitude of the industrial combinations that were formed in all lines of trade.[24]

And of 1899:

> In every industry, in every line and branch of trade, great consolidations and amalgamations were planned, and in most cases carried into effect....This incorporation of industrial undertakings on an enormous and unprecedented scale was the distinctive feature of the year.[25]

To a large degree, these combinations were promoted by financial capitalists. For the most part these were New Yorkers, with an intimate knowledge of Wall Street and only an incidental appreciation of the production functions of the industries they were consolidating.

At this time, the trust companies participated in the merger wave mainly by financing the syndicates that were

---

[24] Commercial and Financial Chronicle, January 7, 1899, 6. The editors estimate that 38 major combinations were formed in 1898, representing a capital stock value of $873 million.

[25] Ibid., January 6, 1900, 4. For background on the merger movement see: Herman E. Krooss and Charles Gilbert, American Business History, Englewood, N.J., Prentice-Hall, Inc., 1972, Chapter 9.

doing the combinations, and to a lesser extent by taking underwriting positions in the syndicates.[26] As indicated in Chapter III the financing of stock brokers through collateralized call loans was traditionally an important segment of trust company business. Consequently, when the merger wave developed in 1898, the trust companies were in a seasoned market position to meet the stock promoters' demands for funds.

All of this could be and was done by the traditional, old line trust companies. But with the trust company formations of 1898 and 1899, a new element entered into the picture: several of the new trust companies were sponsored by financial capitalists whose orientation was toward the stock market. As a result, several individuals and institutions who were prominently identifed as promoters of industrial combinations--the "trusts," also were identified with trust companies. In 1902, Bankers Magazine stated:

> A considerable part of the increase in the volume of business done by the trust companies has been due to the organization of large industrial corporations,...[27]

---

[26]Of course the trust companies also benefited from the enormous increase in corporate trust business brought about by the consolidation movement.

[27]Bankers Magazine, August, 1902, 150.

And in 1904, an editor of the New York Sun wrote:

> Trust companies and similar institutions sometimes bear the same relation to industrial combinations as manufacturers do to the product of the mechanical or scientific inventor's brain. They produce it, place it on the market, and find purchasers for it. compensating themselves, by getting the largest obtainable profit for the least possible risk or responsibility.[28]

The eventual outcome of the identification between the industrial trusts and the trust companies was that when the industrial trusts suffered in the early 1900's, and became the target of "trust busters," the trust companies also came under critical scrutiny, especially in the New York State "Armstrong Investigation" of 1905 (on the life insurance industry) and the Pujo "Money Trust Investigation" in Washington in 1913.[29] This in turn created a political environment which made difficult the con-

---

[28] L. Walter Sammis, "The Relation of Trust Companies to Industrial Combinations, as Illustrated by the United States Shipbuilding Company," Annals of the American Academy of Political Science, July, 1904, 241.

[29] Larry Neal, "Trust Companies and Financial Innovation, 1847-1914," Business History Review, Spring, 1971, 51. Also: U.S. Congress, 62nd, House of Representatives, Banking and Currency Committee, Report of the Committee Appointed Pursuant to House Resolutions 429 and 504 to Investigate the Concentration of Control of Money and Credit, dated February 28, 1913, especially Sections 5, 6, 7 and 11.

tinuation of the structural privileges enjoyed by the New York City trust companies.

In fact the legislation which mandated minimum reserves for New York trust companies was passed on April 27, 1906, just after the height of the publicity from the Armstrong Investigation concerning the speculative underwriting practices of some trust companies.[30]

Two of the companies formed in the 1898-1899 period are particularly noteworthy in this regard: Fifth Avenue Trust and Morton Trust.

Fifth Avenue Trust was formed in 1898 by Levi P. Morton.[31] Morton, who started working at the age of twelve as a clerk in a general store in Enfield, Massachusetts, later became Vice President of the United States (1889-93) and Governor of New York (1895-7). He was also a senior partner in the prestigious investment firm of Morton, Bliss and Company.

The directors of Fifth Avenue were immensely prominent,

---

[30] There was other restrictive legislation concerning the examination and reporting of trust companies. See: New York State, Laws of 1905, Chapters 394, 416, 418.

[31] Data on Fifth Avenue may be found in Fifth Avenue Trust Company, New York State Banking Department, Albany, N.Y., Archive Number 117980.

including S. D. Babcock, August Belmont, Chauncey Depew, G. G. Haven, J. C. Hendrix, J. H. Hyde, Adrian Islin, A. D. Julliard, F. D. Tappan and Frank Tilford.

Babcock, it will be recalled from Chapter II, was a founder of Guaranty Trust, of Central Trust, of United States Mortgage and was Chairman of the Finance Committee of Mutual Life Insurance Company.

Hendrix was President of the National Bank of Commerce, Tappan of Gallatin National, and Tilford of Bank of New Amsterdam. Three Fifth Avenue directors were also directors of Western National Bank. Fifth Avenue maintained correspondent balances with all four of these commercial banks.

The interlocking directorates with other financial intermediaries were extensive.

Of the eighteen Fifth Avenue directors, sixteen held seats on other New York City trust companies, representing a total of thirty-one seats distributed among fifteen companies, including six with Guaranty Trust, with which it would eventually merge.

Thirteen of the directors held seats on New York City national banks, representing a total of sixteen seats distributed among nine companies, including five with National Bank of Commerce, three with Western National and two with Gallatin. Eventually National Bank of Commerce and Western would also merge into Guaranty Trust.

Seven of the directors held seats on New York City state banks, representing a total of ten seats distributed among six companies, including three each with Bank of America and Bank of New Amsterdam.

Four of the directors held seats on the board of Equitable Life Assurance Society, including Levi P. Morton, and eight other directors held seats on the board of Mutual Life Insurance Company.

The ownership of stock was also in prestigious hands. Mutual Life Insurance held 20% of the stock with another 22% identified directly with Mutual interests. Equitable Life also owned 20%, with another 13% directly identified with its interest. Equitable's holdings were in addition to its better than 50% control of Mercantile Trust and of U.S. Mortgage. In addition to the directors and their relatives, another shareholder was George F. Baker (1%), President of Astor National Bank, but also a director of First National and Liberty National Banks.

With affiliations of this character, Fifth was propitiously launched.

Morton Trust Company was formed a year later (1899) and also by Levi P. Morton. In this case, however, there was a highly unusual twist. The investment firm of Morton, Bliss and Company was dissolved, to "be succeeded by the Morton Trust Company." In a circular to the business community, Morton announced the new formation and suggested:

> ...the transfer to the books of the /Trust/ company on October 1st of your account with us /Morton, Bliss and Co./, and unless advised to the contrary will make this transfer.[32]

In a separate circular of the same date (July 1, 1899) Morton said his...

> ...objective in making this change is to preserve as an inheritance for my children some of the results of a lifetime in the financial world, which would otherwise disappear with the final dissolution of the firm.[33]

Doubtless there were other reasons also, the most probable of which was to gain the limited liability of incorporation. This would be useful in view of the heavy volume of speculative underwriting which the investment community was now undertaking.[34]

---

[32] "Letter from Morton, Bliss and Co., dated July 1, 1899." Levi P. Morton Papers, Letters, 1897-1920, New York Public Library. See also: Morton Trust Company, New York Banking Department, Albany, Archive Number 117979.

[33] "Letter from Levi P. Morton, dated July 1, 1899." Ibid. See also: Morton Bliss and Company, George Bliss, Letter Book 1893-5, New York Historical Society.

[34] Morton's biographer wrote years later that the trust company was founded "to meet competition of a growing financial community." See: Robert McElroy, Levi Parsons Morton--Banker, Diplomat and Statesman, N.Y., G. P. Putnam's Sons, 1930, 315.

Early in 1900, Morton's footings were considerably increased through the acquisition of State Trust Company, which was more than twice Morton's size. State, which had had management succession problems in recent years, was 27% owned by American Surety Company, and 27% owned by a trust of which Morton's former partner (Cornelius Bliss) was a trustee.[35]

Like Fifth Avenue Trust, Morton Trust's directors were immensely important men in the New York financial and industrial establishment, including J. W. Alexander, President of Equitable Assurance, John Jacob Astor, George Banker, by now President of First National Bank, Henry Flagler, Vice President of Standard Oil, Augustus D. Juilliard, R. A. McCurdy, President of Mutual Life Insurance, and W. G. Oakman, President of Guaranty Trust.

Eight of Morton's twenty-four directors held seats on

---

[35]At the time of the merger, State Trust was in the midst of a particularly bitter and highly publicized intra-company dispute. One Abram Kling, an ex-American Surety director, accused Walter Johnston, State Trust's President, of running the company into the ground with syndicate loans. Johnston later accused Kling of trying to ruin State. In response to this accusation Kling replied cryptically: "When you catch a fellow with a chicken under his arm, it is natural that he should cry 'wolf'." New York Times, March 14, 1900, 5. See also: State Trust Company, New York State Banking Department, Albany, Archive Number 117979.

the Guaranty Trust board (including Levi Morton) and six held seats on the Fifth Avenue Trust board. Within the decade these three institutions would be merged into one--Guaranty Trust.

Interlocking directorates were also extensive with national and state banks, especially with the National Bank of Commerce and the Bank of New Amsterdam.

Four of Morton's directors held seats on the Equitable Assurance board and seven on the Mutual Life board.

The directors and their affiliations of the Morton-Fifth Avenue-Guaranty trust company complex were more than enough to inspire confidence on the part of depositors and lift anticipations of investors. Within this grouping of directors, however, were two related spheres of economic interests, the life insurance interests and the Morgan interest, the former of which would be picked up by the Armstrong Investigation (1905) and the latter by the Pujo Investigation (1913) and both of which would involve perjorative exposure for the trust companies.[36]

---

[36] The extent and mechanics of syndicate layoffs from Mutual Life through their affiliated trust companies is brought out by Charles Evans Hughes (Armstrong Committee) in cross examination of Frederic Cromwell. See: New York State, Joint Committee of the Senate and Assembly of the State of New York, Appointed to Investigate the Affairs

Trust Companies and the American Bankers Association

Trade associations are voluntary gatherings of like-minded people for education, entertainment and self-defense. The American Bankers Association (formed in 1875) snugly fitted this definition. Members gathered once a year to hear speeches on banking practices, to place an unholy strain on the social graces of banks domiciled in the host city, and to plead with one voice the political needs of bankers. For the banks in the bigger cities, the annual meetings presented opportunity to reaffirm existing correspondent relationships and to build new ones.

By the end of the nineteenth century, the trust company movement was invited to join the ABA. In 1896, through a special "Trust Company Section," the ABA became the trade association for the trust companies as it had been for many years for the commercial banks.

The importance of this development can best be measured by considering an alternative. One of the functions of a financial trade association is to promote legislative and

---

of Life Insurance Companies, Assembly Document No. 41, Session 129, 1906, especially pp. 564-77. See also: Frederick Lewis Allen, The Great Pierpont Morgan, N. Y. Harper and Row, 1965, 219-24.

regulatory developments which give the industry it represents a superior position vis-a-vis its competitors; and discourages those governmental developments which give competitors an advantage. The trade association strives to obtain for its industry a preferred franchise from the government. This often means entering into an antagonistic relationship with a competing industry, which has its own trade association. The executive of a trade association, a non-profit organization, optimizes his position by especially vigilant behavior toward his industry's competitors.

In the 1890's, between the trust companies and the commercial banks, there was a clear potential for a grass-root antagonism.[37] If the ABA had closed its doors to the trust companies, and the trust companies established their own trade association, then there would have existed in institutionalized form, a primary mechanism by which divergent

---

[37]Willis Paine of New York's State Trust Company remarked at the organizational meeting of the Trust Company Section: "The reason that banks of discount in some commonwealths are hostile to trust companies is that the latter do virtually the same business as the former, and have privileges which banks do not possess. While I was Bank Superintendent of the State of New York, a number of bankers called on me from time to time, and expressed a feeling of dislike by reason of the fact that trust companies were continually increasing in number and made serious inroads upon the business of the banks of discount." American Bankers Association, Proceedings of Annual Meeting, 1896, 107.

interests could be pursued, solidified and perpetuated.

The reasons why the ABA set up a special Trust Company Section were probably three-fold:

1. The trust companies were customers of the commercial banks, on a transactions basis, because the commercial banks controlled the clearing house associations across the country. If an antagonistic relationship were allowed to grow, the trust companies in the bigger cities would eventually set up their own clearing houses, and then be in a position to challenge the correspondent business of the large commercial banks.

2. The trust companies had a powerful advocate high in the ABA councils. In 1896, Joseph C. Hendrix, Chairman of the Executive Committee of the ABA, against some opposition, forced approval of the Trust Company Section through the Committee. Breckenridge Jones, the first Chairman of the Section said a few years later:

   > It may not be known to all of us that the existence of the Trust Company Section is largely due to Mr. Hendrix.[38]

   Hendrix, who had previously founded a Brooklyn

---

[38] _Ibid._, 1899, 88.

trust company, became by 1900, President of the powerful National Bank of Commerce (New York), and a director of Fifth Avenue Trust and Morton Trust.

3. The ABA had historically billed itself as an open organization:

> All National and State Banks, Banking Firms and Financial Institutions in America are cordially invited to become members of the American Bankers Association...the fees are ...ten ($10) dollars for all banks and trust companies whose capital is $100,000 or over.[39]

This was in 1895. And some trust companies were members long before 1896. In 1888, seven New York trust companies were listed as members; in 1890, still seven; in 1895 up to ten; and in 1900, eighteen.

The critical point is, however, that the special Trust Company Section set up in 1896 was specifically devoted to the sharing of experiences and practices concerning personal and corporate trust business. Had the ABA not been willing to undertake this educational function with regard to trust business, the trust companies, especially the regional ones, would have set up their own device for sharing such informa-

---

[39] Ibid., 1895, advertisement on front of Proceedings.

ion, because in the 1890's personal trust business grew rapidly and for the first time became a big business.[40]

Interlocking Directors

The Pujo Investigation in 1913 on the "concentration of the control of money" resulted in celebrated disclosures of the magnitude of interlocking directors, and mutual control and ownership of financial institutions.

This section of Chapter V shows that the interlocking influences were already well-developed by 1900; trust companies were deeply interlocked with each other, with national banks, with state banks, with the New York Stock Exchange, and with insurance companies.[41]

---

[40] Securities held under personal trust administration by the Union Trust Company grew as follows:

April 1, 1878	$ 1,172,000
September 30, 1890	$10,080,000
September 30, 1895	$28,461,000
September 30, 1897	$31,723,000

See: Union Trust Company, Executive Committee Minutes, for respective dates.

[41] This section of Chapter V is built on an examination of interlocking directorates among trust companies, and between trust companies and national banks, state banks, savings banks, the New York Stock Exchange and selected life insurance and fire insurance companies. All companies were located in New York City. The reference date is 1900. Companies included in the analysis were: Trust Companies (30) American Deposit and Loan, Atlantic, Bowl-Green, Central Realty, Central, City, Colonial Continental, Farmers, Fifth Avenue, Guaranty, Holland, Knickerbocker,

At the end of 1900, there were 30 trust companies in New York City; these companies had a total of 645 director

---

Manhattan, Mercantile, Merchants, Metropolitan, Morton, N.Y. Life, N.Y. Security, North American, Real Estate, Standard, Title Guaranty, Trust Company of America, Trust Company of N.Y., Union, U.S. Mortgage, U.S. Trust and Washington; National Banks (44)--American Exchange, Astor, Bank of N.Y., Central, Chase, Chatham, Chemical, Continental, Domestic Exchange, East River, Fifth, First National, Fourth, Gallatin, Garfield, Hanover, Hide and Leather, Importers and Traders, Irving, Leather Manufacturers, Liberty, Lincoln, Market and Fulton, Mechanics, Mercantile, Merchants Exchange, Merchants, National Bank of Commerce, National Bank of North America, National Bank of the Republic, National Broadway, National Butchers and Drovers, National Citizens, National City, National Park, National Shoe and Leather, N.Y. County, N.Y. National Exchange, Ninth, Phenix, Seaboard, Second, Seventh, Western; State Banks (35)--Bank of America, Bank of New Amsterdam, Bank of the Metropolis, Bank of the State of N.Y., Bowery, Colonial, Columbia, Corn Exchange, Eleventh Ward, Fifth, Fourteenth Street, Gansevoort, German-American, German Exchange, Germania, Greenwich, Hamilton, Manhattan, Mechanics and Traders, Mount Morris, Mutual, Nassau, N.Y. Produce Exchange, Nineteenth Ward, Oriental, Pacific, Peoples, Plaza, Riverside, State, Twelfth Ward, Twenty-Third Ward, Union Square, West Side, Yorkville, Savings Banks (27)--American, Bank for Savings, Bowery, Broadway, Citizens, Dollar, Dry Dock, East River, Emigrant, Empire City, Excelsior, Franklin, German, Greenwich, Harlem, Institution of Merchants Clerks, Irving, Italia, Manhattan, Metropolitan, N.Y. Savings, North River, Seamen's, Union Dime, U.S. Savings, Washington, West Side; Life Insurance (5)--Equitable, Home, Manhattan, Mutual, N.Y. Life; Fire Insurance (3)--American Surety, Atlantic,Continental.

The directors of each of these companies were cross-indexed with those of the trust companies to derive schedules of interlocking relationships. The names of the directors were taken from Moody's Industrial Manuals, 1900-2, and Superintendent of Banking New York, Annual Report Relative Savings Banks, 1901.

TABLE 5:5

Summary of Director
Interlock(s) Between Trust
Companies and Financial Industries
(New York: 1900)

	Number of Companies in N.Y.C.	Number of Companies Having Interlock(s) with Trust Companies	Number of Trust Companies Having Interock(s) With:
Trust Companies	30	30	30
National Banks	44	35	30
State Banks	35	17	27
Savings Banks	27	18	27
N.Y. Stock Exchange	1,100*	60*	25
Major Life Ins. Cos.	5	5	26
Major Fire Ins. Cos.	3	3	21

*Representing Seats on New York Stock Exchange.

Source: Moody's Industrial Manuals, 1900-2.

seats, and these seats were distributed among 533 individuals. Tables 5:5-5:6D summarize the interlocks which the trust companies had with each other and with other financial industries.

As Table 5:5 indicates, every trust company in New York City had interlocking directors with at least one other trust company. A high portion of the national banks, as an industry, had interlocking directors with trust companies, and every trust company had at least one interlock with a national bank. The state banks, which on balance were much smaller than the national banks, were noticeably less interlocked as an industry with the trust companies. All but three, however, of the trust companies, had interlocks with the state bank industry. Savings banks in New York City also had extensive interlocks with trust companies, and all but three of the trust companies also had at least one interlock with the savings bank industry. And all but five of the trust companies had at least one member of the New York Stock Exchange sitting on their boards.

The life insurance and fire insurance companies, representing a selected list of the major New York City-based companies in these industries were also extensively interlocked with trust companies, and all but four and nine trust companies had at least one interlock with the life and fire insurance industries respectively.

The conclusions drawn from Table 5:5 are: (1) the trust companies were closely interlocked with each other; (2) that the trust companies were horizontally well-interlocked with other financial industries; and (3) that these horizontal interlocks were representative of a large portion of the trust companies in New York City. Just how intense these interlocks could be, is shown in Tables 5:6A-D.

As Table 5:6A indicates, the degree of multiple interlocks among trust companies was quite high. Two-thirds of the trust companies had interlocks with at least five other trust companies and one-third had interlocks with at least ten other trust companies. Out of a universe of thirty companies, this represents a rather close fraternal design.[42]

---

[42]The high degree of interlocks among trust companies was not representative of other financial industries. Of the 44 national banks in New York City in 1900, 17 had no interlocks with other national banks, 11 had an interlock with one other bank, 8 had two, 3 had three, 2 had four, 2 had six and 1 had seven. To some extent, the high degree of interlocks among trust companies can be traced to the fact that they were multi-functional and not all trust companies emphasized the same function. Consequently, there were degrees of competition among trust companies. Even allowing for this, however, the degree of self-interlocking was much higher than among the national banks.

TABLE 5:6:A

Summary Of Multiple Company Interlocks With Other Trust Companies (New York City: 1900)

Interlocks With Number of Trust Companies	Trust Companies		
	Number	Percent	Cumulative Percent
0	0	0.0%	100.0%
1	1	3.3	100.0
2	2	6.7	96.7
3	4	13.3	90.0
4	3	10.0	76.7
5	2	6.7	66.7
6	0	0.0	60.0
7	6	20.0	60.0
8	2	6.7	40.0
9	0	0.0	33.3
10	1	3.3	33.3
11	3	10.0	30.0
12	2	6.7	20.0
13	1	3.3	13.3
14	2	6.7	10.0
15	1	3.3	3.3
Total	30	100.0%	

Source: Same as Table 5:5.

The degree of multiple interlocks with national banks was also quite high, as Table 5:6:B illustrates. Over half of the trust companies had interlocks with at least six national banks and one-fifth had interlocks with at least nine.

The degree of multiple interlocks with state banks, as Table 5:6:C shows, was considerably lower than was the

TABLE 5:6:B

Summary Of Multiple Company Interlocks
Between Trust Companies and National Banks
(New York City: 1900)

Interlocks With Number of National Banks	Trust Companies		
	Number	Percent	Cumulative Percent
0	0	0.0%	100.0%
1	0	0.0	100.0
2	3	10.0	100.0
3	3	10.0	90.0
4	3	10.0	80.0
5	5	16.7	70.0
6	4	13.3	53.3
7	3	10.0	40.0
8	3	10.0	30.0
9	2	6.7	20.0
10	2	6.7	13.3
11	1	3.3	6.7
12	1	3.3	3.3
Total	30	100.0	

Source: Same as Table 5:5.

case with national banks. Two-thirds of the trust companies had interlocks with at least two state banks and slightly less than one-fourth had interlocks with at least five.

The degree of multiple interlocks with savings banks was about the same as with state banks. Two-thirds of the trust companies had interlocks with at least two savings banks and slightly over one-fourth had interlocks with at least four.

TABLE 5:6:C

Summary of Multiple Company Interlocks
Between Trust Companies and State Banks
(New York City: 1900)

Interlocks With Number of State Banks	Trust Companies Number	Percent	Cumulative Percent
0	3	10.0%	100.0%
1	7	23.3	90.0
2	2	6.7	66.7
3	7	23.3	60.0
4	4	13.3	36.7
5	2	6.7	23.3
6	4	13.3	16.7
7	1	3.3	3.3
Total	30	100.0%	

Source: Same as Table 5:5.

TABLE 5:6:D

Summary of Multiple Company Interlocks
Between Trust Companies and Savings Banks
(New York City: 1900)

Interlocks With Number of Savings Banks	Trust Companies Number	Percent	Cumulative Percent
0	3	10.0%	100.0%
1	7	23.3	90.0
2	6	20.0	66.7
3	6	20.0	46.7
4	6	20.0	26.7
5	2	6.7	6.7
Total	30	100.0%	

Source: Same as Table 5:5.

As Tables 5:6:A-D confirm, the trust companies were extensively interlocked with one another and with other financial industries. The average trust company not only had lines of contact with other industries, it had several lines. How did this network of interlocks come about and what function did it serve?

The first fact that emerges is that the trust companies had a large number of directors relative to other industries.

TABLE 5:7

Comparative Size of Directorates
(New York City: 1900)

Industry	Number of Directors Seats In Industry	Number of Companies	Average Size of Board of Directors
Trust Companies	645	30	21.5
National Banks	489	44	11.1
State Banks	452	35	12.9
Savings Banks	550	27	20.4

Source: Same as Table 5:5

The national banks in New York City had nearly 50% more banks than the trust companies and 60% more assets, yet only 75% as many directors. The average number of directors per company was, as Table 5:7 shows, noticeably smaller for the commercial bank (national and state) than for the trust companies or savings banks. The contrast is even more clear if the distribution of board sizes among industries is compared.

TABLE 5:8

Distribution of Size of Boards of Directors (New York City: 1900)

Size of Board of Directors	Trust Companies	National Banks	State Banks	Savings Banks
0- 5	0.0%	4.5%	0.0%	0.0%
6-10	3.3	40.9	34.3	0.0
11-15	6.7	47.7	45.7	22.2
16-20	20.0	6.9	14.3	44.4
21-25	60.0	0.0	5.7	14.8
26-30	6.7	0.0	0.0	11.2
31- +	3.3	0.0	0.0	7.4
	100.0%	100.0%	100.0%	100.0%

Source: Same as Table 5:5.

The reasons for the difference in board sizes between trust companies and national and state banks appear to be three-fold. First, both national and state banks were chartered under general banking laws. The National Bank Act of 1864 set the minimum number of directors for a national bank at five (Section 9). The State of New York also set five as the minimum number of directors (Laws 1882, Chapter 409, Section 59). The minimum number of directors set by the state, however, for trust companies was thirteen (Laws

1887, Chapter 546, Section 1). While there was no prohibition against having more than the minimum number of directors, clearly there was a legislative bias favoring larger trust company boards.

Second, even those trust companies formed prior to 1887 had large boards. The companies formed prior to 1887 had an average board size of 21.0 and those formed in 1887 and after, 22.1. Those formed prior to 1887, as indicated previously, were chartered by special acts of the Legislature. It is possible that, as a technical nuance of the legislative process, the promoters would strive to gain the approbation of the Legislature through a large list of well-known directors. The larger the list, the greater the likelihood that more legislators would have personal contacts with, or recognize, some of the directors. The commercial banks, chartered by the administrative process of free banking legislation and not by individual acts of the Legislature or Congress, had no such motive to have larger boards.

Third, while trust companies were in the commercial banking business, they were also in the trust business--which the commercial banks were not. It is possible that as a marketing feature of the trust business, a company would want to have a large list of well-known directors.

A common feature of trust company advertising at the time was the prominent display of the names of the directors. This hypothesis has some statistical verification, as Table 5:9 illustrates.

TABLE 5:9

Trust Companies:
Correlation Between Trust Powers
And Size of Directors Boards
(New York City: 1870-3)

	Average Size of Board of Directors of Trust Companies Applying for Charters:	
Year	With Trust Powers	Without Trust Powers
1870	19.0	13.1
1871	18.8	12.4
1872	13.5	10.4
1873	16.0	6.8

Source: Same as Table 1:2.

In Table 5:9, the average size of the boards of those trust companies applying for trust powers in their charters is compared with the average board size of those companies which did not seek these powers. In each year of the sample, those seeking trust powers had noticeably larger boards than those not seeking trust powers.

Moreover, there was a broad recognition that trust companies did have special fiduciary responsibilities. Trust companies were seen to stand in the same fiducial relationship to wealthy individuals as the savings banks stood to the working class. As Table 5:7 shows, the sizes of the average savings bank and trust company boards were nearly equal, and both were considerably larger than the average national or state bank boards, which did not have these fiduciary responsibilities.

There were, then, plausible and specific historical reasons why the trust companies had large boards. The sheer size of these boards and the fiduciary motive to have well-known and prominent directors would both lead to a high degree of interlocks with other financial institutions.

There were other and good economic reasons for a large board of directors:

First, a large board would be considerable help in the development of new business. At a time before business development departments were commonplace in the banking industry, a large and well connected board would be a decided asset.

Second, in a period when the quality and consistency of corporate accounting was just becoming an important issue (paralleling the rise of non-management ownership), a board with extensive business connections would serve as an important vehicle for the transmission of credit information.[43]

Third, a large board would also facilitate the protection of existing account relationships. Since a trust company would normally have account relationships with several commercial and savings banks, this too would tend to promote a high degree of interlocking directors.

The economic advantages of a large and prominent board were recognized by others also. Three of the most aggressive national banks in New York City, National Bank of Commerce (19 directors), National City (19) and Western National (20) had much larger boards than the national bank average; and the two most aggressive life insurance companies, Mutual Life (35) and Equitable (51) both boasted considerably larger boards than was representative of the life insurance industry.

Between Times

By 1900, the success of the trust company movement in

---

[43]Colonial Trust Company, Trust Manual, N.Y.--Colonial Trust ca. 1900, 12. The reference states: "Furthermore, the officers of a Trust Company, because of their connection with railroads, and other corporations, public officials and business men, often know that a security is in danger long before a crisis is reached,..."

New York City was established and recognized, admiringly, by the community. Within a few years, several of these companies would encounter painful financial embarrassment and some others would come under the disapproving eye of public examination. Between times, however, there was an interlude of praise:

> Edward B. Wesley, who is the sole survivor of the original incorporators in 1864 of the Union Trust Company, and is still a trustee, celebrated his ninetieth birthday on Thursday. In recognition of the event the members of the executive committee of the board of trustees adopted congratulatory resolutions and presented him with a gold-headed cane.[44]

[44] Commercial and Financial Chronicle, January 12, 1901.

CHAPTER VI

SUMMARY

An Overview

Object of Dissertation. Between 1875 and 1900, the assets of trust companies in New York City grew at a compound annual rate of 9.6%, compared with 4.1% for national banks and 5.4% for state banks located in the City.

The objective of this dissertation is to bring to light the entrepreneurial, economic and political forces which prompted the high growth rate of the trust companies, resolved the movement into a well-defined financial intermediary, and eventually led to the unification of the trust company movement with the commercial banks.

Although a half a dozen or so trust companies were chartered in the four decades preceding the Civil War, it was not until the years following the Civil War that the formation of trust companies reached the proportion of a major financial movement.

Defining a Trust Company. By the mid-1870's the phrase "trust company" was employed in the titles of specific companies and, to a lesser extent, as a generic term referring to a class of companies. In the early years of the period under examination, "trust company" was a residual classification, denoting financial companies other than national and state banks, savings banks and insurance companies--each of which had specific enabling legilsation. By the mid-1870's the residual classification changed to "other moneyed corporations," of which trust companies were the largest subset.

From about the end of the nineteenth century, the term "trust company" connoted to most observers a bank with authority to engage in personal and corporate trust business. For the 1870-1900 period, however, this definition was entirely too specific. An examination of charter applications to the New York State Legislature in the 1870-3 period, reveals that of the 47 companies seeking charters, only 15 asked for corporate trust powers and only 11 sought personal trust powers.

What, then, did the term "trust company" mean? Overwhelmingly, the term "trust company" referred to a debtor-creditor relationship and this in the function of lending on collateral. Of the 47 trust companies seeking charters in the 1870-3 period, every one asked for authority to lend on collateral.

If trust companies were interested in commercial banking, how was it that they were chartered by special legislation and not under the New York State General Banking Law of 1838. The State Constitution did prohibit the special chartering of financial companies that could be chartered under the Law of 1838. The legal loop-hole was an almost incidental by-product of a case at law in 1855. In this case, (U.S. Trust Company vs. Brady) the State Supreme Court held in effect that as long as a state chartered financial institution did not issue circulating notes, it need not come under the force of the Law of 1838. The trust companies never issued circulating notes, they did not have the authority to do so and they showed no interest in getting such authority.

Statutory and Regulatory Background. In the 1870-1900 period, trust companies were created and regulated by State law. In New York two pieces of legislation were especially important: (1) the Act of 1874, and (2) the Act of 1887.

In 1874, the New York State Legislature passed the first general legislation relating to trust companies. The Act provided in substance, that all trust companies would in the future report to and be examined by the State Superintendent of Banking.

Prior to the Act of 1874, there was no regulatory supervision of trust companies, unless provided for in the charter of a trust company, and even then the "regulation" was of an incidental and passive nature. Of the 47 trust companies applying for charters in the 1870-3 period, 30 made no provision for reporting to any State agency.

One of the factors prompting the State to pass the Act of 1874 was a recognition of the primacy of New York City financial institutions and the nationwide repercussions which could result if one of these institutions failed. The role of the Ohio Life and Trust Company in the Panic of 1857 was well remembered.

Another critical aspect of the Act of 1874 was to bring the trust company movement under the authority of the State Superintendent of Banking. While this seems logical in retrospect, at the time it was not. The Superintendent of Insurance, the Secretary of State, or even a new agency, were then likely alternatives. If any of these alternatives had been adopted, it is unlikely that the trust company movement would have assimilated into the commercial banking industry as smoothly as it did, and that the structure of American financial intermediaries would be different than it is now.

The Act of 1887 provided a "free banking" environment for trust companies in New York State. Prior to this Act, each trust company was chartered by a special act of the State legislature. Powers granted to trust companies could and did vary widely from charter to charter.

The Act of 1887, however, eliminated the special legislation procedure, providing instead that all a trust company had to do to gain a charter was to make application to the Superintendent of Banking and satisfy certain standard, minimum requirements. Hereafter, charter powers were uniform for new companies.

Structurally the Act of 1887 was similar to enabling legislation for national and state banks, with the major distinctions that trust companies could not issue circulating notes and the minimum capital requirements were five times as great for trust companies.

<u>The Formation of Trust Companies</u>. In the 1870-1900 period, 41 trust companies were in operation at one time or another. Trust companies were a highly stable intermediary during this period, only three went out of business involuntarily and in each case the liquidation was orderly.

The factors which influenced the rate of trust company

formations were: (1) prior to 1887, the willingness of the Governor or Legislature to pass charter legislation, and (2) general economic conditions. The years of low or no new company formations were fairly closely correlated with recessionary periods. Beyond this, the entrepreneurs in each new company formation would have particular economic motivations.

The Trust Company Movement Quickens: 1870-73

The first concentrated activity in the trust company movement came in the decade following the end of the Civil War. In the four years from 1870-3 inclusive, the period of most intense activity, 93 bills were introduced in the New York State Legislature bearing on New York City trust companies. Who were the men involved in this stage of the movement, what legislative and political forces shaped the movement, what economic functions were the companies seeking and what was the economic environment of the period?

Entrepreneurs and Incorporators. Of the 93 bills introduced in the 1870-3 period concerning New York City trust companies, 62 were concerned with chartering new companies. Of these 62, 46 moved far enough along the legislative process to get printed, and hence to preserve the list, in each case, of the company's incorporators. These 46 companies had a total of 614 incorporator positions (e.g. trustees or directors), distributed among 553 different individuals.

A survey of these 553 individuals indicates that 11% were lawyers, 8% commercial bankers, 37% engaged in mercantile or commercial pursuits, 10% politicians, 1% other (e.g. doctors, school teacher or priest), and 33% could not be occupationally identified. The involvement of politicians as directors or trustees dropped markedly in 1872 and 1873, following the exposure of the Tweed scandals in 1871.

The supporters of the trust company movement were consequently well distributed in this period, the base of support was quite broad in the New York business community, and while many prominent individuals were involved, the base of the support was the solid middle class mercantile level.

The Legislative and Political Process: 1870-3. The 1870-3 period preceded by several years general trust company legislation. Each trust company was still chartered by a separate act. Each amendment to a trust company charter was by a separate act.

The sponsorship of legislation on the floor of the New York State Senate or Assembly was usually by an individual representing the party in power. In 1870 and 1871, most bills concerning trust companies were sponsored by Democrats and in 1872 and 1873, by Republicans. With the exception of 1871, the peak of Tammany influence in Albany, the sponsorship of trust company bills were widely distributed among the legislators.

The legislative process was in a way a regulatory filter in itself. Of the 93 bills introduced, 50 failed to become law. There were three filters in the legislative process: first, the standing committees (e.g., on Banking, on Insurance). The standing committees killed 19 of the 50 bills which failed. Secondly the Committees of the Whole (the Senate or Assembly sitting as a whole) killed 8 of the bills. And thirdly, the Governors, by veto killed 23 bills.

The legislative process defeated trust company bills for a good many reasons: First, the charter might provide for an interest rate in excess of usurious levels. Second, the "powers" section of the charter might be too general, vague or non-existent. Third, stipulated capital levels could be too low. Fourth, the people listed as corporators were either unknown to the legislators or known to be deficient in character. Fifth, challenges to new company charters by existing companies. Sixth, the threat of economic concentration within the trust company movement. Seventh, uneasiness over the "unregulated" aspect of the movement which still existed in the 1870-3 period. And eighth, concern that some companies requested too many banking functions. Although these eight reasons for defeating trust company bills were not applied consistently by any stage of the legislative process, they were applied often enough to shape the general character of the movement.

The Economic Functions of the Trust Companies. Of the 93 bills concerning trust companies introduced in the 1870-3 period, 47 sought new charters. These 47 companies sought a broad range of powers, some companies more than others. The range of powers included: the right to make mortgages, to engage in mercantile transactions, pawning, debt guaranty, to receive deposits, lending on collateral, personal trust, corporate trust, warehousing, insurance activities, permissable investments, agency powers, borrowing, and branching. Of this list, lending on collateral and receiving deposits were by far the most commonly sought.

Economic Conditions and Trust Company Formations. Of the 47 bills introduced in the New York State legislature in the 1870-3 period which concerned new company formations, only 21 actually became law and of these only 5 charters were actually activated by July 1, 1874. What happened? The answer appears to be that the only major hurdle to activating a charter, once passed, was the capital subscription requirement. As the years moved from 1870-3, monetary conditions eased slightly, then tightened, and the raising of capital progressively became more difficult and expensive. Of the 12 charters granted in the 1870-1 period, 5 successfully raised capital. But of the 9 granted in the 1872-3 period, difficult years in the capital market, none was able to raise capital by July 1, 1874. Ironically, the very excess of economic prosperity which made it attractive in the first place to form a trust company also begat the conditions which would keep most companies from beginning operations.

The Asset Structure

Trust companies grew more rapidly than commercial banks, showed better profits, attracted more capital and a more energetic class of entrepreneurs because their regulatory constraints were more lenient. The trust companies enjoyed a comparative advantage on both the asset and liability sides of the balance sheet.

The major asset items of a New York City trust company were cash, mortgages, investments and loans.

Cash. New York City trust companies carried a substantially lower portion of their assets in cash than did national or state banks located in the City. In 1875, trust companies held 0.8% of assets in cash, compared with 23.7% for national banks and 23.9% for state banks. In 1900, the figure was 12.7% for trust companies, 31.5% for national banks and 35.5% for state banks. Trust companies, consequently had a higher portion of assets actually lent out or invested than the two commercial bank systems; this in turn helped the relative profitability of the trust companies.

Trust companies could hold lower reserves because: (1) unlike the commercial banks, no reserve requirements were then set by law or regulation, and (2) the nature of the deposit structure was believed to be less volatile than that of the commercial banks. This last item refers to the fact that the vast majority of trust company deposits were purchased, thus giving management the ability to stabilize deposit levels by adjusting rates. The vast majority of commercial bank deposits were not purchased, but rather represented transactions balances or compensating balances for present or future loans.

While trust companies did carry lower cash balances, these balances grew at a faster rate than assets in the latter portion of the century. The main reason for this was pressure from the New York Clearing House banks, who cleared for the trust companies, and were fearful that in times of monetary crisis the rapidly growing trust companies would be a heavy burden. This was a reasonable concern, since by 1900, New York City trust company deposits in commercial banks accounted for 9.2% of the Clearing House's deposits.

Most of the trust company cash balances were held on deposit with commercial banks, and these balances often earned interest. Cash itself thereby became an invested asset, indicating another competitive advantage for the trust companies over the commercial banks.

Mortgages. In 1875, trust companies held 8.5% of their assets in mortgages and in 1900, 4.4%. National and state banks were prohibited by law from investing in mortgages. The major investors in mortgages were savings banks and life insurance companies.

A few trust companies did specialize in mortgages, in Western mortgages particularly, usually in the role of mortgage originators. But for most trust companies in the City, funds were only rarely placed in mortgages; and in these cases largely to accommodate preferred existing customers or as a liquidity accommodation for personal trust accounts--which often had real estate property as a principal asset.

Investments. In 1875, New York City trust companies held 31.8% of their assets in investments, compared with 20.8% for national banks and 1.7% for state banks. By 1900, the figure was 24.4% for trust companies, 13.4% for national banks and 3.4% for state banks.

Unlike commercial banks, trust company investments were not limited to certain classes of investments. Trust companies could invest in common and preferred stocks and corporate bonds as well as the U.S. Government and political entity bonds which the commercial banks could invest in.

A cross-section analysis of trust company investment portfolios of 1885 indicates, however, that 98.2% of investments were in long-term bonds and only 1.8% in common stocks. U.S. Government bonds accounted for 74.1% of trust company investments at this time, state and local bonds 6.2%, and railroad bonds 17.7%.

The maturity structure was quite long, 93.5% of the bonds coming due after five years and 76.9% after 10 years. From this maturity structure, it would appear that the investment portfolio did not play a liquidity-buffer role. But appearances are misleading.

If liquidity is seen in terms of credit quality rather than maturity dates, then the heavy holdings of U.S. Governments (the vast majority of U.S. bonds had long maturities at this time) would be considered more liquid than corporate bonds. Moreover, in a secular trend of declining long term interest rates, representative of most of this period, long term bonds would appreciate soon enough, giving a profit buffer to absorb a discount should the seller dispose of the bonds hurriedly.

A case study of the investment portfolio transactions of Central Trust Company, a major financial institution by 1885, indicates a turnover rate (sales/cost value at beginning of the year) of 70%, indicating a fairly active use of the investment account.

The mobility of the trust company investment account was decidedly greater than that of the national banks. This permitted the trust companies to take greater advantage of market conditions. The problem for the national banks centered in the fact that a sizable portion of their investments were deposited with the U.S. Treasury to cover Federal deposits with the banks and to back circulating notes issued by the banks. The regulatory requirements covering the substitution and transportation of these pledged bonds were quite cumbersome and inhibited the investment mobility of the portfolio.

Loans. In 1875, 47.7% of trust company assets were in loans, compared with 51.9% for national banks and 65.3% for state banks. By 1900, the figures were 54.7% for trust companies, 53.3% for national banks and 52.3% for state banks.

The national banks were prohibited by law from lending more than 10% of capital to any one customer. Trust companies had no such constraint; and this was an important comparative advantage. In 1885, only two national banks had lending limits of up to $500,000. But at least six trust companies had the practical capacity to make loans in the $500,000 range. Central Trust, for example, which under the National banking system would have had a lending limit of $100,000, made many loans in 1885 in the $500,000 range, with a few even reaching the $1,000,000 level. With the credit demands of large corporations and stock brokers steadily increasing in the 1870-1900 period, the trust companies were in a more favored position to meet this demand.

Most trust company loans were made on collateral, and this in the form of quality negotiable securities. Loans were usually collateralized at 120%, ranging upward depending on the quality of the credit and the collateral. This type of lending was particularly useful in the call loan market, and was surely also an important factor in the growth of the New York City securities market.

The interest charged on loans was subject to usury rates, varying in New York State between 6% and 7%. These usury limits were often unrealistic in light of supply and demand conditions for money. Lenders, particularly lenders in the call loan market (for which trust companies were the major source of funds), by-passed these limits by adding *per diem* commissions. After considerable political agitation usury limits were removed in 1882 for collateralized loans over $5,000.

Loan Characteristics. From surviving general ledgers

of trust companies and commercial banks, it is possible to gain helpful insights into the characteristics of loan portfolios. Roughly, portfolios were divided into three classes of loans: bills discounted, call loans, and time loans. Commercial banks made mainly bills discounted loans, with some call loans. Trust companies made all three classes of loans, but most characteristically call loans.

The origination of call loans was quite sensitive to stock market conditions and financial crises. In both 1884 and 1893, for example, the number of call loans made by Union Trust Company dropped by more than two-thirds in the months following financial crises.

Bills discounted showed a noticeably heavier origination activity in the third quarter of the year and a heavier repayment activity in the fourth quarter, coinciding with the nation's general liquidity condition before and after the autumn harvest.

In terms of maturities, the average bill discounted tended to mature in three to four months, the average call loan in about two months and the average time loan in about eight months.

With the exception of the trust companies specializing

in Western mortgages, both the commercial banks and the trust companies were basically short-term lenders.

Deposits, Capital and Profitability

The trust companies also enjoyed advantages over the commercial banks in deposits and capital. These advantages also contributed to a brighter profit picture.

Deposits. Over most of the 1875-1900 period, the loan-to-net deposit ratio of trust companies and commercial banks in New York City was approximately one-to-one.

The general deposit classifications were demand deposits, time deposits (including certificates of deposits), certified checks and coupon accounts. Trust companies had deposits in each of these classifications, while the commercial banks normally had only demand deposits and certified checks, although a few had certificates of deposit.

The coupon accounts represented undistributed deposit balances held by trust companies in connection with corporate trust business. While these balances were not exceptionally large, they did give an incremental source of lendable funds. More importantly, the corporate trust business gave direct business connections with major corporations, which in turn paved the way for more profitable loan and deposit relationships with these corporations.

Trust companies paid interest on most deposits, excluding receivership accounts, certain transactions oriented accounts and coupon accounts. On average, slightly more than 90% of the trust companies deposit base was interest bearing in the 1875-1900 period. The rates paid for deposits varied with the maturity of the deposit and general economic conditions.

The average interest bearing deposit account for a trust company was around $6,700 in 1875 and $15,000 in 1900. This contrasts noticeably with the average interest bearing deposit account of a New York City savings bank, which was around $350 in 1875 and $450 in 1900.

The financial and regulatory communities considered the issuance of interest bearing deposits by trust companies as normal and structurally sound. But the same was not held to be true of the commercial banks. Repeatedly during this period, the New York Clearing House and the Comptroller of the Currency expressed disapproval of the practice of paying interest on deposits by commercial banks. Some commercial banks did pay interest, especially on correspondent bank balances, but they were not big purchasers of money market funds until late in the century.

The evidence is persuasive that the ability of the

trust companies to attract deposits over the entire 1875-1900 period without direct or indirect censure must be regarded as a prime contributing factor to their superior growth rate. In effect, the trust companies were virtually alone over most of the 1875-1900 period in offering a safe, liquid, remunerative haven for corporate funds. The failure of commercial banks to develop techniques, instruments and regulatory endorsement to meet the emerging demands of corporate treasurers allowed the trust companies to pre-empt the market and to very quickly become muscular competitors.

Moreover, the ability to pay interest on deposits gave the trust companies immense flexibility in managing the day-to-day money position. This contrasts sharply with the deposit structure of the commercial banks, who were virtually at the mercy of the seasonal and transactional demands of the mercantile community.

The turnover rates of the loans and deposits of the trust companies were very nearly parallel, while those of the commercial banks showed a sharply higher rate of turnover in deposits than in loans. The managements of the trust companies were able to match the principal maturity flows of the two sides of the balance sheet. This in turn gave greater stability to earnings and discretionary control over the rate of growth.

Certified checks, while serving a useful and legitimate purpose, were for a while in the early 1880's used by certain New York City national banks as a means of extending credit to the Wall Street community. The process was called "overcertification," or the certifying of a check when good funds were not on deposit. This process, although illegal under Federal law, was winked at until the volume of overcertification became alarmingly large. After a bitter confrontation, the Comptroller of the Currency forced the national banks to abandon the practice in late 1882. While the Comptroller's action probably promoted sounder banking, at the same time it denied the national banks the right to extend a service which the investment community regarded as essential, and hence increased the reliance of the investment community on funds supplied by the trust companies.

Capital. Over the 1875-1900 period, the trust companies showed a compound annual growth rate in equity capital of 8.1%, compared with 1.2% for national banks and 1.6% for state banks in the City.

The reasons for the trust companies' superior growth

rate are four-fold: first, the trust companies attracted new capital, the commercial banks did not; second, high rates of taxation encouraged an exodus of capital from commercial banks; third, the trust companies were more profitable, thus generating greater earnings to retain; and fourth, the trust companies had a lower payout ratio on dividends.

Profitability. Between 1875 and 1900, the New York City trust companies showed an average rate of return on equity of 10.7%, compared to 7.9% for national banks in the City.

The advantages which the trust companies enjoyed in the asset and liability areas contributed importantly to their higher profitability. Higher profitability, however, was only part of the story. Trust company profitability was consistently high, while the profitability of the commercial banks swung markedly with the business cycle.

Two main factors accounted for the cyclicality of commercial bank earnings: first, credit losses were considerably higher. Credit losses were characteristically 3% of capital per year in the commercial banks, somewhat below this in good years and well above in times of financial and economic troubles. The losses suffered by trust companies were normally less than 1% of capital per year, with surprisingly little cyclical variation. The reason for this difference is that the commercial banks were lending primarily in the personal and mercantile markets, on paper with an endorser who was probably also dependent on the mercantile market. The trust companies, by contrast, lent to much larger industrial and financial customers, and mainly on high quality investment collateral.

Second, since the commercial banks paid very little interest on deposits, the effect on loan income of declining or rising interest rates was transmitted directly to the net income account. In the case of the trust companies, however, changes in the interest rate also influenced the expense side. As a result the net interest income of the trust company tended to be much more stable.

The End of the Century: Signs of Maturity

In the 1890's, developments took place which would eventually guide the trust company movement into the mainstream of the commercial banking system. This was, in retrospect, a significant development because it brought an immense amount of entrepreneurial vitality back into the commercial banking (especially the State) system, as well as the very sizable block of business which the trust companies had captured. The absorption of the trust companies into the commercial banking system was a major formative step in the evolution of American financial intermediaries.

The Formation of Trust Companies: 1898-1899. Approximately fifty New York City based trust companies were chartered in the 1870-1900 period. Thirty-one became operative and of these ten were chartered in the brief span of two years--from 1898 to 1899.

What prompted this wave of trust company formations at the end of the century?

First, it was not due to a sudden relaxation of regulatory barriers. That much had already been done in 1887.

Second, the business environment and money market conditions were noticeably more favorable from mid-1897 to late 1899 than in most of the 1891 to mid-1897 period. No trust companies were formed in New York City in the seven years ending in 1897. As in the 1870-3 period, trust company formations were influenced by general economic conditions.

Third, in the mid-1890's trust companies began to receive wide public acclaim as "growth companies." Emoluments to officers and staffs of the trust companies were high and dividends to shareholders continually increased. But now the capital gain potential of trust company stocks came in for recognition. Over the 1880-1900 period the Trust Company Stock Index increased at a compound annual rate of 9.2%, compared with 3.5% for the Commercial Bank Stock Index.

The significance of the wave of trust company formations in the 1898-9 period was two-fold: first, for the first time a large number of marginally qualified entrepreneurs entered the trust company field, and second, the formations also indicated that major financial capitalists were using trust companies as an instrument in their dealings. Both these developments would eventually lead to an environment whereby the industry's structural advantages were reduced. In the first instance, the marginal entrepreneurs weakened the financial reputation of the movement, leading to tighter regulation and mandatory reserves. In the second case, the involvement of major financial capitalists led to a broad pejorative exposure for the trust companies in the Armstrong Investigation (1905) and the Pujo Investigation (1913).

<u>Trust Companies and the American Bankers Association</u>. In

1896, through a special "Trust Company Section," the American Bankers Association became the trade association for the trust companies as it had been for many years for the commercial banks. The significance of this can be measured by considering an alternative: if the ABA had closed its doors to the trust companies, and the trust companies established their own trade association, then there would have existed in institutionalized form, a primary mechanism by which divergent interests could be pursued, solidified and perpetuated. And this in turn could have had a marked influence in the development of the American financial intermediaries.

The reason why the ABA admitted the trust companies was importantly the fear among commercial bankers that the trust companies, if allowed to follow their separate way, would set up a rival check clearing system, thereby challenging the correspondent business of the large commercial banks.

Interlocking Directors. A cross-section analysis of 1900, reveals that the trust companies in New York City were deeply interlocked with each other, with national banks, with state banks, with the New York Stock Exchange, and with insurance companies.

At the end of 1900, there were 30 trust companies in New York City; these companies had a total of 645 director seats, and these seats were distributed among 533 individuals.

Two-thirds of the trust companies had interlocks with at least five other trust companies, one-third had interlocks with at least ten other trust companies, and every trust company had at least one interlock with another trust company.

Over half of the trust companies had interlocks with at least six national banks, one-fifth had interlocks with at least nine, and every trust company had, at the least, interlocks with two national banks.

Two-thirds of the trust companies had interlocks with at least two state banks, slightly less than one-fourth had interlocks with at least five, and all but three of the trust companies had interlocks with at least one state bank.

Two-thirds of the trust companies had interlocks with at least two savings banks, slightly over one-fourth had interlocks with at least four, and all but three of the trust companies had interlocks with at least one savings bank.

Twenty-five of the trust companies had at least one member of the New York Stock Exchange on the board. Twenty-six had interlocks with major life insurance companies and twenty-one with major fire insurance companies.

The scope and intensiveness of trust company interlocks among themselves and with other financial intermediaries was not duplicated by national and state banks. In part, this was simply a matter of numbers, because the average trust company board of directors was nearly twice as large as the average board of either national or state banks. Trust company boards were larger because of political, regulatory and fiduciary reasons.

Other reasons why trust companies had large boards: to help in the development of new business, to serve as a vehicle for the exchange of credit information, and to protect existing account relationships.

Between Times. By 1900, the trust company movement in New York City was successfully established and recognized, admiringly, by the community. Within a few years, several of these companies would experience painful circumstances. But until that happened, the trust company movement was at its high water mark.

BIBLIOGRAPHY

Manuscripts

Note: Manuscript citations with numbers enclosed in ( ) refer to company folders located at the Archives of the New York State Banking Department at Albany. The Mercantile Trust Company citations are the care of Bankers Trust Company of New York. The Levi P. Morton Papers are located in the Manuscript Division of the New York Public Library, while the George Bliss Letter Book is located at the New York Historical Society. All other manuscript citations are the jurisdiction of Manufacturers Hanover Trust Company, New York City.

Atlantic Trust Company, General Ledger No. 1, 1887-95.

Bowling Green Trust Company, File (117981).

Central Realty Bond and Trust Company, File (117972).

Central Trust Company, Semi-Annual Statements from July 1, 1876 (to June 30, 1915).

___________, Miscellaneous Historical Papers.

___________, George W. Davidson, The Story of Central Hanover. Typed, unpublished manuscript, ca. 1932.

___________, General Ledgers: A-C, 1875-1901, 3 volumes.

___________, Trustee's Minutes: April 20, 1875-September 17, 1901, 2 volumes.

___________, Executive Committee Minutes: August 21, 1875-March 12, 1912, 5 volumes.

Chatham National Bank, General Ledgers: Nos. 9 and 10, 1882-5, 2 volumes.

City Trust Company, File (117977).

Continental Trust Company, File (117971).

Fifth Avenue Trust Company, _File_ (117980).

Hanover National Bank, _Directors Minutes: May 22, 1863-March 10, 1914_, 5 volumes.

__________, _General Ledgers: Nos. 6-49, 1879-1900_, 44 volumes.

Holland Trust Company, _File_ (117974).

Mercantile Trust Company, _Minutes of Stockholders Meetings Beginning January 1, 1875_.

__________, _Minutes of Executive Committee: February 10, 1874-December 24, 1907_, 6 volumes.

Merchants Trust Company, _File_ (117975).

Metropolitan Trust Company, _General Ledger No. 1, 1881-91_.

Levi P. Morton Papers, _Letters: 1897-1920_.

Morton, Bliss and Company, _George Bliss, Letter Book, 1893-5_.

Morton Trust Company, _File_ (117979).

North American Trust Company, _File_ (117977).

Phenix National Bank, _General Ledgers, 1880-90_, 2 volumes.

Standard Trust Company, _File_ (117978).

State Trust Company, _File_ (117979).

Trust Company of America, _File_ (117977).

Trust Company of New York, _File_ (117973).

United States Transfer and Exchange Company, _File_ (117970).

Union Trust Company, _Executive Committee Minutes: May 10, 1865-March 31, 1899_, 4 volumes.

__________, _General Ledgers: C-H, 1875-90_, 6 volumes.

Union Trust Company, Miscellaneous Data Pertaining to History of Bank.

__________, Trustees Minutes: May 1, 1864-September 6, 1900, 2 volumes.

Washington Trust Company, File (117976).

Government Publications

Federal Publications

Banking and Currency Committee, House of Representatives, United States Congress, Sixty-second Session, Report of the Committee Appointed Pursuant to House Resolutions 429 and 504 to Investigate the Concentration of Control of Money and Credit, February 28, 1913, Washington, D.C., 1913.

Comptroller of the Currency, Annual Report, Washington, D.C., 1870-1900.

New York State Publications

Banks Committee, Senate, New York State, Testimony Taken before the Senate on Charges against John F. Smyth, Superintendent of the Insurance Department, Albany, 1878.

__________, Testimony Taken before the Senate Committee on Banks and the Senate of the State of New York, in Reference to the Charges Preferred by William J. Best, Receiver, Etc., Edward Mallon and John Mack, Against DeWitt C. Ellis, Superintendent of the Banking Department of the State of New York, Albany, 1878.

Constitutional Convention of the State of New York, Journal, Albany, 1873.

Governor, New York State, Annual Message to the Legislature, Assembly Documents, Albany, 1870-1900.

__________, Messages from the Governors Comprising Executive Communications to the Legislature, and Other Papers Relating to Legislation, from the Organization of the

First Colonial Assembly in 1683, to and including the Year 1906, C. Z. Lincoln (ed.), Albany, 1909.

Joint Committee, Senate and Assembly, New York State, Appointed to Investigate the Affairs of Life Insurance Companies, Report, February 22, 1906, Assembly Document No. 41-Session 129, Albany, 1906.

Legislature, New York State, Bills Introduced into Assembly and Senate, Albany, 1867-1900.

____________, Assembly and Senate Documents, Albany, 1867-1900.

____________, Assembly and Senate Journals, Albany, 1868-1900.

McElory, W. C., and A. McBride, Life Sketches of Executive Officers and Members of the Legislature of the State of New York for 1873, Albany, 1873.

New York State, Laws, Albany, 1867-1900.

Special Committee on Banks, New York State, Letter from A. B. Hepburn, Stephen Baun, Andrew Mills, Edward W. Sheldon and E. S. Marsten to Governor Charles E. Hughes, December 16, 1907, Albany, 1907.

Superintendent of Banking Department, New York State, Annual Reports, Assembly Documents, Albany, 1867-1900.

____________, Annual Reports Relative to Savings Banks, Assembly Documents, Albany, 1867-1900.

New York City Publications

Board of Aldermen, New York City, Document Number 6, April 8, 1872, New York City, 1872.

Department of Taxes and Assessments, New York City, Report of the Commissioners, May 1, 1871, New York City, 1871.

Books

Allen, Frederick Lewis, The Great Pierpont Morgan. New York, Harper & Row, 1965.

Barnett, G. S., State Banks and Trust Companies. National Monetary Commission (1911), New York, Augustus M. Kelly, 1969.

Bouvier, John, Law Dictionary. Philadelphia, J. B. Lippincott, 1874.

Buley, R. Carlyle, The Equitable Life Assurance Society of the United States. New York, Appleton Century Croft, 1959.

Central Trust Company of New York, Charter and By-Laws. New York, 1875

Chaplin, Stewart, A Treatise on Express Trusts and Powers. New York, Banker, Voorhis, 1897.

Colonial Trust Company, Trust Manual. New York, ca. 1900.

Cross, William T., The Making of a Trust Company: Twenty-one Years Experience of Chicago Trust Company. Chicago, 1923.

Gest, William P., The Rise and Business of the Modern Trust Company. Philadelphia, 1905.

Gibbons, J. S., The Bank of New York, Their Dealers, the Clearing House and the Panic of 1857. New York, Appleton, 1858.

Goodyear, Lloyd E., Bank Accounting. Cedar Rapids, Iowa, Goodyear Marshall Publishing, 1906.

Guaranty Trust Company, One Hundred Years of Banking Service: 1839-1939. New York, 1939.

Hedges, Joseph E., Commercial Banking and the Stock Market before 1863. Baltimore, Johns Hopkins Press, 1938.

Herrick, Clay, Trust Companies, Their Organization, Growth and Management. New York, Bankers Publishing, 1909.

Krooss, Herman E. and Charles Gilbert, American Business History. Englewood Cliffs, N.J., Prentice-Hall, 1972.

March, Christopher C., The Theory and Practice of Bank Bookkeeping. New York, Appleton, 1856.

McElroy, Robert, Levi P. Morton--Banker, Diplomat and Statesman. New York, G. P. Putnam, 1930.

Moore, G. H. (ed.), Business Cycle Indicators, Volume I. National Bureau of Economic Research, Princeton, Princeton University Press, 1961.

Myers, Margaret G., The New York Money Market: Volume I, Origins and Development. New York, Columbia University Press, 1931.

Neal, F. Virgil, Modern Banking and Bank Accounting. New York, William and Rogers, 1899.

Packard, S. S., Bank Bookkeeping. New York, 1897.

Paine, Willis S., The Laws of the State of New York Relating to Banks, Banking, Trust, Investment, Safe Deposit, Personal Loan Companies and Brokers, Private Banks, Savings and Loan Associations, Credit Unions and the Land Bank. New York, Baker Voorhis, 1914.

Perine, Edward T. B., The Story of the Trust Companies. New York, Riverside Press, 1916.

Robertson, Ross M., The Comptroller and Bank Supervision: A Historical Appraisal. McCall Printing, 1968.

Schaffner, Margaret A., Trust Company Reserves, Comparative Legislation Bulletin No. 6. Wisconsin Free Library Commission, 1906.

Smith, James G., The Development of Trust Companies in the United States. New York, Henry Holt, 1927.

Spahr, Walter E., The Clearing and Collection of Checks. New York, Bankers Publishing, 1926.

Stedman, Edmund C. (ed.), The New York Stock Exchange. New York, Stock Exchange Historical Company, 1905.

Studenski, Paul and Herman E. Krooss, Financial History of the United States. New York, McGraw Hill, 1963.

Union Trust Company of New York, Charter and By-Laws. New York, 1891.

Walker, Guy M., Trust Companies: A Study of the Nature of Their Business and the Source of Their Great Earning Power. Boston, Press of Boston, 1903.

Articles

Gilman, Theodore, "Trust Company Reserves," Bankers Magazine, April, 1904.

Kilburn, Frederick D., "Control and Supervision of Trust Companies," Annals of the American Academy of Political Science, July, 1904.

Neal, Larry, "Trust Companies and Financial Innovations, 1847-1914," Business History Review, Spring, 1971.

Nourse, B. F., "The Crises of 1837 and 1873," Commercial and Financial Chronicle, April 7, 1875.

Sammis, L. Walter, "The Relation of Trust Companies to Industrial Combinations, as Illustrated by the United States Shipbuilding Company," Annals of the American Academy of Political Science, July, 1904.

Newspapers, Periodicals and Serial Publications

American Bankers Association Proceedings.

Bankers Magazine.

Commercial and Financial Chronicle.

Directory of Directors in New York City.

Financier.

Moody's Industrial Manual.

Nation.

New York Times.

Rand McNally's Bankers Directory.

Trow's New York City Directory.

Trust Companies.

United States Investor.

Court Cases

Henry Clews et al., Respondents, Bank of New York National Banking Association, Appellant, 89 _New York Reports_ (New York State Court of Appeals).

Mercantile Bank v. New York, 121 _United States_ (United States District Court).

Merchants Bank v. State Bank, 10 _Wallace_ (United States Supreme Court).

The People ex rel. the Gallatin National Bank et al., Appellants, v. the Commissioner of Taxes and Assessments, respondents, 22 _Sickles_ (New York State Court of Appeals).

United States Trust v. Brady, 20 _Barbour_ (New York State Supreme Court).

Van Allen v. The Assessors, 3 _Wallace_ (United States Supreme Court).